CEH™
Certified Ethical Hacker
Study Guide

CEH™
Certified Ethical Hacker
Study Guide

Kimberly Graves

WILEY

Wiley Publishing, Inc.

Acquisitions Editor: Jeff Kellum
Development Editor: Pete Gaughan
Technical Editors: Keith Parsons, Chris Carson
Production Editor: Angela Smith
Copy Editor: Liz Welch
Editorial Manager: Pete Gaughan
Production Manager: Tim Tate
Vice President and Executive Group Publisher: Richard Swadley
Vice President and Publisher: Neil Edde
Media Project Manager 1: Laura Moss-Hollister
Media Associate Producer: Josh Frank
Media Quality Assurance: Shawn Patrick
Book Designers: Judy Fung and Bill Gibson
Compositor: Craig Johnson, Happenstance Type-O-Rama
Proofreader: Publication Services, Inc.
Indexer: Ted Laux
Project Coordinator, Cover: Lynsey Stanford
Cover Designer: Ryan Sneed

Library of Congress Cataloging-in-Publication Data

Graves, Kimberly, 1974-

  CEH : certified ethical hacker study guide / Kimberly Graves. — 1st ed.

    p. cm.

  Includes bibliographical references and index.

  ISBN 978-0-470-52520-3 (paper/cd-rom : alk. paper)
1. Electronic data processing personnel—Certification. 2. Computer security—Examinations—Study guides.
3. Computer hackers—Examinations—Study guides. 4. Computer networks—Examinations—Study guides. I. Title.
  QA76.3.G6875 2010
  005.8—dc22

                              2010003135

10 9 8 7 6 5 4 3

Dear Reader,

Thank you for choosing *CEH: Certified Ethical Hacker Study Guide*. This book is part of a family of premium-quality Sybex books, all of which are written by outstanding authors who combine practical experience with a gift for teaching.

Sybex was founded in 1976. More than 30 years later, we're still committed to producing consistently exceptional books. With each of our titles, we're working hard to set a new standard for the industry. From the paper we print on, to the authors we work with, our goal is to bring you the best books available.

I hope you see all that reflected in these pages. I'd be very interested to hear your comments and get your feedback on how we're doing. Feel free to let me know what you think about this or any other Sybex book by sending me an email at nedde@wiley.com. If you think you've found a technical error in this book, please visit http://sybex.custhelp.com. Customer feedback is critical to our efforts at Sybex.

Best regards,

Neil Edde
Vice President and Publisher
Sybex, an Imprint of Wiley

To all my former and future students who have embarked on the path to greater knowledge. Remember the ethical hacker motto is to do no harm and leave no tracks.

Acknowledgments

To my family and friends, who have been so supportive through countless hours spent writing and editing this book. All your comments and critiques were invaluable and I appreciate your efforts. Most importantly, I want to thank my husband Ed for his support in this endeavor. It has been no small task and I appreciate his understanding every step of the way.

I want to thank my technical editor, Keith Parsons, for his attention to detail and continual quest for excellence from himself and everyone he works with, this book being no exception. Thanks, Keith, I know it was a long road and you stuck with it until the very end.

Also thanks to the team at Sybex: Jeff Kellum, Pete Gaughan, and Angela Smith. Thank you for following through on this book and keeping me motivated.

About the Author

Graduating in 1995 from American University, with a major in political science and a minor in computer information technology, Kimberly Graves quickly learned that the technical side of her degree was going to be a far more interesting and challenging career path than something that kept her "inside the Beltway."

Starting with a technical instructor position at a computer training company in Arlington, Virginia, Kimberly used the experience and credentials gained from that position to begin the steady accumulation of the other certifications that she now uses in her day-to-day interactions with clients and students. Since gaining her Certified Novell Engineer Certification (CNE) in a matter of a few months at her first job, Kimberly's expertise in networking and security has grown to encompass certifications by Microsoft, Intel, Aruba Networks, EC-Council, Cisco Systems, and CompTIA.

With over 15 cumulative years invested in the IT industry, Kimberly has amassed more than 25 instructor grade networking and security certifications. She has served various educational institutions in Washington, DC, as an adjunct professor while simultaneously serving as a subject matter expert for several security certification programs. Recently Kimberly has been utilizing her Security+, Certified Wireless Network Associate (CWNA), Certified Wireless Security Professional (CWSP), Certified Ethical Hacker (CEH), and Certified Information Systems Security Professional (CISSP) certificates to teach and develop course material for the Department of Veterans Affairs, U.S. Air Force, and the NSA. Kimberly currently works with leading wireless vendors across the country to train the next generation of wireless security professionals. In 2007, Kimberly founded Techsource Network Solutions to better serve the needs of her clients and offer additional network and security consulting services.

Contents at a Glance

Contents

Table of Exercises

Introduction

The Certified Ethical Hacker (CEH) exam was developed by the International Council of E-Commerce Consultants (EC-Council) to provide an industry-wide means of certifying the competency of security professionals. The CEH certification is granted to those who have attained the level of knowledge and security skills needed to perform security audits and penetration testing of systems and network.

The CEH exam is periodically updated to keep the certification applicable to the most recent hacking tools and vulnerabilities. This is necessary because a CEH must be familiar with the latest attacks and exploits. The most recent revisions to the exam as of this writing are found in version 6. The version 6 exam objectives are reflected in this book.

What Is CEH Certification?

The CEH certification was created to offer a wide-ranging certification, in the sense that it's intended to certify competence with many different makers/vendors. This certification is designed for security officers, auditors, security professionals, site administrators, and anyone who deals with the security of the network infrastructure on a day-to-day basis.

The goal of ethical hackers is to help organizations take preemptive measures against malicious attacks by attacking systems themselves, all the while staying within legal limits. This philosophy stems from the proven practice of trying to catch a thief by thinking like a thief. As technology advances, organizations increasingly depend on technology and information assets have evolved into critical components of survival.

The definition of an ethical hacker is similar to a penetration tester. The ethical hacker is an individual who is usually employed with the organization and who can be trusted to undertake an attempt to penetrate networks and/or computer systems using the same methods as a hacker. Hacking is a felony in the United States and most other countries. When it is done by request and under a contract between an ethical hacker and an organization, it is legal.

You need to pass only a single exam to become a CEH. But obtaining this certification doesn't mean you can provide services to a company—this is just the first step. By obtaining your CEH certification, you'll be able to obtain more experience, build on your interest in networks, and subsequently pursue more complex and in-depth network knowledge and certifications.

For the latest exam pricing and updates to the registration procedures, call either Thomson Prometric at (866) 776-6387 or (800) 776-4276, or Pearson VUE at (877) 680-3926. You can also go to either www.2test.com or www.prometric.com (for Thomson Prometric) or www.vue.com (for Pearson VUE) for additional information or to register online. If you have further questions about the scope of the exams or related EC-Council programs, refer to the EC-Council website at www.eccouncil.org.

Who Should Buy This Book?

Certified Ethical Hacker Study Guide is designed to be a study tool for experienced security professionals seeking the information necessary to successfully pass the certification exam. The study guide can be used either in conjunction with a more complete study program, computer-based training courseware, or classroom/lab environment, or as an exam review tool for those want to brush up before taking the exam. It isn't our goal to give away the answers, but rather to identify those topics on which you can expect to be tested.

If you want to become a CEH, this book is definitely what you need. However, if you just want to attempt to pass the exam without really understanding the basics of ethical hacking, this guide isn't for you. It's written for people who want to create a foundation of the skills and knowledge necessary to pass the exam, and then take what they learned and apply it to the real world.

How to Use This Book and the CD

We've included several testing features in the book and on the CD. These tools will help you retain vital exam content as well as prepare to sit for the actual exam:

Chapter Review Questions   To test your knowledge as you progress through the book, there are review questions at the end of each chapter. As you finish each chapter, answer the review questions and then check your answers—the correct answers appear on the page following the last review question. You can go back to reread the section that deals with each question you got wrong to ensure that you answer correctly the next time you're tested on the material.

Electronic Flashcards   You'll find flashcard questions on the CD for on-the-go review. These are short questions and answers, just like the flashcards you probably used to study in school. You can answer them on your PC or download them onto a Palm device for quick and convenient reviewing.

Test Engine   The CD also contains the Sybex Test Engine. Using this custom test engine, you can identify weak areas up front and then develop a solid studying strategy using each of these robust testing features. Our thorough readme file will walk you through the quick, easy installation process.

In addition to taking the chapter review questions, you'll find sample exams. Take these practice exams just as if you were taking the actual exam (without any reference material). When you've finished the first exam, move on to the next one to solidify your test-taking skills. If you get more than 90 percent of the answers correct, you're ready to take the certification exam.

Searchable Book in PDF   The CD contains the entire book in PDF (Adobe Acrobat) format so you can easily read it on any computer. If you have to travel and brush up on any key terms, and you have a laptop with a CD-ROM drive, you can do so with this resource.

Tips for Taking the CEH Exam

Here are some general tips for taking your exam successfully:

- Bring two forms of ID with you. One must be a photo ID, such as a driver's license. The other can be a major credit card or a passport. Both forms must include a signature.

- Arrive early at the exam center so you can relax and review your study materials, particularly tables and lists of exam-related information.

- Read the questions carefully. Don't be tempted to jump to an early conclusion. Make sure you know exactly what the question is asking.

- Don't leave any unanswered questions. Unanswered questions are scored against you.

- There will be questions with multiple correct responses. When there is more than one correct answer, a message at the bottom of the screen will prompt you to either "Choose two" or "Choose all that apply." Be sure to read the messages displayed to know how many correct answers you must choose.

- When answering multiple-choice questions you're not sure about, use a process of elimination to get rid of the obviously incorrect answers first. Doing so will improve your odds if you need to make an educated guess.

- For the latest pricing on the exams and updates to the registration procedures, visit EC-Council's website at www.eccouncil.org.

The CEH Exam Objectives

At the beginning of each chapter in this book, we have included the complete listing of the CEH objectives as they appear on EC-Council's website. These are provided for easy reference and to assure you that you are on track with the objectives.

Exam objectives are subject to change at any time without prior notice and at EC-Council's sole discretion. Please visit the CEH Certification page of EC-Council's website (www.eccouncil.org/certification/certified_ethical_hacker.aspx) for the most current listing of exam objectives.

Ethics and Legality

- Understand ethical hacking terminology.
- Define the job role of an ethical hacker.
- Understand the different phases involved in ethical hacking.

- Identify different types of hacking technologies.
- List the five stages of ethical hacking.
- What is hacktivism?
- List different types of hacker classes.
- Define the skills required to become an ethical hacker.
- What is vulnerability research?
- Describe the ways of conducting ethical hacking.
- Understand the legal implications of hacking.
- Understand 18 U.S.C. § 1030 US Federal Law.

Footprinting

- Define the term footprinting.
- Describe information-gathering methodology.
- Describe competitive intelligence.
- Understand DNS enumeration.
- Understand Whois, ARIN lookup.
- Identify different types of DNS records.
- Understand how traceroute is used in footprinting.
- Understand how email tracking works.
- Understand how web spiders work.

Scanning

- Define the terms port scanning, network scanning, and vulnerability scanning.
- Understand the CEH scanning methodology.
- Understand ping sweep techniques.
- Understand nmap command switches.
- Understand SYN, stealth, XMAS, NULL, IDLE, and FIN scans.
- List TCP communication flag types.
- Understand war dialing techniques.
- Understand banner grabbing and OF fingerprinting techniques.
- Understand how proxy servers are used in launching an attack.
- How do anonymizers work?
- Understand HTTP tunneling techniques.
- Understand IP spoofing techniques.

Enumeration

- What is enumeration?
- What is meant by null sessions?
- What is SNMP enumeration?
- What are the steps involved in performing enumeration?

System Hacking

- Understanding password cracking techniques.
- Understanding different types of passwords.
- Identify various password cracking tools.
- Understand escalating privileges.
- Understanding keyloggers and other spyware technologies.
- Understand how to hide files.
- Understand rootkits.
- Understand steganography technologies.
- Understand how to cover your tracks and erase evidence.

Trojans and Backdoors

- What is a Trojan?
- What is meant by overt and covert channels?
- List the different types of Trojans.
- What are the indications of a Trojan attack?
- Understand how Netcat Trojan works.
- What is meant by wrapping?
- How do reverse connecting Trojans work?
- What are the countermeasure techniques in preventing Trojans?
- Understand Trojan evading techniques.

Sniffers

- Understand the protocols susceptible to sniffing.
- Understand active and passive sniffing.
- Understand ARP poisoning.
- Understand ethereal capture and display filters.
- Understand MAC flooding.
- Understand DNS spoofing techniques.
- Describe sniffing countermeasures.

Denial of Service

- Understand the types of DoS attacks.
- Understand how a DDoS attack works.
- Understand how BOTs/BOTNETs work.
- What is a Smurf attack?
- What is SYN flooding?
- Describe the DoS/DDoS countermeasures.

Social Engineering

- What is social engineering?
- What are the common types of attacks?
- Understand dumpster diving.
- Understand reverse social engineering.
- Understand insider attacks.
- Understand identity theft.
- Describe phishing attacks.
- Understand online scams.
- Understand URL obfuscation.
- Social engineering countermeasures.

Session Hijacking

- Understand spoofing vs. hijacking.
- List the types of session hijacking.
- Understand sequence prediction.
- What are the steps in performing session hijacking?
- Describe how you would prevent session hijacking.

Hacking Web Servers

- List the types of web server vulnerabilities.
- Understand the attacks against web servers.
- Understand IIS Unicode exploits.
- Understand patch management techniques.
- Understand Web Application Scanner.
- What is the Metasploit Framework?
- Describe web server hardening methods.

Web Application Vulnerabilities

- Understand how a web application works.
- Objectives of web application hacking.
- Anatomy of an attack.
- Web application threats.
- Understand Google hacking.
- Understand web application countermeasures.

Web-Based Password-Cracking Techniques

- List the authentication types.
- What is a password cracker?
- How does a password cracker work?
- Understand password attacks—classification.
- Understand password cracking countermeasures.

SQL Injection

- What is SQL injection?
- Understand the steps to conduct SQL injection.
- Understand SQL Server vulnerabilities.
- Describe SQL injection countermeasures.

Wireless Hacking

- Overview of WEP, WPA authentication systems, and cracking techniques.
- Overview of wireless sniffers and SSID, MAC spoofing.
- Understand rogue access points.
- Understand wireless hacking techniques.
- Describe the methods in securing wireless networks.

Virus and Worms

- Understand the difference between a virus and a worm.
- Understand the types of viruses.
- How a virus spreads and infects the system.
- Understand antivirus evasion techniques.
- Understand virus detection methods.

Physical Security

- Physical security breach incidents.
- Understand physical security.
- What is the need for physical security?
- Who is accountable for physical security?
- Factors affecting physical security.

Linux Hacking

- Understand how to compile a Linux kernel.
- Understand GCC compilation commands.
- Understand how to install LKM modules.
- Understand Linux hardening methods.

Evading IDS, Honeypots, and Firewalls

- List the types of intrusion detection systems and evasion techniques.
- List firewall and honeypot evasion techniques.

Buffer Overflows

- Overview of stack based buffer overflows.
- Identify the different types of buffer overflows and methods of detection.
- Overview of buffer overflow mutation techniques.

Cryptography

- Overview of cryptography and encryption techniques.
- Describe how public and private keys are generated.
- Overview of MD5, SHA, RC4, RC5, Blowfish algorithms.

Penetration Testing Methodologies

- Overview of penetration testing methodologies.
- List the penetration testing steps.
- Overview of the Pen-Test legal framework.
- Overview of the Pen-Test deliverables.
- List the automated penetration testing tools.

Hardware and Software Requirements

This book contains numerous lab exercises to practice the skills of ethical hacking. In order to be able to perform all the lab exercises, you must have an extensive lab setup of many different types of operating systems and servers. The lab should have the following operating systems:

- Windows 2000 Professional
- Windows 2000 Server
- Windows NT Server 4.0
- Windows XP
- Windows Vista
- Linux (Backtrack recommended)

The purpose of the diverse OS types is to test the hacking tools against both patched and unpatched versions of each OS. The best way to do that is to use a virtual machine setup: you do not need to have actual systems for each OS, but they can be loaded as needed to test hacking tools. At a minimum, your lab should include test systems running the following services:

- FTP
- Telnet
- Web (HTTP)
- SSL (HTTPS)
- POP
- SMTP
- SNMP
- Active Directory

Additionally, the benefit of using a virtual machine setup is that the systems can be restored without affecting the host system. By using a virtual environment, malware such as rootkits, Trojans, and viruses can be run without endangering any real production data. The tools in the book should *never* be used on production servers or systems because real and immediate data loss could occur.

In addition to the host system necessary to run the virtual server environment, a USB drive will be needed. This book includes lab instructions to create a bootable Linux Backtrack installation on a USB drive.

How to Contact the Publisher

Sybex welcomes feedback on all of its titles. Visit the Sybex website at www.sybex.com for book updates and additional certification information. You'll also find forms you can use to submit comments or suggestions regarding this or any other Sybex title.

Assessment Test

1. In which type of attack are passwords never cracked?

   A. Cryptography attacks

   B. Brute-force attacks

   C. Replay attacks

   D. John the Ripper attacks

2. If the password is 7 characters or less, then the second half of the LM hash is always:

   A. 0xAAD3B435B51404EE

   B. 0xAAD3B435B51404AA

   C. 0xAAD3B435B51404BB

   D. 0xAAD3B435B51404CC

3. What defensive measures will you take to protect your network from password brute-force attacks? (Choose all that apply.)

   A. Never leave a default password.

   B. Never use a password that can be found in a dictionary.

   C. Never use a password related to the hostname, domain name, or anything else that can be found with Whois.

   D. Never use a password related to your hobbies, pets, relatives, or date of birth.

   E. Use a word that has more than 21 characters from a dictionary as the password.

4. Which of the following is the act intended to prevent spam emails?

   A. 1990 Computer Misuse Act

   B. Spam Prevention Act

   C. US-Spam 1030 Act

   D. CANSPAM Act

5. _____ is a Cisco IOS mechanism that examines packets on Layers 4 to 7.

   A. Network-Based Application Recognition (NBAR)

   B. Denial-of-Service Filter (DOSF)

   C. Rule Filter Application Protocol (RFAP)

   D. Signature-Based Access List (SBAL)

6. What filter in Ethereal will you use to view Hotmail messages?

   A. (http contains "e-mail") && (http contains "hotmail")

   B. (http contains "hotmail") && (http contains "Reply-To")

   C. (http = "login.passport.com") && (http contains "SMTP")

   D. (http = "login.passport.com") && (http contains "POP3")

SMURF attacks on the Internet?

)NS servers directly?

:acks

:tacks

n attacks

plification attack

s carried out in which OSI layer?

n serving different types of web pages based on the user's IP

C. II a⸺   ⸺de

D. Website cloaking

11. True or False: Data is sent over the network as cleartext (unencrypted) when Basic Authentication is configured on web servers.

    A. True

    B. False

12. What is the countermeasure against XSS scripting?

    A. Create an IP access list and restrict connections based on port number.

    B. Replace < and > characters with < and > using server scripts.

    C. Disable JavaScript in Internet Explorer and Firefox browsers.

    D. Connect to the server using HTTPS protocol instead of HTTP.

13. How would you prevent a user from connecting to the corporate network via their home computer and attempting to use a VPN to gain access to the corporate LAN?

    A. Enforce Machine Authentication and disable VPN access to all your employee accounts from any machine other than corporate-issued PCs.

    B. Allow VPN access but replace the standard authentication with biometric authentication.

    C. Replace the VPN access with dial-up modem access to the company's network.

    D. Enable 25-character complex password policy for employees to access the VPN network.

14. How would you compromise a system that relies on cookie-based security?

   A. Inject the cookie ID into the web URL and connect back to the server.

   B. Brute-force the encryption used by the cookie and replay it back to the server.

   C. Intercept the communication between the client and the server and change the cookie to make the server believe that there is a user with higher privileges.

   D. Delete the cookie, reestablish connection to the server, and access higher-level privileges.

15. Windows is dangerously insecure when unpacked from the box; which of the following must you do before you use it? (Choose all that apply.)

   A. Make sure a new installation of Windows is patched by installing the latest service packs.

   B. Install the latest security patches for applications such as Adobe Acrobat, Macromedia Flash, Java, and WinZip.

   C. Install a personal firewall and lock down unused ports from connecting to your computer.

   D. Install the latest signatures for antivirus software.

   E. Create a non-admin user with a complex password and log onto this account.

   F. You can start using your computer since the vendor, such as Dell, Hewlett-Packard, and IBM, already has installed the latest service packs.

16. Which of these is a patch management and security utility?

   A. MBSA

   B. BSSA

   C. ASNB

   D. PMUS

17. How do you secure a GET method in web page posts?

   A. Encrypt the data before you send using the GET method.

   B. Never include sensitive information in a script.

   C. Use HTTPS SSLv3 to send the data instead of plain HTTPS.

   D. Replace GET with the POST method when sending data.

18. What are two types of buffer overflow?

   A. Stack-based buffer overflow

   B. Active buffer overflow

   C. Dynamic buffer overflow

   D. Heap-based buffer overflow

19. How does a polymorphic shellcode work?

- **A.** It reverses the working instructions into opposite order by masking the IDS signatures.
- **B.** It converts the shellcode into Unicode, uses a loader to convert back to machine code, and then executes the shellcode.
- **C.** It encrypts the shellcode by XORing values over the shellcode, using loader code to decrypt the shellcode, and then executing the decrypted shellcode.
- **D.** It compresses the shellcode into normal instructions, uncompresses the shellcode using loader code, and then executes the shellcode.

20. Where are passwords kept in Linux?

- **A.** /etc/shadow
- **B.** /etc/passwd
- **C.** /bin/password
- **D.** /bin/shadow

21. What of the following is an IDS defeating technique?

- **A.** IP routing or packet dropping
- **B.** IP fragmentation or session splicing
- **C.** IDS spoofing or session assembly
- **D.** IP splicing or packet reassembly

22. True or False: A digital signature is simply a message that is encrypted with the public key instead of the private key.

- **A.** True
- **B.** False

23. Every company needs which of the following documents?

- **A.** Information Security Policy (ISP)
- **B.** Information Audit Policy (IAP)
- **C.** Penetration Testing Policy (PTP)
- **D.** User Compliance Policy (UCP)

24. What does the hacking tool Netcat do?

- **A.** Netcat is a flexible packet sniffer/logger that detects attacks. Netcat is a library packet capture (libpcap)-based packet sniffer/logger that can be used as a lightweight network intrusion detection system.
- **B.** Netcat is a powerful tool for network monitoring and data acquisition. This program allows you to dump the traffic on a network. It can be used to print out the headers of packets on a network interface that matches a given expression.
- **C.** Netcat is called the TCP/IP Swiss army knife. It is a simple Unix utility that reads and writes data across network connections using the TCP or UDP protocol.
- **D.** Netcat is a security assessment tool based on SATAN (Security Administrator's Integrated Network Tool).

25. Which tool is a file and directory integrity checker that aids system administrators and users in monitoring a designated set of files for any changes?

   A. Hping2

   B. DSniff

   C. Cybercop Scanner

   D. Tripwire

26. Which of the following Nmap commands launches a stealth SYN scan against each machine in a class C address space where `target.example.com` resides and tries to determine what operating system is running on each host that is up and running?

   A. `nmap -v target.example.com`

   B. `nmap -sS -O target.example.com/24`

   C. `nmap -sX -p 22,53,110,143,4564 198.116.*.1-127`

   D. `nmap -XS -O target.example.com`

27. Snort is a Linux-based intrusion detection system. Which command enables Snort to use network intrusion detection (NIDS) mode assuming snort.conf is the name of your rules file and the IP address is 192.168.1.0 with Subnet Mask:255.255.255.0?

   A. `./snort -c snort.conf 192.168.1.0/24`

   B. `./snort 192.168.1.0/24 -x snort.conf`

   C. `./snort -dev -l ./log -a 192.168.1.0/8 -c snort.conf`

   D. `./snort -dev -l ./log -h 192.168.1.0/24 -c snort.conf`

28. Buffer overflow vulnerabilities are due to applications that do not perform bound checks in the code. Which of the following C/C++ functions do not perform bound checks?

   A. `gets()`

   B. `memcpy()`

   C. `strcpr()`

   D. `scanf()`

   E. `strcat()`

29. How do you prevent SMB hijacking in Windows operating systems?

   A. Install WINS Server and configure secure authentication.

   B. Disable NetBIOS over TCP/IP in Windows NT and 2000.

   C. The only effective way to block SMB hijacking is to use SMB signing.

   D. Configure 128-bit SMB credentials key-pair in TCP/IP properties.

30. Which type of hacker represents the highest risk to your network?

   A. Disgruntled employees

   B. Black-hat hackers

   C. Gray-hat hackers

   D. Script kiddies

31. Which of the following command-line switches would you use for OS detection in Nmap?

   A. -X

   B. -D

   C. -O

   D. -P

32. LM authentication is not as strong as Windows NT authentication so you may want to disable its use, because an attacker eavesdropping on network traffic will attack the weaker protocol. A successful attack can compromise the user's password. How do you disable LM authentication in Windows XP?

   A. Download and install the LMSHUT.EXE tool from Microsoft's website'

   B. Disable LM authentication in the Registry.

   C. Stop the LM service in Windows XP.

   D. Disable the LSASS service in Windows XP.

33. You have captured some packets in Ethereal. You want to view only packets sent from 10.0.0.22. What filter will you apply?

   A. ip.equals 10.0.0.22

   B. ip = 10.0.0.22

   C. ip.address = 10.0.0.22

   D. ip.src == 10.0.0.22

34. What does FIN in a TCP flag define?

   A. Used to abort a TCP connection abruptly

   B. Used to close a TCP connection

   C. Used to acknowledge receipt of a previous packet or transmission

   D. Used to indicate the beginning of a TCP connection

35. What does ICMP (type 11, code 0) denote?

   A. Time Exceeded

   B. Source Quench

   C. Destination Unreachable

   D. Unknown Type

Answers to Assessment Test

1. C. Replay attacks involve capturing passwords, most likely encrypted, and playing them back to fake authentication. For more information, see Chapter 4.

2. A. An LM hash splits a password into two sections. If the password is 7 characters or less, then the blank portion of the password will always be a hex value of AAD3B435B51404EE. 0x preceding the value indicates it is in Hex. For more information, see Chapter 4.

3. A,B,C,D. A dictionary word can always be broken using brute force. For more information, see Chapter 4.

4. D. The CANSPAM Act is an acronym for Controlling the Assault of Non-Solicited Pornography and Marketing Act; the act attempts to prevent unsolicited spam. For more information, see Chapter 1.

5. A. Network-Based Application Recognition is a Cisco IOS mechanism for controlling traffic through network ingress points. For more information, see Chapter 6.

6. B. A way of locating Hotmail messages in Ethereal is to use a filter of email and Reply-to to find actual email messages. For more information, see Chapter 6.

7. A. In a Smurf attack a large amount of ICMP echo request (ping) traffic is send to an IP broadcast address, with a spoofed source IP address of the intended victim. IRC servers are commonly used to perpetuate this attack so they are considered primary victims. For more information, see Chapter 7.

8. D. The DNS reflector and amplification type attacks DNS servers directly. By adding amplification to the attack, many hosts send the attack and results in a denial-of-service to the DNS servers. For more information, see Chapter 8.

9. A. TCP operates at the Transport layer, or Layer 4 of the OSI model, and consequently a TCP/IP session hijack occurs at the Transport layer. For more information, see Chapter 7.

10. D. Website cloaking is serving different web pages based on the source IP address of the user. For more information, see Chapter 8.

11. A. Basic Authentication uses cleartext passwords. For more information, see Chapter 8.

12. B. A protection against cross-site scripting is to secure the server scripts. For more information, see Chapter 8.

13. A. Machine Authentication would require the host system to have a domain account that would only be valid for corporate PCs. For more information, see Chapter 13.

14. C. Privilege escalation can be done through capturing and modifying cookies. For more information, see Chapter 8.

15. A,B,C,D. Installing service packs, personal firewall software, and antivirus signatures should all be done prior to using a new computer on the network. For more information, see Chapter 5.

16. A. Microsoft Baseline Security Analyzer is a patch management utility built into Windows for analyzing security. For more information, see Chapter 15.

17. D. POST should be used instead of GET for web page posts. For more information, see Chapter 8.

18. A,D. Stack- and heap-based are the two types of buffer overflow attacks. For more information, see Chapter 9.

19. C. Polymorphic shellcode changes by using the XOR process to encrypt and decrypt the shellcode. For more information, see Chapter 5.

20. A. Passwords are stored in the /shadow file in Linux. For more information, see Chapter 3.

21. B. IP fragmentation or session splicing is a way of defeating an IDS. For more information, see Chapter 13.

22. A. A message is encrypted with a user's private key so that only the user's public key can decrypt the signature and the user's identity can be verified. For more information, see Chapter 14.

23. A. Every company should have an Information Security Policy. For more information, see Chapter 15.

24. C. Netcat is a multiuse Unix utility for reading and writing across network connections. For more information, see Chapter 4.

25. D. Tripwire is a file and directory integrity checker. For more information, see Chapter 4.

26. B. nmap -sS creates a stealth scan and the -O switch performs operating system detection. For more information, see Chapter 3.

27. A. snort -c snort.conf indicates snort.conf is the config file containing snort rules. For more information, see Chapter 13.

28. E. strcat() does not perform bounds checking and creates a buffer overflow vulnerability. For more information, see Chapter 9.

29. C. SMB signing prevents SMB hijacking. For more information, see Chapter 4.

30. A. Disgruntled employees are the biggest threat to a network. For more information, see Chapter 1.

31. C. -O performs OS detection in Nmap. For more information, see Chapter 3.

32. B. LM authentication can be disabled in the Windows Registry. For more information, see Chapter 4.

33. D. ip.src== is the syntax to filter on a source IP address. For more information, see Chapter 6.

34. B. The FIN flag is used to close a TCP/IP connection. For more information, see Chapter 6.

35. A. ICMP Time Exceeded is type 11, code 0. For more information, see Chapter 3.

Chapter

1

Introduction to Ethical Hacking, Ethics, and Legality

CEH EXAM OBJECTIVES COVERED IN THIS CHAPTER:

- ✓ Understand ethical hacking terminology
- ✓ Define the job role of an ethical hacker
- ✓ Understand the different phases involved in ethical hacking
- ✓ Identify different types of hacking technologies
- ✓ List the five stages of ethical hacking
- ✓ What is hacktivism?
- ✓ List different types of hacker classes
- ✓ Define the skills required to become an ethical hacker
- ✓ What is vulnerability research?
- ✓ Describe the ways of conducting ethical hacking
- ✓ Understand the legal implications of hacking
- ✓ Understand 18 USC §1030 US federal law

Most people think hackers have extraordinary skill and knowledge that allow them to hack into computer systems and find valuable information. The term *hacker* conjures up images of a young computer whiz who types a few commands at a computer screen—and poof! The computer spits out passwords, account numbers, or other confidential data. In reality, a good hacker, or security professional acting as an ethical hacker, just has to understand how a computer system works and know what tools to employ in order to find a security weakness. This book will teach you the same techniques and software tools that many hackers use to gather valuable data and attack computer systems.

The realm of hackers and how they operate is unknown to most computer and security professionals. Hackers use specialized computer software tools to gain access to information. By learning the same skills and employing the software tools used by hackers, you will be able to defend your computer networks and systems against malicious attacks.

The goal of this first chapter is to introduce you to the world of the hacker and to define the terminology used in discussing computer security. To be able to defend against malicious hackers, security professionals must first understand how to employ ethical hacking techniques. This book will detail the tools and techniques used by hackers so that you can use those tools to identify potential risks in your systems. This book will guide you through the hacking process as a *good guy*.

Most ethical hackers are in the business of hacking for profit, an activity known as *penetration testing*, or *pen testing* for short. Pen testing is usually conducted by a security professional to identify security risks and vulnerabilities in systems and networks. The purpose of identifying risks and vulnerabilities is so that a countermeasure can be put in place and the risk mitigated to some degree. Ethical hackers are in the business of hacking and as such need to conduct themselves in a professional manner.

Additionally, state, country, or international laws must be understood and carefully considered prior to using hacking software and techniques. Staying within the law is a must for the ethical hacker. An ethical hacker is acting as a security professional when performing pen tests and must always act in a professional manner.

Defining Ethical Hacking

The next section will explain the purpose of ethical hacking and exactly what ethical hackers do. As mentioned earlier, ethical hackers must always act in a professional manner to differentiate themselves from malicious hackers. Gaining the trust of the client and taking all precautions to do no harm to their systems during a pen test are critical to being a professional. Another key component of ethical hacking is to always gain permission from the data owner prior to accessing the computer system. This is one of the ways ethical hackers can overcome the stereotype of hackers and gain the trust of clients.

The goals ethical hackers are trying to achieve in their hacking attempts will be explained as well in this section.

Understanding the Purpose of Ethical Hacking

When I tell people that I am an ethical hacker, I usually hear snickers and comments like "That's an oxymoron." Many people ask, "Can hacking be ethical?" Yes! That best describes what I do as a security professional. I use the same software tools and techniques as malicious hackers to find the security weakness in computer networks and systems. Then I apply the necessary fix or patch to prevent the malicious hacker from gaining access to the data. This is a never-ending cycle as new weaknesses are constantly being discovered in computer systems and patches are created by the software vendors to mitigate the risk of attack.

Ethical hackers are usually security professionals or network penetration testers who use their hacking skills and toolsets for defensive and protective purposes. Ethical hackers who are security professionals test their network and systems security for vulnerabilities using the same tools that a hacker might use to compromise the network. Any computer professional can learn the skills of ethical hacking.

The term *cracker* describes a hacker who uses their hacking skills and toolset for destructive or offensive purposes such as disseminating viruses or performing denial-of-service (DoS) attacks to compromise or bring down systems and networks. No longer just looking for fun, these hackers are sometimes paid to damage corporate reputations or steal or reveal credit card information, while slowing business processes and compromising the integrity of the organization.

    Another name for a cracker is a *malicious hacker.*

Hackers can be divided into three groups:

White Hats   Good guys, ethical hackers

Black Hats   Bad guys, malicious hackers

Gray Hats   Good or bad hacker; depends on the situation

Ethical hackers usually fall into the white-hat category, but sometimes they're former gray hats who have become security professionals and who *now* use their skills in an ethical manner.

White Hats

White hats are the good guys, the ethical hackers who use their hacking skills for defensive purposes. White-hat hackers are usually security professionals with knowledge of hacking and the hacker toolset and who use this knowledge to locate weaknesses and implement countermeasures. White-hat hackers are prime candidates for the exam. White hats are those who hack with permission from the data owner. It is critical to get permission prior to beginning any hacking activity. This is what makes a security professional a white hat versus a malicious hacker who cannot be trusted.

Black Hats

Black hats are the bad guys: the malicious hackers or *crackers* who use their skills for illegal or malicious purposes. They break into or otherwise violate the system integrity of remote systems, with malicious intent. Having gained unauthorized access, black-hat hackers destroy vital data, deny legitimate users service, and just cause problems for their targets. Black-hat hackers and crackers can easily be differentiated from white-hat hackers because their actions are malicious. This is the traditional definition of a hacker and what most people consider a hacker to be.

Gray Hats

Gray hats are hackers who may work offensively or defensively, depending on the situation. This is the dividing line between hacker and cracker. Gray-hat hackers may just be interested in hacking tools and technologies and are not malicious black hats. Gray hats are self-proclaimed ethical hackers, who are interested in hacker tools mostly from a curiosity standpoint. They may want to highlight security problems in a system or educate victims so they secure their systems properly. These hackers are doing their "victims" a favor. For instance, if a weakness is discovered in a service offered by an investment bank, the hacker is doing the bank a favor by giving the bank a chance to rectify the vulnerability.

From a more controversial point of view, some people consider the act of hacking itself to be unethical, like breaking and entering. But the belief that "ethical" hacking excludes destruction at least moderates the behavior of people who see themselves as "benign" hackers. According to this view, it may be one of the highest forms of "hackerly" courtesy to break into a system and then explain to the system operator exactly how it was done and how the hole can be plugged; the hacker is acting as an unpaid—and unsolicited—*tiger team* (a group that conducts security audits for hire). This approach has gotten many ethical hackers in legal trouble. Make sure you know the law and your legal liabilities when engaging in ethical hacking activity.

Many self-proclaimed ethical hackers are trying to break into the security field as consultants. Most companies don't look favorably on someone who appears on their doorstep with confidential data and offers to "fix" the security holes "for a price." Responses range from "thank you for this information, we'll fix the problem" to calling the police to arrest the self-proclaimed ethical hacker.

The difference between white hats and gray hats is that *permission* word. Although gray hats might have good intentions, without the correct permission they can no longer be considered ethical.

Now that you understand the types of hackers, let's look at what hackers do. This may seem simple—they hack into computer systems—but sometimes it's not that simple or nebulous. There is a process that should be followed and information that needs to be documented. In the next section, we'll look at what hackers, and most importantly ethical hackers, do.

What Do Ethical Hackers Do?

Ethical hackers are motivated by different reasons, but their purpose is usually the same as that of crackers: they're trying to determine what an intruder can see on a targeted network or system, and what the hacker can do with that information. This process of testing the security of a system or network is known as a *penetration test,* or *pen test.*

Hackers break into computer systems. Contrary to widespread myth, doing this doesn't usually involve a mysterious leap of hackerly brilliance, but rather persistence and the dogged repetition of a handful of fairly well-known tricks that exploit common weaknesses in the security of target systems. A pen test is no more than just performing those same steps with the same tools used by a malicious hacker to see what data could be exposed using hacking tools and techniques.

Many ethical hackers detect malicious hacker activity as part of the security team of an organization tasked with defending against malicious hacking activity. When hired, an ethical hacker asks the organization what is to be protected, from whom, and what resources the company is willing to expend in order to gain protection. A penetration test plan can then be built around the data that needs to be protected and potential risks.

Documenting the results of various tests is critical in producing the end product of the pen test: the pen test report. Taking screenshots of potentially valuable information or saving log files is critical to presenting the findings to a client in a pen test report. The pen test report is a compilation of all the potential risks in a computer or system. More detail about the contents of the pen test report will be covered in the last chapter of this book.

Goals Attackers Try to Achieve

Whether perpetuated by an ethical hacker or malicious hacker, all attacks are an attempt to breach computer system security. Security consists of four basic elements:

- Confidentiality
- Authenticity
- Integrity
- Availability

A hacker's goal is to exploit vulnerabilities in a system or network to find a weakness in one or more of the four elements of security. For example, in performing a *denial-of-service (DoS)* attack, a hacker attacks the *availability* elements of systems and networks. Although a DoS attack can take many forms, the main purpose is to use up system resources or bandwidth. A flood of incoming messages to the target system essentially forces it to shut down, thereby denying service to legitimate users of the system. Although the media focuses on the target of DoS attacks, in reality such attacks have many victims—the final target and the systems the intruder controls.

Information theft, such as stealing passwords or other data as it travels in cleartext across trusted networks, is a *confidentiality* attack, because it allows someone other than the intended recipient to gain access to the data. This theft isn't limited to data on network servers. Laptops, disks, and backup tapes are all at risk. These company-owned devices are loaded with confidential information and can give a hacker information about the security measures in place at an organization.

Bit-flipping attacks are considered *integrity* attacks because the data may have been tampered with in transit or at rest on computer systems; therefore, system administrators are unable to verify the data is as the sender intended it. A bit-flipping attack is an attack on a cryptographic cipher: the attacker changes the cipher text in such a way as to result in a predictable change of the plain text, although the attacker doesn't learn the plain text itself. This type of attack isn't directed against the cipher but against a message or series of messages. In the extreme, this can become a DoS attack against all messages on a particular channel using that cipher. The attack is especially dangerous when the attacker knows the format of the message. When a bit-flipping attack is applied to digital signatures, the attacker may be able to change a promissory note stating "I owe you $10.00" into one stating "I owe you $10,000."

MAC address spoofing is an *authentication* attack because it allows an unauthorized device to connect to the network when Media Access Control (MAC) filtering is in place, such as on a wireless network. By spoofing the MAC address of a legitimate wireless station, an intruder can take on that station's identity and use the network.

An Ethical Hacker's Skill Set

Ethical hackers who stay a step ahead of malicious hackers must be computer systems experts who are very knowledgeable about computer programming, networking, and operating systems. In-depth knowledge about highly targeted platforms (such as Windows, Unix, and Linux) is also a requirement. Patience, persistence, and immense perseverance are important qualities for ethical hackers because of the length of time and level of concentration required for most attacks to pay off. Networking, web programming, and database skills are all useful in performing ethical hacking and vulnerability testing.

Most ethical hackers are well rounded with wide knowledge on computers and networking. In some cases, an ethical hacker will act as part of a "tiger team" who has been hired to test network and computer systems and find vulnerabilities. In this case, each member of the team will have distinct specialties, and the ethical hacker may need more specialized skills in one area of computer systems and networking. Most ethical hackers are knowledgeable about security areas and related issues but don't necessarily have a strong command of the countermeasures that can prevent attacks.

Ethical Hacking Terminology

Being able to understand and define terminology is an important part of a CEH's responsibility. This terminology is how security professionals acting as ethical hackers communicate. This "language" of hacking is necessary as a foundation to the follow-on concepts in later chapters of this book. In this section, we'll discuss a number of terms you need to be familiar with for the CEH certification exam:

Threat   An environment or situation that could lead to a potential breach of security. Ethical hackers look for and prioritize threats when performing a security analysis. Malicious hackers and their use of software and hacking techniques are themselves threats to an organization's information security.

Exploit   A piece of software or technology that takes advantage of a bug, glitch, or vulnerability, leading to unauthorized access, privilege escalation, or denial of service on a computer system. Malicious hackers are looking for exploits in computer systems to open the door to an initial attack. Most exploits are small strings of computer code that, when executed on a system, expose vulnerability. Experienced hackers create their own exploits, but it is not necessary to have any programming skills to be an ethical hacker as many hacking software programs have ready-made exploits that can be launched against a computer system or network. An exploit is a defined way to breach the security of an IT system through a vulnerability.

Vulnerability   The existence of a software flaw, logic design, or implementation error that can lead to an unexpected and undesirable event executing bad or damaging instructions to the system. Exploit code is written to target a vulnerability and cause a fault in the system in order to retrieve valuable data.

Target of Evaluation (TOE)   A system, program, or network that is the subject of a security analysis or attack. Ethical hackers are usually concerned with high-value TOEs, systems that contain sensitive information such as account numbers, passwords, Social Security numbers, or other confidential data. It is the goal of the ethical hacker to test hacking tools against the high-value TOEs to determine the vulnerabilities and patch them to protect against exploits and exposure of sensitive data.

Attack   An attack occurs when a system is compromised based on a vulnerability. Many attacks are perpetuated via an exploit. Ethical hackers use tools to find systems that may be vulnerable to an exploit because of the operating system, network configuration, or applications installed on the systems, and to prevent an attack.

There are two primary methods of delivering exploits to computer systems:

Remote   The exploit is sent over a network and exploits security vulnerabilities without any prior access to the vulnerable system. Hacking attacks against corporate computer systems or networks initiated from the outside world are considered remote. Most people think of this type of attack when they hear the term *hacker*, but in reality most attacks are in the next category.

Local   The exploit is delivered directly to the computer system or network, which requires prior access to the vulnerable system to increase privileges. Information security policies should be created in such a way that only those who need access to information should be allowed access and they should have the lowest level of access to perform their job function. These concepts are commonly referred as "need to know" and "least privilege" and, when used properly, would prevent local exploits. Most hacking attempts occur from within an organization and are perpetuated by employees, contractors, or others in a trusted position. In order for an insider to launch an attack, they must have higher privileges than necessary based on the concept of "need to know." This can be accomplished by privilege escalation or weak security safeguards.

The Phases of Ethical Hacking

The process of ethical hacking can be broken down into five distinct phases. Later in this book, hacking software programs and tools will be categorized into each of these steps.

An ethical hacker follows processes similar to those of a malicious hacker. The steps to gain and maintain entry into a computer system are similar no matter what the hacker's intentions are. Figure 1.1 illustrates the five phases that hackers generally follow in hacking a computer system.

FIGURE 1.1   Phases of hacking

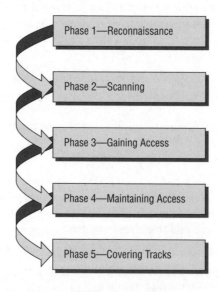

Phase 1—Reconnaissance

Phase 2—Scanning

Phase 3—Gaining Access

Phase 4—Maintaining Access

Phase 5—Covering Tracks

Phase 1: Passive and Active Reconnaissance

Passive reconnaissance involves gathering information about a potential target without the targeted individual's or company's knowledge. Passive reconnaissance can be as simple as watching a building to identify what time employees enter the building and when they leave. However, most reconnaissance is done sitting in front of a computer.

When hackers are looking for information on a potential target, they commonly run an Internet search on an individual or company to gain information. I'm sure many of you have performed the same search on your own name or a potential employer, or just to gather information on a topic. This process when used to gather information regarding a TOE is generally called *information gathering.* Social engineering and dumpster diving are also considered passive information-gathering methods. These two methods will be discussed in more detail later in this chapter.

Sniffing the network is another means of passive reconnaissance and can yield useful information such as IP address ranges, naming conventions, hidden servers or networks, and other available services on the system or network. Sniffing network traffic is similar to building monitoring: a hacker watches the flow of data to see what time certain transactions take place and where the traffic is going. Sniffing network traffic is a common hook for many ethical hackers. Once they use some of the hacking tools and are able to see all the data that is transmitted in the clear over the communication networks, they are eager to learn and see more.

Sniffing tools are simple and easy to use and yield a great deal of valuable information. An entire chapter in this book (Chapter 6, "Gathering Data from Networks: Sniffers") is dedicated to these tools, which literally let you see all the data that is transmitted on the network. Many times this includes usernames and passwords and other sensitive data. This is usually quite an eye-opening experience for many network administrators and security professionals and leads to serious security concerns.

Active reconnaissance involves probing the network to discover individual hosts, IP addresses, and services on the network. This process involves more risk of detection than passive reconnaissance and is sometimes called *rattling the doorknobs.* Active reconnaissance can give a hacker an indication of security measures in place (is the front door locked?), but the process also increases the chance of being caught or at least raising suspicion. Many software tools that perform active reconnaissance can be traced back to the computer that is running the tools, thus increasing the chance of detection for the hacker.

Both passive and active reconnaissance can lead to the discovery of useful information to use in an attack. For example, it's usually easy to find the type of web server and the operating system (OS) version number that a company is using. This information may enable a hacker to find a vulnerability in that OS version and exploit the vulnerability to gain more access.

Phase 2: Scanning

Scanning involves taking the information discovered during reconnaissance and using it to examine the network. Tools that a hacker may employ during the scanning phase include

- Dialers
- Port scanners
- Internet Control Message Protocol (ICMP) scanners

- Ping sweeps
- Network mappers
- Simple Network Management Protocol (SNMP) sweepers
- Vulnerability scanners

Hackers are seeking any information that can help them perpetrate an attack on a target, such as the following:

- Computer names
- Operating system (OS)
- Installed software
- IP addresses
- User accounts

 The methods and tools used in scanning are discussed in detail in Chapter 3, "Gathering Network and Host Information: Scanning and Enumeration."

Phase 3: Gaining Access

Phase 3 is when the real hacking takes place. Vulnerabilities exposed during the reconnaissance and scanning phase are now exploited to gain access to the target system. The hacking attack can be delivered to the target system via a local area network (LAN), either wired or wireless; local access to a PC; the Internet; or offline. Examples include stack-based buffer overflows, denial of service, and session hijacking. These topics will be discussed in later chapters. Gaining access is known in the hacker world as *owning* the system because once a system has been hacked, the hacker has control and can use that system as they wish.

Phase 4: Maintaining Access

Once a hacker has gained access to a target system, they want to keep that access for future exploitation and attacks. Sometimes, hackers *harden* the system from other hackers or security personnel by securing their exclusive access with backdoors, rootkits, and Trojans. Once the hacker owns the system, they can use it as a base to launch additional attacks. In this case, the owned system is sometimes referred to as a *zombie* system.

Phase 5: Covering Tracks

Once hackers have been able to gain and maintain access, they cover their tracks to avoid detection by security personnel, to continue to use the owned system, to remove evidence of hacking, or to avoid legal action. Hackers try to remove all traces of the attack, such as log files or intrusion detection system (IDS) alarms. Examples of activities during this phase of the attack include

- Steganography
- Using a tunneling protocol
- Altering log files

Steganography, using tunneling protocols, and altering log files for purposes of hacking will be discussed in later chapters.

Identifying Types of Hacking Technologies

Many methods and tools exist for locating vulnerabilities, running exploits, and compromising systems. Once vulnerabilities are found in a system, a hacker can exploit that vulnerability and install malicious software. Trojans, backdoors, and rootkits are all forms of malicious software, or *malware*. Malware is installed on a hacked system after a vulnerability has been exploited.

Buffer overflows and SQL injection are two other methods used to gain access into computer systems. Buffer overflows and SQL injection are used primarily against application servers that contain databases of information.

These technologies and attack methods will each be discussed in later chapters. Many are so complex that an entire chapter (Chapter 9, "Attacking Applications: SQL Injection and Buffer Overflows") is devoted to explaining the attack and applicable technologies.

Most hacking tools exploit weaknesses in one of the following four areas:

Operating Systems Many system administrators install operating systems with the default settings, resulting in potential vulnerabilities that remain unpatched.

Applications Applications usually aren't thoroughly tested for vulnerabilities when developers are writing the code, which can leave many programming flaws that a hacker can exploit. Most application development is "feature-driven," meaning programmers are under a deadline to turn out the most robust application in the shortest amount of time.

Shrink-Wrap Code Many off-the-shelf programs come with extra features the common user isn't aware of, and these features can be used to exploit the system. The macros in Microsoft Word, for example, can allow a hacker to execute programs from within the application.

Misconfigurations Systems can also be misconfigured or left at the lowest common security settings to increase ease of use for the user; this may result in vulnerability and an attack.

 This book will cover all these technologies and hacking tools in depth in later chapters. It's necessary to understand the types of attacks and basics of security before you learn all the technologies associated with an attack.

Identifying Types of Ethical Hacks

Ethical hackers use many different methods to breach an organization's security during a simulated attack or penetration test. Most ethical hackers have a specialty in one or a few of the following attack methods. In the initial discussion with the client, one of the questions that should be asked is whether there are any specific areas of concern, such as wireless networks or social engineering. This enables the ethical hacker to customize the test to be performed to the needs of the client. Otherwise, security audits should include attempts to access data from all of the following methods.

Here are the most common entry points for an attack:

Remote Network   A remote network hack attempts to simulate an intruder launching an attack over the Internet. The ethical hacker tries to break or find vulnerability in the outside defenses of the network, such as firewall, proxy, or router vulnerabilities. The Internet is thought to be the most common hacking vehicle, while in reality most organizations have strengthened their security defenses sufficient to prevent hacking from the public network.

Remote Dial-Up Network   A remote dial-up network hack tries to simulate an intruder launching an attack against the client's modem pools. *War dialing* is the process of repetitive dialing to find an open system and is an example of such an attack. Many organizations have replaced dial-in connections with dedicated Internet connections so this method is less relevant than it once was in the past.

Local Network   A local area network (LAN) hack simulates someone with physical access gaining additional unauthorized access using the local network. The ethical hacker must gain direct access to the local network in order to launch this type of attack. Wireless LANs (WLANs) fall in this category and have added an entirely new avenue of attack as radio waves travel through building structures. Because the WLAN signal can be identified and captured outside the building, hackers no longer have to gain physical access to the building and network to perform an attack on the LAN. Additionally, the huge growth of WLANs has made this an increasing source of attack and potential risk to many organizations.

Stolen Equipment   A stolen-equipment hack simulates theft of a critical information resource such as a laptop owned by an employee. Information such as usernames, passwords, security settings, and encryption types can be gained by stealing a laptop. This is usually a commonly overlooked area by many organizations. Once a hacker has access to a laptop authorized in the security domain, a lot of information, such as security configuration, can be gathered. Many times laptops disappear and are not reported quickly enough to allow the security administrator to lock that device out of the network.

Social Engineering   A social-engineering attack checks the security and integrity of the organization's employees by using the telephone or face-to-face communication to gather information for use in an attack. Social-engineering attacks can be used to acquire usernames, passwords, or other organizational security measures. Social-engineering scenarios usually consist of a hacker calling the help desk and talking the help desk employee into giving out confidential security information.

Physical Entry   A physical-entry attack attempts to compromise the organization's physical premises. An ethical hacker who gains physical access can plant viruses, Trojans, rootkits, or hardware key loggers (physical device used to record keystrokes) directly on systems in the target network. Additionally, confidential documents that are not stored in a secure location can be gathered by the hacker. Lastly, physical access to the building would allow a hacker to plant a rogue device such as a wireless access point on the network. These devices could then be used by the hacker to access the LAN from a remote location.

Understanding Testing Types

When performing a security test or penetration test, an ethical hacker utilizes one or more types of testing on the system. Each type simulates an attacker with different levels of knowledge about the target organization. These types are as follows:

Black Box   Black-box testing involves performing a security evaluation and testing with no prior knowledge of the network infrastructure or system to be tested. Testing simulates an attack by a malicious hacker outside the organization's security perimeter. Black-box testing can take the longest amount of time and most effort as no information is given to the testing team. Therefore, the information-gathering, reconnaissance, and scanning phases will take a great deal of time. The advantage of this type of testing is that it most closely simulates a real malicious attacker's methods and results. The disadvantages are primarily the amount of time and consequently additional cost incurred by the testing team.

White Box   White-box testing involves performing a security evaluation and testing with complete knowledge of the network infrastructure such as a network administrator would have. This testing is much faster than the other two methods as the ethical hacker can jump right to the attack phase, thus bypassing all the information-gathering, reconnaissance, and scanning phases. Many security audits consist of white-box testing to avoid the additional time and expense of black-box testing.

Gray Box   Gray-box testing involves performing a security evaluation and testing internally. Testing examines the extent of access by insiders within the network. The purpose of this test is to simulate the most common form of attack, those that are initiated from within the network. The idea is to test or audit the level of access given to employees or contractors and see if those privileges can be escalated to a higher level.

In addition to the various types of technologies a hacker can use, there are different types of attacks. Attacks can be categorized as either *passive* or *active*. Passive and active attacks are used on both network security infrastructures and on hosts. Active attacks alter the system or network they're attacking, whereas passive attacks attempt to gain information from the system. Active attacks affect the availability, integrity, and authenticity of data; passive attacks are breaches of confidentiality.

In addition to the active and passive categories, attacks are categorized as either *inside attacks* or *outside attacks*. Figure 1.2 shows the relationship between passive and active attacks, and inside and outside attacks. An attack originating from within the security perimeter of an organization is an inside attack and usually is caused by an "insider" who gains access to more resources than expected. An outside attack originates from a source outside the security perimeter, such as the Internet or a remote access connection.

FIGURE 1.2   Types of attacks

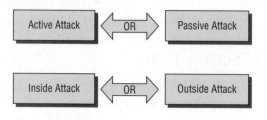

Most network security breaches originate from within an organization—usually from the company's own employees or contractors.

Security, Functionality, and Ease of Use Triangle

As a security professional, it's difficult to strike a balance between adding security barriers to prevent an attack and allowing the system to remain functional for users. The security, functionality, and ease of use triangle is a representation of the balance between security and functionality and the system's ease of use for users (see Figure 1.3). In general, as security increases, the system's functionality and ease of use decrease for users.

FIGURE 1.3   Security, functionality, and ease of use triangle

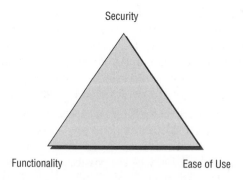

In an ideal world, security professionals would like to have the highest level of security on all systems; however, sometimes this isn't possible. Too many security barriers make it difficult for users to use the system and impede the system's functionality.

Real World Scenario

Usability vs. Security

Suppose that in order to gain entry to your office at work, you had to first pass through a guard checkpoint at the entrance to the parking lot to verify your license plate number, then show a badge as you entered the building, then use a passcode to gain entry to the elevator, and finally use a key to unlock your office door. You might feel the security checks were too stringent! Any one of those checks could cause you to be detained and consequently miss an important meeting—for example, if your car was in the repair shop and you had a rental car, or you forgot your key or badge to access the building, elevator, or office door. This is an example of tension between usability and security.

In many cases, if security checks are too stringent people will bypass them completely. For example, people might prop open a door so they can get back in the building. When I am doing a physical security audit during a penetration test, I just carry a box toward the door of the building; invariably people will hold the door open for someone carrying something. It is just human nature and is an easy way for a hacker to bypass security measures.

Vulnerability Research and Tools

Vulnerability research is the process of discovering vulnerabilities and design weaknesses that could lead to an attack on a system. Several websites and tools exist to aid the ethical hacker in maintaining a current list of vulnerabilities and possible exploits against systems or networks. It's essential that system administrators keep current on the latest viruses, Trojans, and other common exploits in order to adequately protect their systems and network. Also, by becoming familiar with the newest threats, an administrator can learn how to detect, prevent, and recover from an attack.

Vulnerability research is different from ethical hacking in that research is passively looking for possible security holes whereas ethical hacking is trying to see what information can be gathered. It is similar to an intruder casing a building and seeing a window at ground level and thinking "Well, maybe I can use that as an entry point." An ethical hacker would go and try to open the window to see if it is unlocked and provide access to the building. Next they would look around the room they entered through the building for any valuable information. Each entry into a system and additional level of access gives a foothold to additional exploits or attacks.

Ethical Hacking Report

The result of a network penetration test or security audit is an ethical hacking, or pen test report. Either name is acceptable, and they can be used interchangeably. This report details the results of the hacking activity, the types of tests performed, and the hacking methods used. The results are compared against the expectations initially agreed upon with the customer. Any vulnerabilities identified are detailed, and countermeasures are suggested. This document is usually delivered to the organization in hard-copy format, for security reasons.

The details of the ethical hacking report must be kept confidential, because they highlight the organization's security risks and vulnerabilities. If this document falls into the wrong hands, the results could be disastrous for the organization. It would essentially give someone the roadmap to all the security weaknesses of an organization.

How to Be Ethical

Ethical hacking is usually conducted in a structured and organized manner, usually as part of a penetration test or security audit. The depth and breadth of the systems and applications to be tested are usually determined by the needs and concerns of the client. Many ethical hackers are members of a tiger team. A tiger team works together to perform a full-scale test covering all aspects of network, physical, and systems intrusion.

The ethical hacker must follow certain rules to ensure that all ethical and moral obligations are met. An ethical hacker must do the following:

- Gain authorization from the client and have a signed contract giving the tester permission to perform the test.

- Maintain and follow a nondisclosure agreement (NDA) with the client in the case of confidential information disclosed during the test.

- Maintain confidentiality when performing the test. Information gathered may contain sensitive information. No information about the test or company confidential data should ever be disclosed to a third party.

- Perform the test up to but not beyond the agreed-upon limits. For example, DoS attacks should only be run as part of the test if they have previously been agreed upon with the client. Loss of revenue, goodwill, and worse could befall an organization whose servers or applications are unavailable to customers as a result of the testing.

The following steps (shown in Figure 1.4) are a framework for performing a security audit of an organization and will help to ensure that the test is conducted in an organized, efficient, and ethical manner:

1. Talk to the client, and discuss the needs to be addressed during the testing.
2. Prepare and sign NDA documents with the client.
3. Organize an ethical hacking team, and prepare a schedule for testing.
4. Conduct the test.

5. Analyze the results of the testing, and prepare a report.

6. Present the report findings to the client.

FIGURE 1.4 Security audit steps

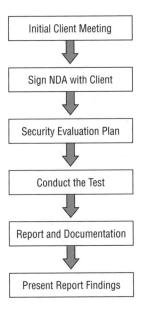

 In-depth penetration testing and security auditing information is discussed in EC-Council's Licensed Penetration Tester (LPT) certification.

Performing a Penetration Test

Many ethical hackers acting in the role of security professionals use their skills to perform security evaluations or penetration tests. These tests and evaluations have three phases, generally ordered as follows:

Preparation   This phase involves a formal agreement between the ethical hacker and the organization. This agreement should include the full scope of the test, the types of attacks (inside or outside) to be used, and the testing types: white, black, or gray box.

Conduct Security Evaluation   During this phase, the tests are conducted, after which the tester prepares a formal report of vulnerabilities and other findings.

Conclusion   The findings are presented to the organization in this phase, along with any recommendations to improve security.

Notice that the ethical hacker does not "fix" or patch any of the security holes they may find in the target of evaluation. This is a common misconception of performing security audits or penetration tests. The ethical hacker usually does not perform any patching or implementation of countermeasures. The final goal or deliverable is really the findings of the test and an analysis of the associated risks. The test is what leads to the findings in the final report and must be well documented.

Contrary to popular belief, ethical hackers performing a penetration test must be very organized and efficient, and they must document every finding by taking screenshots, copying the hacking tool output, or printing important log files. Ethical hackers must be very professional and present a well-documented report to be taken seriously in their profession. More information on performing a penetration test can be found in Chapter 15, "Performing a Penetration Test."

Defining Hacktivism

Hacktivism refers to hacking for a cause. These hackers usually have a social or political agenda. Their intent is to send a message through their hacking activity while gaining visibility for their cause and themselves.

Many of these hackers participate in activities such as defacing websites, creating viruses, and implementing DoS or other disruptive attacks to gain notoriety for their cause. Hacktivism commonly targets government agencies, political groups, and any other entities these groups or individuals perceive as "bad" or "wrong."

Keeping It Legal

An ethical hacker should know the penalties of unauthorized hacking into a system. No ethical hacking activities associated with a network-penetration test or security audit should begin until a signed legal document giving the ethical hacker express permission to perform the hacking activities is received from the target organization. Ethical hackers need to be judicious with their hacking skills and recognize the consequences of misusing those skills.

Computer crimes can be broadly categorized into two categories: crimes facilitated by a computer and crimes where the computer is the target.

The most important U.S. laws regarding computer crimes are described in the following sections. Although the CEH exam is international in scope, make sure you familiarize yourself with these U.S. statutes and the punishment for hacking. Remember, intent doesn't make a hacker above the law; even an ethical hacker can be prosecuted for breaking these laws.

Cyber Security Enhancement Act and SPY ACT

The Cyber Security Enhancement Act of 2002 mandates life sentences for hackers who "recklessly" endanger the lives of others. Malicious hackers who create a life-threatening situation by attacking computer networks for transportation systems, power companies, or other public services or utilities can be prosecuted under this law.

The Securely Protect Yourself Against Cyber Trespass Act of 2007 (SPY ACT) deals with the use of spyware on computer systems and essentially prohibits the following:

- Taking remote control of a computer when you have not been authorized to do so
- Using a computer to send unsolicited information to people (commonly known as spamming)
- Redirecting a web browser to another site that is not authorized by the user
- Displaying advertisements that cause the user to have to close out of the web browser (pop-up windows)
- Collecting personal information using keystroke logging

- Changing the default web page of the browser
- Misleading users so they click on a web page link or duplicating a similar web page to mislead a user

The SPY ACT is important in that it starts to recognize annoying pop-ups and spam as more than mere annoyances and as real hacking attempts. The SPY ACT lays a foundation for prosecuting hackers that use spam, pop-ups, and links in emails.

18 USC §1029 and 1030

The U.S. Code categorizes and defines the laws of the United States by titles. Title 18 details "Crimes and Criminal Procedure." Section 1029, "Fraud and related activity in connection with access devices," states that if you produce, sell, or use counterfeit access devices or telecommunications instruments with intent to commit fraud and obtain services or products with a value over $1,000, you have broken the law. Section 1029 criminalizes the misuse of computer passwords and other access devices such as token cards.

Section 1030, "Fraud and related activity in connection with computers," prohibits accessing protected computers without permission and causing damage. This statute criminalizes the spreading of viruses and worms and breaking into computer systems by unauthorized individuals.

 The full text of the Section 1029 and 1030 laws is included as an appendix in this book for your reference.

U.S. State Laws

In addition to federal laws, many states have their own laws associated with hacking and auditing computer networks and systems. When performing penetration testing, review the applicable state laws to ensure that you are staying on the right side of the law. In many cases, a signed testing contract and NDA will suffice as to the intent and nature of the testing.

The National Security Institute has a website listing all the state laws applicable to computer crimes. The URL is

```
http://nsi.org/Library/Compsec/computerlaw/statelaws.html
```

Federal Managers Financial Integrity Act

The Federal Managers Financial Integrity Act of 1982 (FMFIA) is basically a responsibility act to ensure that those managing financial accounts are doing so with the utmost responsibility and are ensuring the protection of the assets. This description can be construed to encompass all measurable safeguards to protect the assets from a hacking attempt. The act essentially ensures that

- Funds, property, and other assets are safeguarded against waste, loss, unauthorized use, or misappropriation.
- Costs are in compliance with applicable laws.

The FMFIA is important to ethical hacking as it places the responsibility on an organization for the appropriate use of funds and other assets. Consequently, this law requires management to be responsible for the security of the organization and to ensure the appropriate safeguards against hacking attacks.

Freedom of Information Act (FOIA)

The Freedom of Information Act (5 USC 552), or FoIA, makes many pieces of information and documents about organizations public. Most records and government documents can be obtained via the FoIA. Any information gathered using this act is fair game when you are performing reconnaissance and information gathering about a potential target.

Federal Information Security Management Act (FISMA)

The Federal Information Security Management Act (FISMA) basically gives ethical hackers the power to do the types of testing they perform and makes it a mandatory requirement for government agencies.

FISMA requires that each federal agency develop, document, and implement an agency-wide information security program to provide information security for the information and information systems that support the operations and assets of the agency, including those provided or managed by another agency, contractor, or other source. The information security program must include the following:

- Periodic assessments of the risk and magnitude of the harm that could result from the unauthorized access, use, disclosure, disruption, modification, or destruction of information and information systems that support the operations and assets of the agency
- Policies and procedures that are based on risk assessments, cost-effectively reduce information security risks to an acceptable level, and ensure that information security is addressed throughout the life cycle of each agency information system
- Subordinate plans for providing adequate information security for networks, facilities, information systems, or groups of information systems, as appropriate
- Security awareness training to inform personnel (including contractors and other users of information systems that support the operations and assets of the agency) of the information security risks associated with their activities and their responsibilities in complying with agency policies and procedures designed to reduce these risks

- Periodic testing and evaluation of the effectiveness of information security policies, procedures, and practices (including the management, operational, and technical controls of every agency information system identified in their inventory) with a frequency depending on risk, but no less than annually

- A process for planning, implementing, evaluating, and documenting remedial action to address any deficiencies in the information security policies, procedures, and practices of the agency

- Procedures for detecting, reporting, and responding to security incidents (including mitigating risks associated with such incidents before substantial damage is done and notifying and consulting with the federal information security incident response center, and as appropriate, law enforcement agencies, relevant Offices of Inspector General, and any other agency or office, in accordance with law or as directed by the President

- Plans and procedures to ensure continuity of operations for information systems that support the operations and assets of the agency

This act is guaranteed job security for ethical white hat hackers to perform continual security audits of government agencies and other organizations.

Privacy Act of 1974

The Privacy Act of 1974 (5 USC 552a) ensures nondisclosure of personal information and ensures that government agencies are not disclosing information without the prior written consent of the person whose information is in question.

USA PATRIOT Act

This act, with the official name Uniting and Strengthening America by Providing Appropriate Tools Required to Intercept and Obstruct Terrorism (USA PATRIOT) Act of 2001, gives the government the authority to intercept voice communications in computer hacking and other types of investigations. The Patriot Act was enacted primarily to deal with terrorist activity but can also be construed as a wiretap mechanism to discover and prevent hacking attempts.

Government Paperwork Elimination Act (GPEA)

The Government Paperwork Elimination Act (GPEA) of 1998 requires federal agencies to allow people the option of using electronic communications when interacting with a government agency. GPEA also encourages the use of electronic signatures. When valuable government information is stored in electronic format, the targets and stakes for hackers is increased.

Cyber Laws in Other Countries

Other countries each have their own applicable laws regarding protection of information and hacking attacks. When you're performing penetration testing for international organizations, it is imperative to check the laws of the governing nation to make sure the testing is legal in the country. With the use of the Internet and remote attacks, regional and international borders can be crossed very quickly. When you're performing an outside remote attack, the data may be stored on servers in another country and the laws of that country may apply. It is better to be safe than sorry, so do the research prior to engaging in a penetration test for an international entity. In some countries, laws may be more lenient than in the United States, and this fact may work to your advantage as you perform information gathering.

Summary

Ethical hacking is more than just running hacking tools and gaining unauthorized access to systems just to see what is accessible. When performed by a security professional, ethical hacking encompasses all aspects of reconnaissance and information gathering, a structured approach, and postattack analysis. Ethical hackers require in-depth knowledge of systems and tools as well as a great deal of patience and restraint to ensure no damage is done to the target systems. Hacking can be performed ethically and in fact is being mandated by government and the private sector to ensure systems security.

Exam Essentials

Understand essential hacker terminology.   Make sure you're familiar with and can define the terms *threat, exploit, vulnerability, target of evaluation,* and *attack.*

Understand the difference between ethical hackers and crackers.   Ethical hackers are security professionals who act defensively. Crackers are malicious hackers who choose to inflict damage on a target system.

Know the classes of hackers.   It's critical to know the differences among black-hat, white-hat, and gray-hat hackers for the exam. Know who the good guys are and who the bad guys are in the world of hacking.

Know the phases of hacking.   Passive and active reconnaissance, scanning, gaining access, maintaining access, and covering tracks are the five phases of hacking. Know the order of the phases and what happens during each phase.

Be aware of the types of attacks.   Understand the differences between active and passive and inside and outside attacks. The ability to be detected is the difference between active and passive attacks. The location of the attacker is the difference between inside and outside attacks.

Know the ethical hacking types.   Hackers can attack the network from a remote network, a remote dial-up network, or a local network, or through social engineering, stolen equipment, or physical access.

Understand the security testing types.   Ethical hackers can test a network using black-box, white-box, or gray-box testing techniques.

Know the contents of an ethical hacking report.   An ethical hacking report contains information on the hacking activities performed, network or system vulnerabilities discovered, and countermeasures that should be implemented.

Know the legal implications involved in hacking.   The Cyber Security Enhancement Act of 2002 can be used to prosecute ethical hackers who recklessly endanger the lives of others.

Be aware of the laws and punishment applicable to computer intrusion.   Title 18 sections 1029 and 1030 of the US Code carry strict penalties for hacking, no matter what the intent.

Review Questions

1. Which of the following statements best describes a white-hat hacker?

    A. Security professional

    B. Former black hat

    C. Former gray hat

    D. Malicious hacker

2. A security audit performed on the internal network of an organization by the network administration is also known as _____.

    A. Gray-box testing

    B. Black-box testing

    C. White-box testing

    D. Active testing

    E. Passive testing

3. What is the first phase of hacking?

    A. Attack

    B. Maintaining access

    C. Gaining access

    D. Reconnaissance

    E. Scanning

4. What type of ethical hack tests access to the physical infrastructure?

    A. Internal network

    B. Remote network

    C. External network

    D. Physical access

5. The security, functionality, and ease of use triangle illustrates which concept?

    A. As security increases, functionality and ease of use increase.

    B. As security decreases, functionality and ease of use increase.

    C. As security decreases, functionality and ease of use decrease.

    D. Security does not affect functionality and ease of use.

6. Which type of hacker represents the highest risk to your network?

    A. Disgruntled employees

    B. Black-hat hackers

    C. Gray-hat hackers

    D. Script kiddies

7. What are the three phases of a security evaluation plan? (Choose three answers.)
- **A.** Security evaluation
- **B.** Preparation
- **C.** Conclusion
- **D.** Final
- **E.** Reconnaissance
- **F.** Design security
- **G.** Vulnerability assessment

8. Hacking for a cause is called _____.
- **A.** Active hacking
- **B.** Hacktivism
- **C.** Activism
- **D.** Black-hat hacking

9. Which federal law is most commonly used to prosecute hackers?
- **A.** Title 12
- **B.** Title 18
- **C.** Title 20
- **D.** Title 2

10. When a hacker attempts to attack a host via the Internet, it is known as what type of attack?
- **A.** Remote attack
- **B.** Physical access
- **C.** Local access
- **D.** Internal attack

11. Which law allows for gathering of information on targets?
- **A.** Freedom of Information Act
- **B.** Government Paperwork Elimination Act
- **C.** USA PATRIOT Act of 2001
- **D.** Privacy Act of 1974

12. The Securely Protect Yourself Against Cyber Trespass Act prohibits which of the following? (Choose all that apply.)
- **A.** Sending spam
- **B.** Installing and using keystroke loggers
- **C.** Using video surveillance
- **D.** Implementing pop-up windows

13. Which step in the framework of a security audit is critical to protect the ethical hacker from legal liability?

   A. Talk to the client prior to the testing.

   B. Sign an ethical hacking agreement and NDA with the client prior to the testing.

   C. Organize an ethical hacking team and prepare a schedule prior to testing.

   D. Analyze the testing results and prepare a report.

14. Which of the following is a system, program, or network that is the subject of a security analysis?

   A. Owned system

   B. Vulnerability

   C. Exploited system

   D. Target of evaluation

15. Which term best describes a hacker who uses their hacking skills for destructive purposes?

   A. Cracker

   B. Ethical hacker

   C. Script kiddie

   D. White-hat hacker

16. MAC address spoofing is which type of attack?

   A. Encryption

   B. Brute-force

   C. Authentication

   D. Social engineering

17. Which law gives authority to intercept voice communications in computer hacking attempts?

   A. Patriot Act

   B. Telecommunications Act

   C. Privacy Act

   D. Freedom of Information Act

18. Which items should be included in an ethical hacking report? (Choose all that apply.)

   A. Testing type

   B. Vulnerabilities discovered

   C. Suggested countermeasures

   D. Router configuration information

19. Which type of person poses the most threat to an organization's security?

   A. Black-hat hacker

   B. Disgruntled employee

   C. Script kiddie

   D. Gray-hat hacker

20. Which of the following should be included in an ethical hacking report? (Choose all that apply.)

   A. Findings of the test

   B. Risk analysis

   C. Documentation of laws

   D. Ethics disclosure

Answers to Review Questions

1. A. White-hat hackers are "good" guys who use their skills for defensive purposes.

2. C. White-box testing is a security audit performed with internal knowledge of the systems.

3. D. Reconnaissance is gathering information necessary to perform the attack.

4. D. Physical access tests access to the physical infrastructure.

5. B. As security increases, it makes it more difficult to use and less functional.

6. A. Disgruntled employees have information that can allow them to launch a powerful attack.

7. A, B, C. The three phases of a security evaluation plan are preparation, security evaluation, and conclusion.

8. B. Hacktivism is performed by individuals who claim to be hacking for a political or social cause.

9. B. Title 18 of the US Code is most commonly used to prosecute hackers.

10. A. An attack from the Internet is known as a remote attack.

11. A. The Freedom of Information Act ensures public release of many documents and records and can be a rich source of information on potential targets.

12. A, B, D. Sending spam, installing and using keystroke loggers, and implementing pop-up windows are all prohibited by the SPY ACT.

13. B. Signing an NDA agreement is critical to ensuring the testing is authorized and the ethical hacker has the right to access the client's systems.

14. D. A target of evaluation is a system, program, or network that is the subject of a security analysis. It is the target of the ethical hacker's attacks.

15. A. A cracker is a hacker who uses their hacking skills for destructive purposes.

16. C. MAC address spoofing is an authentication attack used to defeat MAC address filters.

17. A. The Patriot Act gives authority to intercept voice communications in many cases, including computer hacking.

18. A, B, C. All information about the testing process, vulnerabilities discovered in the network or system, and suggested countermeasures should be included in the ethical hacking report.

19. B. Disgruntled employees pose the biggest threat to an organization's security because of the information and access that they possess.

20. A, B. Findings of the test and risk analysis should both be included in an ethical hacking report.

Chapter
2

Gathering Target Information: Reconnaissance, Footprinting, and Social Engineering

- ✓ Understand insider attacks
- ✓ Understand identity theft
- ✓ Describe phishing attacks
- ✓ Understand online scams
- ✓ Understand URL obfuscation
- ✓ Social-engineering countermeasures

The first step of the hacking process is gathering information on a target. Information gathering, also known as *footprinting*, is the process of gathering all available information about an organization. In the age of the Internet, information is available in bits and pieces from many different sources. Seemingly insignificant bits of information can be enlightening when pieced together—which is the purpose of information gathering. Footprinting can be effective in identifying high-value targets, which is what hackers will be looking for to focus their efforts.

A hacker uses information-gathering techniques to determine organizations' high-value targets, where the most valuable information resides. Not only does information gathering help identify where the information is located, but it also helps determine the best way to gain access to the targets. This information can then be used to identify and eventually hack target systems. Many people jump right into running hacking tools, but information gathering is critical in minimizing the chance of detection and assessing where to spend the most time and effort.

Social engineering can also be used to obtain more information about an organization, which can ultimately lead to an attack. Social engineering as an information-gathering tool is highly effective at exploiting the most vulnerable asset in an organization: the people. Human interaction and the willingness to give out information make people an excellent source of information. Good social-engineering techniques can speed up the hacking process and in most cases will yield information much more easily.

In this chapter, we'll look at information gathering as the first step in hacking target systems.

Reconnaissance

The term *reconnaissance* comes from the military and means to actively seek an enemy's intentions by collecting and gathering information about an enemy's composition and capabilities via direct observation, usually by scouts or military intelligence personnel trained in surveillance. In the world of ethical hacking, reconnaissance applies to the process of information gathering. Reconnaissance is a catchall term for watching the hacking target and gathering information about how, when, and where they do things. By identifying patterns of behavior, of people or systems, an enemy could find and exploit a loophole.

Real World Scenario

Using Reconnaissance to Gain Physical Access

Every weekday at 3 p.m. the Federal Express driver stops at the loading dock of a building where the offices of Medical Associates, Inc. are located. When the driver backs the truck up to the rear door of the building, he presses the buzzer and lets the security guard know he is at the door. Because the building's security personnel recognize the driver—as he comes to the door every day around the same time for pickup and drop-off—they remotely unlock the door and allow the driver to enter. A hacker is watching this process from a car in the parking lot and takes note of the procedure to gain physical entry into the building.

The next day, the hacker carries a large cardboard box toward the door just as the Federal Express driver has been given entry to the building. The driver naturally holds the door for the hacker because he is carrying what appears to be a heavy, large box. They exchange pleasantries and the hacker heads for the elevator up to Medical Associates' offices. The hacker leaves the box in the hallway of the building as he heads to his target office.

Once he reaches the front desk of the Medical Associates office, he asks to speak with the office manager whose name he previously looked up on the company website. The receptionist leaves her desk to go get the office manager, and the hacker reaches over the desk and plugs a USB drive containing hacking tools into the back of her computer. Because the computer is not locked with a password, he double-clicks on the USB drive icon and it silently installs the hacking software on the receptionist's computer. He removes the USB drive and quickly exits the office suite and building undetected.

This is an example of how reconnaissance and understanding the pattern of people's behavior can enable a hacker to gain physical access to a target—in this case the Medical Associates network via a Trojaned system—and circumvent security checkpoints.

Understanding Competitive Intelligence

Competitive intelligence means information gathering about competitors' products, marketing, and technologies. Most competitive intelligence is nonintrusive to the company being investigated and is benign in nature—it's used for product comparison or as a sales and marketing tactic to better understand how competitors are positioning their products or services. Several tools exist for the purpose of competitive intelligence gathering and can be used by hackers to gather information about a potential target.

In Exercises 2.1 through 2.3, I will show you how to use the SpyFu and KeywordSpy online tools to gather information about a target website. SpyFu and KeywordSpy will give keywords for websites. This allows you to perform some information gathering regarding a website. I use these two tools because they are easy to use and completely passive, meaning a potential target could not detect the information gathering.

Using SpyFu

To use the SpyFu online tool to gather competitive intelligence information:

1. Go to the www.spyfu.com website and enter the website address of the target in the search field:

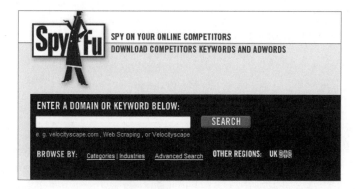

2. Review the report and determine valuable keywords, links, or other information.

Using KeywordSpy

To use the KeywordSpy online tool to gather competitive intelligence information:

1. Go to the www.keywordspy.com website and enter the website address of the target in the search field:

2. Review the report and determine valuable keywords, links, or other information.

Another useful tool to perform competitive intelligence and information gathering is the EDGAR database. This is a database of all the SEC filings for public companies. Information can be gathered by reviewing the SEC filings for contact names and addresses. In Exercise 2.3 I will show you how to use the EDGAR database for gathering information on potential targets.

EXERCISE 2.3

Using the EDGAR Database to Gather Information

1. Determine the company's stock symbol using Google.

2. Open a web browser to www.sec.gov.

3. On the right side of the page, click the link EDGAR Filers.

4. Click the Search For Filings menu and enter the company name or stock symbol to search the filings for information. You can learn, for example, where the company is registered and who reported the filing.

5. Use the Yahoo! yellow pages (http://yp.yahoo.com) to see if an address or phone number is listed for any of the employee names you have located.

6. Use Google Groups and job-posting websites to search on the names you have found. Are there any IT jobs posted or other information in the newsgroups that would indicate the type of network or systems the organization has?

The website www.Netcraft.com is another good source for passive information gathering. The website will attempt to determine the operating system and web server version running on a web server. This tool will be further discussed in the following chapter.

Information-Gathering Methodology

Information gathering can be broken into seven logical steps (see Figure 2.1). Footprinting is performed during the first two steps of unearthing initial information and locating the network range.

FIGURE 2.1   Seven steps of information gathering

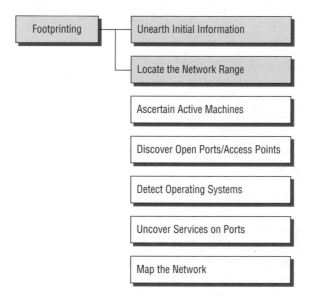

The other information-gathering steps are covered in Chapter 3, "Gathering Network and Host Information: Scanning and Enumeration."

Footprinting

Footprinting is defined as the process of creating a blueprint or map of an organization's network and systems. Information gathering is also known as footprinting an organization. Footprinting begins by determining the target system, application, or physical location of the target. Once this information is known, specific information about the organization is gathered using nonintrusive methods. For example, the organization's own web page may provide a personnel directory or a list of employee bios, which may prove useful if the hacker needs to use a social-engineering attack to reach the objective.

The information the hacker is looking for during the footprinting phase is anything that gives clues as to the network architecture, server, and application types where valuable data is stored. Before an attack or exploit can be launched, the operating system and version as well as application types must be uncovered so the most effective attack can be launched against the target. Here are some of the pieces of information to be gathered about a target during footprinting:

- Domain name
- Network blocks
- Network services and applications
- System architecture
- Intrusion detection system
- Authentication mechanisms
- Specific IP addresses
- Access control mechanisms
- Phone numbers
- Contact addresses

Once this information is compiled, it can give a hacker better insight into the organization, where valuable information is stored, and how it can be accessed.

Footprinting Tools

Footprinting can be done using hacking tools, either applications or websites, which allow the hacker to locate information passively. By using these footprinting tools, a hacker can gain some basic information on, or "footprint," the target. By first footprinting the target, a hacker can eliminate tools that will not work against the target systems or network. For example, if a graphics design firm uses all Macintosh computers, then all hacking software that targets Windows systems can be eliminated. Footprinting not only speeds up the hacking process by eliminating certain toolsets but also minimizes the chance of detection as fewer hacking attempts can be made by using the right tool for the job.

For the exercises in this chapter, you will perform reconnaissance and information gathering on a target company. I recommend you use your own organization, but because these tools are passive, any organization name can be used.

Some of the common tools used for footprinting and information gathering are as follows:

- Domain name lookup
- Whois
- NSlookup
- Sam Spade

Before we discuss these tools, keep in mind that open source information can also yield a wealth of information about a target, such as phone numbers and addresses. Performing Whois requests, searching domain name system (DNS) tables, and using other lookup web tools are forms of open source footprinting. Most of this information is fairly easy to get and legal to obtain.

Footprinting a Target

Footprinting is part of the preparatory preattack phase and involves accumulating data regarding a target's environment and architecture, usually for the purpose of finding ways to intrude into that environment. Footprinting can reveal system vulnerabilities and identify the ease with which they can be exploited. This is the easiest way for hackers to gather information about computer systems and the companies they belong to. The purpose of this preparatory phase is to learn as much as you can about a system, its remote access capabilities, its ports and services, and any specific aspects of its security.

Using Google to Gather Information

A hacker may also do a Google search or a Yahoo! People search to locate information about employees or the organization itself.

The Google search engine can be used in creative ways to perform information gathering. The use of the Google search engine to retrieve information has been termed Google hacking. Go to http://groups.google.com to search the Google newsgroups. The following commands can be used to have the Google search engine gather target information:

site   Searches a specific website or domain. Supply the website you want to search after the colon.

filetype   Searches only within the text of a particular type of file. Supply the file type you want to search after the colon. Don't include a period before the file extension.

link   Searches within hyperlinks for a search term and identifies linked pages.

cache   Identifies the version of a web page. Supply the URL of the site after the colon.

intitle   Searches for a term within the title of a document.

inurl   Searches only within the URL (web address) of a document. The search term must follow the colon.

For example, a hacker could use the following command to locate certain types of vulnerable web applications:

`INURL:["parameter="] with FILETYPE:[ext] and INURL:[scriptname]`

Or a hacker could use the search string `intitle: "BorderManager information alert"` to look for Novell BorderManager proxy/firewall servers.

> For more syntax on performing Google searches, visit `www.google.com/help/refinesearch.html`.

Blogs, newsgroups, and press releases are also good places to find information about the company or employees. Corporate job postings can provide information as to the type of servers or infrastructure devices a company may be using on its network.

Other information obtained may include identification of the Internet technologies being used, the operating system and hardware being used, active IP addresses, email addresses and phone numbers, and corporate policies and procedures.

> Generally, a hacker spends 90 percent of the time profiling and gathering information on a target and 10 percent of the time launching the attack.

Understanding DNS Enumeration

DNS enumeration is the process of locating all the DNS servers and their corresponding records for an organization. A company may have both internal and external DNS servers that can yield information such as usernames, computer names, and IP addresses of potential target systems.

NSlookup, DNSstuff, the American Registry for Internet Numbers (ARIN), and Whois can all be used to gain information that can then be used to perform DNS enumeration.

NSlookup and DNSstuff

One powerful tool you should be familiar with is NSlookup (see Figure 2.2). This tool queries DNS servers for record information. It's included in Unix, Linux, and Windows operating systems. Hacking tools such as Sam Spade also include NSlookup tools.

Building on the information gathered from Whois, you can use NSlookup to find additional IP addresses for servers and other hosts. Using the authoritative name server information from Whois (`AUTH1.NS.NYI.NET`), you can discover the IP address of the mail server.

FIGURE 2.2   NSlookup

DNS Lookup: eccouncil.org A record

Generated by www.DNSstuff.com at 13:01:51 GMT on 12 Apr 2006.

```
How I am searching:
Searching for eccouncil.org A record at 1.root-servers.net [198.32.64.12]: Got referral to TLD4.ULTRADNS.org. [took 94 ms]
Searching for eccouncil.org A record at TLD4.ULTRADNS.org. [199.7.67.1]: Got referral to AUTH2.NS.NYI.NET. [took 7 ms]
Searching for eccouncil.org A record at AUTH2.NS.NYI.NET. [66.111.15.154]: Reports eccouncil.org. [took 9 ms]

Answer:
```

Domain	Type	Class	TTL	Answer
eccouncil.org.	A	IN	3600	64.90.176.10
eccouncil.org.	NS	IN	3600	auth2.ns.nyi.net.
eccouncil.org.	NS	IN	3600	auth1.ns.nyi.net.
auth2.ns.nyi.net.	A	IN	7765	66.111.15.154

```
There is no need to refresh the page -- to see the DNS traversal, to make sure that all DNS servers are reporting
the same results, you can Click Here.

Note that these results are obtained in real-time, meaning that these are not cached results.
These results are what DNS resolvers all over the world will see right now (unless they have cached information).
```

The explosion of easy-to-use tools has made hacking easy, if you know which tools to use. DNSstuff is another of those tools. Instead of using the command-line NSlookup tool with its cumbersome switches to gather DNS record information, just access the website www.dnsstuff.com, and you can do a DNS record search online. Figure 2.3 shows a sample DNS record search on www.eccouncil.org using DNSstuff.com.

FIGURE 2.3   DNS record search of www.eccouncil.org

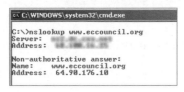

```
C:\WINDOWS\system32\cmd.exe

C:\>nslookup www.eccouncil.org
Server:
Address:

Non-authoritative answer:
Name:    www.eccouncil.org
Address: 64.90.176.10
```

This search reveals all the alias records for www.eccouncil.org and the IP address of the web server. You can even discover all the name servers and associated IP addresses.

The exploits available to you because you have this information are discussed in Chapter 4, "System Hacking: Password Cracking, Escalating Privileges, and Hiding Files."

Understanding Whois and ARIN Lookups

Whois evolved from the Unix operating system, but it can now be found in many operating systems as well as in hacking toolkits and on the Internet. This tool identifies who has registered domain names used for email or websites. A uniform resource locator (URL), such as www.Microsoft.com, contains the domain name (Microsoft.com) and a hostname or alias (www).

The Internet Corporation for Assigned Names and Numbers (ICANN) requires registration of domain names to ensure that only a single company uses a specific domain name. The Whois tool queries the registration database to retrieve contact information about the individual or organization that holds a domain registration.

Hacking Tool

SmartWhois is an information-gathering program that allows you to find all available information about an IP address, hostname, or domain, including country, state or province, city, name of the network provider, administrator, and technical support contact information. SmartWhois is a graphical version of the basic Whois program.

In Exercise 2.4, I will show you how to use a free Whois tool.

EXERCISE 2.4

Using Whois

To use the Whois tool to gather information on the registrar or a domain name:

1. Go to the DNSStuff.com website and scroll down to the free tools at the bottom of the page.

2. Enter your target company URL in the WHOIS Lookup field and click the WHOIS button.

3. Examine the results and determine the following:

     Registered address

     Technical and DNS contacts

     Contact email

EXERCISE 2.4 *(continued)*

Contact phone number

Expiration date

4. Visit the company website and see if the contact information from WHOIS matches up to any contact names, addresses, and email addresses listed on the website.

5. If so, use Google to search on the employee names or email addresses. You can learn the email naming convention used by the organization, and whether there is any information that should not be publicly available.

ARIN is a database that includes such information as the owners of static IP addresses. The ARIN database can be queried using the Whois tool, such as the one located at www.arin.net.

Figure 2.4 shows an ARIN Whois search for www.yahoo.com. Notice that addresses, emails, and contact information are all contained in this Whois search. This information can be used by an ethical hacker to find out who is responsible for a certain IP address and which organization owns that target system, or it can be used by a malicious hacker to perform a social-engineering attack against the organization. As a security professional, you need to be aware of the information available to the public in searchable databases such as ARIN and ensure that a malicious hacker can't use this information to launch an attack against the network.

FIGURE 2.4 ARIN output for www.Yahoo.com

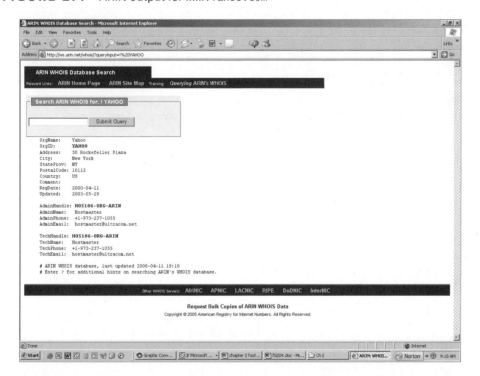

Be aware that other geographical regions outside North American have their own Internet registries, such as RIPE NCC (Europe, the Middle East, and parts of Central Asia), LACNIC (Latin American and Caribbean Internet Addresses Registry), and APNIC (Asia Pacific Network Information Centre).

Analyzing Whois Output

A simple way to run Whois is to connect to a website (for instance, www.networksolutions.com) and conduct the Whois search. Listing 2.1 is the output of a Whois search of the site www.eccouncil.org.

The contact names and server names in this book have been changed.

Listing 2.1

WHOIS OUTPUT FOR WWW.ECCOUNCIL.ORG

```
Domain ID:D81180127-LROR
Domain Name:ECCOUNCIL.ORG
Created On:14-Dec-2001 10:13:06 UTC
Last Updated On:19-Aug-2004 03:49:53 UTC
Expiration Date:14-Dec-2006 10:13:06 UTC
Sponsoring Registrar:Tucows Inc. (R11-LROR)
Status:OK
Registrant ID:tuTv2ItRZBMNd41A
```
Registrant Name: John Smith
```
Registrant Organization:International Council of E-Commerce Consultants
Registrant Street1:67 Wall Street, 22nd Floor
Registrant Street2:
Registrant Street3:
Registrant City:New York
Registrant State/Province:NY
Registrant Postal Code:10005-3198
Registrant Country:US
Registrant Phone:+1.2127098253
Registrant Phone Ext.:
Registrant FAX:+1.2129432300
```

```
Registrant FAX Ext.:
Registrant Email:forum@eccouncil.org
Admin ID:tus9DYvpp5mrbLNd
```
Admin Name: Susan Johnson
```
Admin Organization:International Council of E-Commerce Consultants
Admin Street1:67 Wall Street, 22nd Floor
Admin Street2:
Admin Street3:
Admin City:New York
Admin State/Province:NY
Admin Postal Code:10005-3198
Admin Country:US
Admin Phone:+1.2127098253
Admin Phone Ext.:
Admin FAX:+1.2129432300
Admin FAX Ext.:
Admin Email:ethan@eccouncil.org
Tech ID:tuE1cgAfi1VnFkpu
Tech Name:Jacob Eckel
Tech Organization:International Council of E-Commerce Consultants
Tech Street1:67 Wall Street, 22nd Floor
Tech Street2:
Tech Street3:
Tech City:New York
Tech State/Province:NY
Tech Postal Code:10005-3198
Tech Country:US
Tech Phone:+1.2127098253
Tech Phone Ext.:
Tech FAX:+1.2129432300
Tech FAX Ext.:
Tech Email:forum@eccouncil.org
```
Name Server: ns1.xyz.net
Name Server: ns2.xyz.net

Notice the four highlighted lines. The first shows the target company or person (as well as their physical address, email address, phone number, and so on). The next shows the administration or technical contact (and their contact information). The last two highlighted lines show the names of domain name servers.

Finding the Address Range of the Network

Every ethical hacker needs to understand how to find the network range and subnet mask of the target system. IP addresses are used to locate, scan, and connect to target systems. You can find IP addresses in Internet registries such as ARIN or the Internet Assigned Numbers Authority (IANA).

An ethical hacker may also need to find the geographic location of the target system or network. This task can be accomplished by tracing the route a message takes as it's sent to the destination IP address. You can use tools like traceroute, VisualRoute, and NeoTrace to identify the route to the target.

Additionally, as you trace your target network, other useful information becomes available. For example, you can obtain internal IP addresses of host machines; even the Internet IP gateway of the organization may be listed. These addresses can then be used later in an attack or further scanning processes.

Identifying Types of DNS Records

The following list describes the common DNS record types and their use:

A (Address)   Maps a hostname to an IP address

SOA (Start of Authority)   Identifies the DNS server responsible for the domain information

CNAME (Canonical Name)   Provides additional names or aliases for the address record

MX (Mail Exchange)   Identifies the mail server for the domain

SRV (Service)   Identifies services such as directory services

PTR (Pointer)   Maps IP addresses to hostnames

NS (Name Server)   Identifies other name servers for the domain

Using Traceroute in Footprinting

Traceroute is a packet-tracking tool that is available for most operating systems. It operates by sending an Internet Control Message Protocol (ICMP) echo to each hop (router or gateway) along the path, until the destination address is reached. When ICMP messages are sent back from the router, the time to live (TTL) is decremented by one for each router along the path. This allows a hacker to determine how many hops a router is from the sender.

One problem with using the traceroute tool is that it times out (indicated by an asterisk) when it encounters a firewall or a packet-filtering router. Although a firewall stops the traceroute tool from discovering internal hosts on the network, it can alert an ethical hacker to the presence of a firewall; then, techniques for bypassing the firewall can be used.

These techniques are part of system hacking, which is discussed in Chapter 4.

Sam Spade and many other hacking tools include a version of traceroute. The Windows operating systems use the syntax `tracert` *hostname* to perform a traceroute. Figure 2.5 is an example of traceroute output for a trace of www.yahoo.com.

FIGURE 2.5   Traceroute output for www.yahoo.com

```
Select C:\WINDOWS\system32\cmd.exe                                          _ □

C:\>tracert www.yahoo.com

Tracing route to www.yahoo.akadns.net [68.142.226.42]
over a maximum of 30 hops:

  1     1 ms     1 ms     1 ms   192.168.1.1
  2    55 ms    32 ms    10 ms
  3    27 ms     9 ms     9 ms
  4    30 ms     9 ms     9 ms   mrfddsrj02gex070003.rd.dc.cox.net [68.100.0.149]

  5    22 ms    11 ms    11 ms   mrfdbbrj02-ge020.rd.dc.cox.net [68.1.1.6]
  6    12 ms    11 ms    12 ms   ashbbbrj01-pos020100.r2.as.cox.net [68.1.1.232]

  7    14 ms    11 ms    13 ms   68.105.30.98
  8    43 ms    12 ms    12 ms   vlan260-msr2.re1.yahoo.com [216.115.96.173]
  9    28 ms    11 ms    10 ms   t-2-1.bas2.re2.yahoo.com [206.190.33.93]
 10    28 ms    11 ms    11 ms   p11.www.re2.yahoo.com [68.142.226.42]

Trace complete.
```

Notice in Figure 2.5 that the message first encounters the outbound ISP to reach the Yahoo! web server, and that the server's IP address is revealed as 68.142.226.42. Knowing this IP address enables the ethical hacker to perform additional scanning on that host during the scanning phase of the attack.

The `tracert` command identifies routers located en route to the destination's network. Because routers are generally named according to their physical location, `tracert` results help you locate these devices.

Hacking Tools

NeoTrace, VisualRoute, and VisualLookout are all packet-tracking tools with a GUI or visual interface. They plot the path the packets travel on a map and can visually identify the locations of routers and other internetworking devices. These tools operate similarly to traceroute and perform the same information gathering; however, they provide a visual representation of the results.

Understanding Email Tracking

Email-tracking programs allow the sender of an email to know whether the recipient reads, forwards, modifies, or deletes an email. Most email-tracking programs work by appending a domain name to the email address, such as readnotify.com. A single-pixel graphic file that isn't noticeable to the recipient is attached to the email. Then, when an action is performed on the email, this graphic file connects back to the server and notifies the sender of the action.

Hacking Tool

Visualware's eMailTrackerPro (www.emailtrackerpro.com/) and MailTracking (http://mailtracking.com/) are tools that allow an ethical hacker to track email messages. When you use these tools to send an email, forward an email, reply to an email, or modify an email, the resulting actions and tracks of the original email are logged. The sender is notified of all actions performed on the tracked email by an automatically generated email.

Understanding Web Spiders

Spammers and anyone else interested in collecting email addresses from the Internet can use *web spiders*. A web spider combs websites collecting certain information such as email addresses. The web spider uses syntax such as the @ symbol to locate email addresses and then copies them into a list. These addresses are then added to a database and may be used later to send unsolicited emails.

Web spiders can be used to locate all kinds of information on the Internet. A hacker can use a web spider to automate the information-gathering process. A method to prevent web spidering of your website is to put the robots.txt file in the root of your website with a listing of directories that you want to protect from crawling.

Social Engineering

Social engineering is a nontechnical method of breaking into a system or network. It's the process of deceiving users of a system and convincing them to perform acts useful to the hacker, such as giving out information that can be used to defeat or bypass security mechanisms. Social engineering is important to understand because hackers can use it to attack the human element of a system and circumvent technical security measures. This method can be used to gather information before or during an attack.

A social engineer commonly uses the telephone or Internet to trick people into revealing sensitive information or to get them to do something that is against the security policies of the organization. By this method, social engineers exploit the natural tendency of a person to trust their word, rather than exploiting computer security holes. It's generally agreed that users are the weak link in security; this principle is what makes social engineering possible.

The following is an example of social engineering recounted by Kapil Raina, currently a security expert at VeriSign, based on an actual workplace experience with a previous employer:

> One morning a few years back, a group of strangers walked into a large shipping firm and walked out with access to the firm's entire corporate network. How did they do it? By obtaining small amounts of access, bit by bit, from a number of different employees in that firm. First, they did research about the company for two days before even attempting to set foot on the premises. For example, they learned key employees' names by calling HR. Next, they pretended to lose their key to the front door, and a man let them in. Then they "lost" their identity badges when entering the third floor secured area, smiled, and a friendly employee opened the door for them.

> The strangers knew the CFO was out of town, so they were able to enter his office and obtain financial data off his unlocked computer. They dug through the corporate trash, finding all kinds of useful documents. They asked a janitor for a garbage pail in which to place their contents and carried all of this data out of the building in their hands. The strangers had studied the CFO's voice, so they were able to phone, pretending to be the CFO, in a rush, desperately in need of his network password. From there, they used regular technical hacking tools to gain super-user access into the system.

> In this case, the strangers were network consultants performing a security audit for the CFO without any other employees' knowledge. They were never given any privileged information from the CFO but were able to obtain all the access they wanted through social engineering.

The most dangerous part of social engineering is that companies with authentication processes, firewalls, virtual private networks, and network-monitoring software are still wide open to attacks, because social engineering doesn't assault the security measures directly. Instead, a social-engineering attack bypasses the security measures and goes after the human element in an organization.

The Art of Manipulation

Social engineering includes the acquisition of sensitive information or inappropriate access privileges by an outsider, based on the building of inappropriate trust relationships. The goal of a social engineer is to trick someone into providing valuable information or access to that information. Social engineering preys on qualities of human nature, such as the desire to be helpful, the tendency to trust people, and the fear of getting in trouble. Hackers who are able to blend in and appear to be a part of the organization are the most successful at social-engineering attacks. This ability to blend in is commonly referred to as the *art of manipulation*.

People are usually the weakest link in the security chain. A successful defense depends on having good policies in place and teaching employees to follow the policies. Social engineering is the hardest form of attack to defend against because a company can't protect itself with hardware or software alone.

Types of Social Engineering-Attacks

Social engineering can be broken into two common types:

Human-Based   Human-based social engineering refers to person-to-person interaction to retrieve the desired information. An example is calling the help desk and trying to find out a password.

Computer-Based   Computer-based social engineering refers to having computer software that attempts to retrieve the desired information. An example is sending a user an email and asking them to reenter a password in a web page to confirm it. This social-engineering attack is also known as *phishing*.

We'll look at each of these more closely in the following sections.

Human-Based Social Engineering

Human-based social engineering techniques can be broadly categorized as follows:

Impersonating an Employee or Valid User   In this type of social-engineering attack, the hacker pretends to be an employee or valid user on the system. A hacker can gain physical access by pretending to be a janitor, employee, or contractor. Once inside the facility, the hacker gathers information from trashcans, desktops, or computer systems.

Posing as an Important User   In this type of attack, the hacker pretends to be an important user such as an executive or high-level manager who needs immediate assistance to gain access to a computer system or files. The hacker uses intimidation so that a lower-level employee such as a help desk worker will assist them in gaining access to the system. Most low-level employees won't question someone who appears to be in a position of authority.

Using a Third Person   Using the third-person approach, a hacker pretends to have permission from an authorized source to use a system. This attack is especially effective if the supposed authorized source is on vacation or can't be contacted for verification.

Calling Technical Support   Calling tech support for assistance is a classic social-engineering technique. Help desk and technical support personnel are trained to help users, which makes them good prey for social-engineering attacks.

Shoulder Surfing   Shoulder surfing is a technique of gathering passwords by watching over a person's shoulder while they log in to the system. A hacker can watch a valid user log in and then use that password to gain access to the system.

Dumpster Diving   Dumpster diving involves looking in the trash for information written on pieces of paper or computer printouts. The hacker can often find passwords, filenames, or other pieces of confidential information.

A more advanced method of gaining illicit information is known as *reverse social engineering*. Using this technique, a hacker creates a persona that appears to be in a position of authority so that employees ask the hacker for information, rather than the other way around. For example, a hacker can impersonate a help desk employee and get the user to give them information such as a password.

 Real World Scenario

Social-Engineering Demonstration

The facilitator of a live Computer Security Institute demonstration showed the vulnerability of help desks when he dialed up a phone company, got transferred around, and reached the help desk. "Who's the supervisor on duty tonight?" "Oh, it's Betty." "Let me talk to Betty." [He's transferred.] "Hi Betty, having a bad day?" "No, why?" "Your systems are down." Betty said, "My systems aren't down, we're running fine." He said, "You better sign off." She signed off. He said, "Now sign on again." She signed on again. He said, "We didn't even show a blip, we show no change." He said, "Sign off again." She did. "Betty, I'm going to have to sign on as you here to figure out what's happening with your ID. Let me have your user ID and password."

So this senior supervisor at the help desk tells him her user ID and password. In a few minutes a hacker is able to get information that might have taken him days to get by capturing traffic and cracking the password. It is much easier to gain information by social engineering than by technical methods.

Computer-Based Social Engineering

Computer-based social-engineering attacks can include the following:

- Email attachments
- Fake websites
- Pop-up windows

Insider Attacks

If a hacker can't find any other way to hack an organization, the next best option is to infiltrate the organization by getting hired as an employee or finding a disgruntled employee to assist in the attack. Insider attacks can be powerful because employees have physical access and are able to move freely about the organization. An example might be someone posing as a delivery person by wearing a uniform and gaining access to a delivery room or loading dock. Another possibility is someone posing as a member of the cleaning crew who has access to the inside of the building and is usually able to move about the offices. As a last resort, a hacker might bribe or otherwise coerce an employee to participate in the attack by providing information such as passwords.

Identity Theft

A hacker can pose as an employee or steal the employee's identity to perpetrate an attack. Information gathered in dumpster diving or shoulder surfing in combination with creating fake ID badges can gain the hacker entry into an organization. Creating a persona that can enter the building unchallenged is the goal of identity theft.

Phishing Attacks

Phishing involves sending an email, usually posing as a bank, credit card company, or other financial organization. The email requests that the recipient confirm banking information or reset passwords or PINs. The user clicks the link in the email and is redirected to a fake website. The hacker is then able to capture this information and use it for financial gain or to perpetrate other attacks. Emails that claim the senders have a great amount of money but need your help getting it out of the country are examples of phishing attacks. These attacks prey on the common person and are aimed at getting them to provide bank account access codes or other confidential information to the hacker.

Online Scams

Some websites that make free offers or other special deals can lure a victim to enter a username and password that may be the same as those they use to access their work system. The hacker can use this valid username and password once the user enters the information in the website form.

Mail attachments can be used to send malicious code to a victim's system, which could automatically execute something like a software keylogger to capture passwords. Viruses, Trojans, and worms can be included in cleverly crafted emails to entice a victim to open the attachment. Mail attachments are considered a computer-based social-engineering attack.

Here is an example of an email that which tries to convince the receiver to open an unsafe attachment:

```
Mail server report.
```

```
Our firewall determined the e-mails containing worm copies are being sent from
your computer.
```

Nowadays it happens from many computers, because this is a new virus type (Network Worms).

Using the new bug in the Windows, these viruses infect the computer unnoticeably. After the penetrating into the computer the virus harvests all the e-mail addresses and sends the copies of itself to these e-mail addresses

Please install updates for worm elimination and your computer restoring.

Best regards,
Customer support service

Pop-up windows can also be used in computer-based engineering attacks, in a similar manner to email attachments. Pop-up windows with special offers or free stuff can encourage a user to unintentionally install malicious software.

URL Obfuscation

The URL (uniform resource locator) is commonly used in the address bar of a web browser to access a particular website. In lay terms, it is the website address. URL obfuscation consists of hiding a fake URL in what appear to be a legitimate website address. For example, a website of 204.13.144.2/Citibank may appear to be a legitimate web address for Citibank but in fact is not. URL obfuscation is used in phishing attacks and some online scams to make the scam seem more legitimate. A website address may be seen as an actual financial institution name or logo, but the link leads to a fake website or IP address. When users click the link, they're redirected to the hacker's site.

Addresses can be obfuscated in malicious links by the use of hexadecimal or decimal notations. For example, the address 192.168.10.5 looks like 3232238085 as a decimal. The same address looks like C0A80A05 in IP hex. This conversion requires that you divide 3232238085 by 16 multiple times. Each time the remainder reveals the address, starting from the least significant value.

Here's the explanation:

$3232238085/16 = 202014880.3125\ (.3125 \times 16 = 5)$

$202014880/16 = 12625930.0\ (.0 \times 16 = 0)$

$12625930/16 = 789120.625\ (.625 \times 16 = 10 = A)$

$789120/16 = 49320.0\ (.0 \times 16 = 0)$

$49320.0/16 = 3082.5\ (.5 \times 16 = 8)$

$3082/16 = 192.625\ (.625 \times 16 = 10 = A)$

$192/16 = 12 = C$

Social-Engineering Countermeasures

Knowing how to combat social engineering is critical for any certified ethical hacker. There are a number of ways to do this.

Documented and enforced security policies and security awareness programs are the most critical component in any information security program. Good policies and procedures aren't effective if they aren't taught and reinforced to employees. The policies need to be communicated to employees to emphasize their importance and then enforced by management. After receiving security awareness training, employees will be committed to supporting the security policies of the organization.

The corporate security policy should address how and when accounts are set up and terminated, how often passwords are changed, who can access what information, and how policy violations are to be handled. Also, the policy should spell out help desk procedures for the previous tasks as well as a process for identifying employees—for example, using an employee number or other information to validate a password change. The destruction of paper documents and physical access restrictions are additional areas the security policy should address. Lastly, the policy should address technical areas, such as use of modems and virus control.

One of the advantages of a strong security policy is that it removes the responsibility of employees to make judgment calls regarding a hacker's request. If the requested action is prohibited by the policy, the employee has guidelines for denying it.

The most important countermeasure for social engineering is employee education. All employees should be trained on how to keep confidential data safe. Management teams are involved in the creation and implementation of the security policy so that they fully understand it and support it throughout the organization. The company security awareness policy should require all new employees to go through a security orientation. Annual classes should be required to provide refreshers and updated information for employees.

Another way to increase involvement is through a monthly newsletter with security awareness articles.

Summary

In this chapter, you learned how to take the first steps toward ethical hacking. Information gathering, in the form of reconnaissance, footprinting, and social engineering, is necessary to learn as much about the target as possible. By following the information-gathering methodology, ethical hackers can ensure they are not missing any steps and valuable information. Time spent in the information-gathering phase is well worth it to speed up and produce successful hacking exploits.

Exam Essentials

Know how to search for a company's news, press releases, blogs, and newsgroup postings.
Search job postings from the target company or organization to determine system versions
and other vital pieces of information such as firewall or IDS types and server types. Google
hacking can be used to gather information from these locations, making it easy for a hacker
to quickly locate information about a target.

Use all available public resources to locate information about a target company and gather
data about its network and system security.

Use Yahoo! People search or other Internet search engines to find employees of the target
company.

Know how to query DNS for specific record information. Know how to use DNSstuff,
NSlookup, or Sam Spade to query a DNS server for record information, such as hosts and
IP addresses.

Understand how to perform Whois lookups for personal or company information. Know
how to use the ARIN, LACNIC, RIPE NCC, APNIC, and Whois databases to locate registrar and company contact information.

Know how to find the name of a target company's external and internal domain names.
You should be able to use the Whois and Sam Spade tools to locate the domain information
for a given company. Knowledge of the ARIN database is also necessary for the exam.

**Know how to physically locate a target company's web server and other network infra-
structure devices.** Use NeoTrace, VisualRoute, or VisualLookout to get a graphical view
of the route to a target company's network. These tools enable you to physically locate the
servers.

Know how to track email to or from a company. You should be able to use email tracking
programs to track an email to a target organization and gain additional information to be
used in an attack.

**Understand the difference between human-based and computer-based social-engineering
attacks.** Human-based social engineering uses nontechnical methods to initiate an attack,
whereas computer-based social engineering employs a computer.

Impersonation, posing as important user, the third-person approach, posing as technical
support, shoulder surfing, and dumpster diving are types of human-based social engineering.

Email attachments, fake websites, pop-up windows, and reverse social engineering are all
computer-based social-engineering methods.

Understand the importance of employee education. Educating employees on the signs of
social engineering and the company's security policy is key to preventing social-engineering
attacks.

Review Questions

1. Which are the four regional Internet registries?
   A. APNIC, PICNIC, NANIC, RIPE NCC
   B. APNIC, MOSTNIC, ARIN, RIPE NCC
   C. APNIC, PICNIC, NANIC, ARIN
   D. APNIC, LACNIC, ARIN, RIPE NCC

2. Which of the following is a tool for performing footprinting undetected?
   A. Whois search
   B. Traceroute
   C. Ping sweep
   D. Host scanning

3. Which of the following tools are used for footprinting? (Choose 3.)
   A. Whois
   B. Sam Spade
   C. NMAP
   D. SuperScan
   E. NSlookup

4. What is the next immediate step to be performed after footprinting?
   A. Scanning
   B. Enumeration
   C. System hacking
   D. Bypassing an IDS

5. Which are good sources of information about a company or its employees? (Choose all that apply.)
   A. Newsgroups
   B. Job postings
   C. Company website
   D. Press releases

6. How does traceroute work?

    A. It uses an ICMP destination-unreachable message to elicit the name of a router.

    B. It sends a specially crafted IP packet to a router to locate the number of hops from the sender to the destination network.

    C. It uses a protocol that will be rejected by the gateway to determine the location.

    D. It uses the TTL value in an ICMP message to determine the number of hops from the sender to the router.

7. What is footprinting?

    A. Measuring the shoe size of an ethical hacker

    B. Accumulation of data by gathering information on a target

    C. Scanning a target network to detect operating system types

    D. Mapping the physical layout of a target's network

8. NSlookup can be used to gather information regarding which of the following?

    A. Hostnames and IP addresses

    B. Whois information

    C. DNS server locations

    D. Name server types and operating systems

9. Which of the following is a type of social engineering?

    A. Shoulder surfing

    B. User identification

    C. System monitoring

    D. Face-to-face communication

10. Which is an example of social engineering?

    A. A user who holds open the front door of an office for a potential hacker

    B. Calling a help desk and convincing them to reset a password for a user account

    C. Installing a hardware keylogger on a victim's system to capture passwords

    D. Accessing a database with a cracked password

11. What is the best way to prevent a social-engineering attack?

    A. Installing a firewall to prevent port scans

    B. Configuring an IDS to detect intrusion attempts

    C. Increasing the number of help desk personnel

    D. Employee training and education

12. Which of the following is the best example of reverse social engineering?

A. A hacker pretends to be a person of authority in order to get a user to give them information.

B. A help desk employee pretends to be a person of authority.

C. A hacker tries to get a user to change their password.

D. A user changes their password.

13. Using pop-up windows to get a user to give out information is which type of social-engineering attack?

A. Human-based

B. Computer-based

C. Nontechnical

D. Coercive

14. What is it called when a hacker pretends to be a valid user on the system?

A. Impersonation

B. Third-person authorization

C. Help desk

D. Valid user

15. What is the best reason to implement a security policy?

A. It increases security.

B. It makes security harder to enforce.

C. It removes the employee's responsibility to make judgments.

D. It decreases security.

16. Faking a website for the purpose of getting a user's password and username is which type of social-engineering attack?

A. Human-based

B. Computer-based

C. Web-based

D. User-based

17. Dumpster diving can be considered which type of social-engineering attack?

A. Human-based

B. Computer-based

C. Physical access

D. Paper-based

18. What information-gathering tool will give you information regarding the operating system of a web server?

    A. NSlookup

    B. DNSlookup

    C. tracert

    D. Netcraft

19. What tool is a good source of information for employee's names and addresses?

    A. NSlookup

    B. Netcraft

    C. Whois

    D. tracert

20. Which tool will only work on publicly traded companies?

    A. EDGAR

    B. NSlookup

    C. Netcraft

    D. Whois

Answers to Review Questions

1. **D.** The four Internet registries are ARIN (American Registry of Internet Numbers), RIPE NCC (Europe, the Middle East, and parts of Central Asia), LACNIC (Latin American and Caribbean Internet Addresses Registry), and APNIC (Asia Pacific Network Information Centre).

2. **A.** Whois is the only tool listed that won't trigger an IDS alert or otherwise be detected by an organization.

3. **A, B, E.** Whois, Sam Spade, and NSlookup are all used to passively gather information about a target. NMAP and SuperScan are host and network scanning tools.

4. **A.** According to CEH methodology, scanning occurs after footprinting. Enumeration and system hacking are performed after footprinting. Bypassing an IDS would occur later in the hacking cycle.

5. **A, B, C, D.** Newsgroups, job postings, company websites, and press releases are all good sources for information gathering.

6. **D.** Traceroute uses the TTL values to determine how many hops the router is from the sender. Each router decrements the TTL by one under normal conditions.

7. **B.** Footprinting is gathering information about a target organization. Footprinting is not scanning a target network or mapping the physical layout of a target network.

8. **A.** NSlookup queries a DNS server for DNS records such as hostnames and IP addresses.

9. **A.** Of the choices listed here, shoulder surfing is considered a type of social engineering.

10. **B.** Calling a help desk and convincing them to reset a password for a user account is an example of social engineering. Holding open a door and installing a keylogger are examples of physical access intrusions. Accessing a database with a cracked password is system hacking.

11. **D.** Employee training and education is the best way to prevent a social-engineering attack.

12. **A.** When a hacker pretends to be a person of authority in order to get a user to ask them for information, it's an example of reverse social engineering.

13. **B.** Pop-up windows are a method of getting information from a user utilizing a computer. The other options do not require access to a computer.

14. **A.** Impersonation involves a hacker pretending to be a valid user on the system.

15. **C.** Security policies remove the employee's responsibility to make judgments regarding a potential social-engineering attack.

16. B. Website faking is a form of computer-based social-engineering attack because it requires a computer to perpetuate the attack.

17. A. Dumpster diving is a human-based social-engineering attack because it is performed by a human being.

18. D. The Netcraft website will attempt to determine the operating system and web server type of a target.

19. C. Whois will list a contact name address and phone number for a given website.

20. A. EDGAR is the SEC database of filings and will only work on publicly traded firms.

Chapter 3

Gathering Network and Host Information: Scanning and Enumeration

CEH EXAM OBJECTIVES COVERED IN THIS CHAPTER:

- ✓ Define the terms port scanning, network scanning, and vulnerability scanning
- ✓ Understand the CEH scanning methodology
- ✓ Understand ping sweep techniques
- ✓ Understand nmap command switches
- ✓ Understand SYN, stealth, XMAS, NULL, IDLE, and FIN scans
- ✓ List TCP communication flag types
- ✓ Understand war-dialing techniques
- ✓ Understand banner grabbing and OS fingerprinting techniques
- ✓ Understand how proxy servers are used in launching an attack
- ✓ How do anonymizers work?
- ✓ Understand HTTP tunneling techniques
- ✓ Understand IP spoofing techniques
- ✓ What is enumeration?
- ✓ What is meant by null sessions?
- ✓ What is SNMP enumeration?
- ✓ What are the steps involved in performing enumeration?

Scanning is the first phase of active hacking and is used to locate target systems or networks for later attack. Enumeration is the follow-on step once scanning is complete and is used to identify computer names, usernames, and shares. Scanning and enumeration are discussed together in this chapter because many hacking tools perform both steps simultaneously.

Scanning

After the reconnaissance and information-gathering stages have been completed, scanning is performed. It is important that the information-gathering stage be as complete as possible to identify the best location and targets to scan. During scanning, the hacker continues to gather information regarding the network and its individual host systems. Information such as IP addresses, operating system, services, and installed applications can help the hacker determine which type of exploit to use in hacking a system.

Scanning is the process of locating systems that are alive and responding on the network. Ethical hackers use scanning to identify target systems' IP addresses. Scanning is also used to determine whether a system is on the network and available. Scanning tools are used to gather information about a system such as IP addresses, the operating system, and services running on the target computer.

Table 3.1 lists the three types of scanning.

TABLE 3.1   Types of scanning

Scanning type	Purpose
Port scanning	Determines open ports and services
Network scanning	Identifies IP addresses on a given network or subnet
Vulnerability scanning	Discovers presence of known weaknesses on target systems

Port Scanning   Port scanning is the process of identifying open and available TCP/IP ports on a system. Port-scanning tools enable a hacker to learn about the services available on a given system. Each service or application on a machine is associated with a *well-known* port number. Port Numbers are divided into three ranges:

- Well-Known Ports: 0-1023
- Registered Ports: 1024-49151
- Dynamic Ports: 49152-65535

For example, a port-scanning tool that identifies port 80 as open indicates a web server is running on that system. Hackers need to be familiar with well-known port numbers.

Common Port Numbers

On Windows systems, well-known port numbers are located in the C:\windows\system32\ drivers\etc\services file. Services is a hidden file. To view it, show hidden files in Windows Explorer, and double-click the filename to open it with Notepad. The CEH exam expects you to know the well-known port numbers for common applications; familiarize yourself with the port numbers for the following applications:

- FTP, 21
- Telnet, 23
- HTTP, 80
- SMTP, 25
- POP3, 110
- HTTPS, 443

The following list contains additional port numbers not necessarily on the CEH exam but useful for real-world penetration testing:

- Global Catalog Server (TCP), 3269 and 3268
- LDAP Server (TCP/UDP), 389
- LDAP SSL (TCP/UDP), 636
- IPsec ISAKMP (UDP), 500
- NAT-T (UDP), 4500
- RPC (TCP), 135
- ASP.NET Session State (TCP), 42424
- NetBIOS Datagram Service (UDP), 137 and 138
- NetBIOS Session Service (TCP), 139

- DHCP Server (UDP), 67

- LDAP Server (TCP/UDP), 389

- SMB (TCP), 445

- RPC (TCP), 135

- DNS (TCP/UDP), 53

- IMAP (TCP), 143

- IMAP over SSL (TCP), 993

- POP3 (TCP), 110

- POP3 over SSL (TCP), 995

- RPC (TCP), 135

- RPC over HTTPS (TCP), 443 or 80

- SMTP (TCP/UDP), 25

Network Scanning   Network scanning is a procedure for identifying active hosts on a network, either to attack them or as a network security assessment. Hosts are identified by their individual IP addresses. Network-scanning tools attempt to identify all the *live* or responding hosts on the network and their corresponding IP addresses.

Vulnerability Scanning   Vulnerability scanning is the process of proactively identifying the vulnerabilities of computer systems on a network. Generally, a vulnerability scanner first identifies the operating system and version number, including service packs that may be installed. Then, the scanner identifies weaknesses or vulnerabilities in the operating system. During the later attack phase, a hacker can exploit those weaknesses in order to gain access to the system.

Although scanning can quickly identify which hosts are listening and active on a network, it is also a quick way to be identified by an intrusion detection system (IDS). Scanning tools probe TCP/IP ports looking for open ports and IP addresses, and these probes can be recognized by most security intrusion detection tools. Network and vulnerability scanning can usually be detected as well, because the scanner must interact with the target system over the network.

Depending on the type of scanning application and the speed of the scan, an IDS will detect the scanning and flag it as an IDS event. Some of the tools for scanning have different modes to attempt to defeat an IDS and are more likely to be able to scan undetected. As a CEH it is your job to gather as much information as possible and try and remain undetected.

The CEH Scanning Methodology

As a CEH, you're expected to be familiar with the scanning methodology presented in Figure 3.1. This methodology is the process by which a hacker scans the network. It ensures that no system or vulnerability is overlooked and that the hacker gathers all necessary information to perform an attack.

We'll look at the various stages of this scanning methodology throughout this book, starting with the first three steps—checking for systems that are live and for open ports and service identification—in the following section.

FIGURE 3.1   CEH scanning methodology

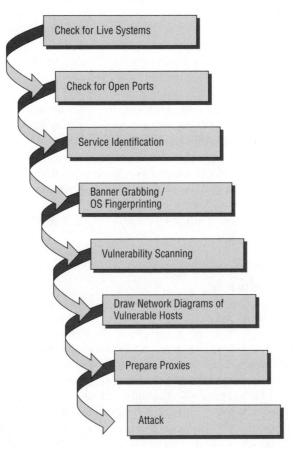

Ping Sweep Techniques

The CEH scanning methodology starts with checking for systems that are live on the network, meaning that they respond to probes or connection requests. The simplest, although not necessarily the most accurate, way to determine whether systems are live is to perform a *ping sweep* of the IP address range. All systems that respond with a ping reply are considered live on the network. A ping sweep is also known as Internet Control Message Protocol (ICMP) scanning, as ICMP is the protocol used by the `ping` command.

ICMP scanning, or a ping sweep, is the process of sending an ICMP request or ping to all hosts on the network to determine which ones are up and responding to pings. ICMP began as a protocol used to send test and error messages between hosts on the Internet. It has evolved as a protocol utilized by every operating system, router, switch or Internet Protocol (IP)-based device. The ability to use the ICMP Echo request and Echo reply as a connectivity test between hosts is built into every IP-enabled device via the `ping` command. It is a quick and dirty test to see if two hosts have connectivity and is used extensively for troubleshooting.

A benefit of ICMP scanning is that it can be run in *parallel*, meaning all systems are scanned at the same time; thus it can run quickly on an entire network. Most hacking tools include a ping sweep option, which essentially means performing an ICMP request to every host on the network. Systems that respond with a ping response are alive and listening on the network. Exercise 3.1 shows how to perform a ping sweep using built-in windows tools.

One considerable problem with this method is that personal firewall software and network-based firewalls can block a system from responding to ping sweeps. More and more systems are configured with firewall software and will block the ping attempt and notify the user that a scanning program is running on the network. Another problem is that the computer must be on to be scanned.

 Real World Scenario

Indications of a Scanning Attack

Bob is working on his laptop while connected on a business trip away from the office. He is using the hotel's free wireless Internet access from his computer. As he is sending an email he notices a pop-up window on the system tray of his Windows XP computer. It says "Windows has detected and blocked an intrusion attempt to your computer." He just closes the pop-up window and goes back to finish writing his email. He then notices another pop-up window with a similar message. He begins to get concerned that his computer is being hacked. He decides to shut down his laptop so that no other connection attempts can be made to his computer.

Hacking Tools

Pinger, Friendly Pinger, and WS_Ping_Pro are all tools that perform ICMP queries. You should be familiar with all these tools for the exam.

EXERCISE 3.1

Using a Windows Ping

To use the built-in `ping` command in Windows to test connectivity to another system:

1. Open a command prompt in Windows.

2. Type **ping www.microsoft.com**.

```
Microsoft Windows [Version 6.0.6001]
Copyright (c) 2006 Microsoft Corporation.  All rights reserved.

C:\Users\kimberly>ping www.microsoft.com

Pinging lb1.www.ms.akadns.net [207.46.19.190] with 32 bytes of data:
Request timed out.
Request timed out.
Request timed out.
Request timed out.

Ping statistics for 207.46.19.190:
    Packets: Sent = 4, Received = 0, Lost = 4 (100% loss),
```

A timeout indicates that the remote system is not responding or turned off or that the ping was blocked. A reply indicates that the system is alive and responding to ICMP requests.

Detecting Ping Sweeps

Almost any IDS or intrusion prevention system (IPS) system will detect and alert the security administrator to a ping sweep occurring on the network. Most firewall and proxy servers block ping responses so a hacker can't accurately determine whether systems are available using a ping sweep alone. More intense port scanning must be used if systems don't respond to a ping sweep. Just because a ping sweep doesn't return any active hosts on the network doesn't mean they aren't available—you need to try an alternate method of identification. Remember, hacking takes time, patience, and persistence.

Scanning Ports and Identifying Services

Checking for open ports is the second step in the CEH scanning methodology. *Port scanning* is the method used to check for open ports. The process of port scanning involves probing each port on a host to determine which ports are open. Port scanning generally yields more valuable information than a ping sweep about the host and vulnerabilities on the system.

Service identification is the third step in the CEH scanning methodology; it's usually performed using the same tools as port scanning. By identifying open ports, a hacker can usually also identify the services associated with that port number. Remember the well-known port numbers discussed earlier in this chapter.

Port-Scan Countermeasures

Countermeasures are processes or toolsets used by security administrators to detect and possibly thwart port scanning of hosts on their network. The following list of countermeasures should be implemented to prevent a hacker from acquiring information during a port scan:

- Proper security architecture, such as implementation of IDS and firewalls, should be followed.

- Ethical hackers use their toolset to test the scanning countermeasures that have been implemented. Once a firewall is in place, a port-scanning tool should be run against hosts on the network to determine whether the firewall correctly detects and stops the port-scanning activity.

- The firewall should be able to detect the probes sent by port-scanning tools. The firewall should carry out *stateful inspections*, which means it examines the data of the packet and not just the TCP header to determine whether the traffic is allowed to pass through the firewall.

- Network IDS should be used to identify the OS-detection method used by some common hackers tools.

- Only needed ports should be kept open. The rest should be filtered or blocked.

- The staff of the organization using the systems should be given appropriate training on security awareness. They should also know the various security policies they're required to follow.

nmap Command Switches

Nmap is a free, open source tool that quickly and efficiently performs ping sweeps, port scanning, service identification, IP address detection, and operating system detection. Nmap has the benefit of scanning a large number of machines in a single session. It's supported by many operating systems, including Unix, Windows, and Linux.

The state of the port as determined by an nmap scan can be open, filtered, or unfiltered. *Open* means that the target machine accepts incoming request on that port. *Filtered* means a firewall or network filter is screening the port and preventing nmap from discovering whether it's open. *Unfiltered* mean the port is determined to be closed, and no firewall or filter is interfering with the nmap requests.

Nmap supports several types of scans. Table 3.2 details some of the common scan methods.

TABLE 3.2   Nmap scan types

Nmap scan type	Description
TCP connect	The attacker makes a full TCP connection to the target system. The most reliable scan type but also the most detectable. Open ports reply with a SYN/ACK while closed ports reply with a RST/ACK.
XMAS tree scan	The attacker checks for TCP services by sending XMAS-tree packets, which are named as such because all the "lights" are on, meaning the FIN, URG, and PSH flags are set (the meaning of the flags will be discussed later in this chapter). Closed ports reply with a RST flag.
SYN stealth scan	This is also known as *half-open scanning*. The hacker sends a SYN packet and receives a SYN-ACK back from the server. It's stealthy because a full TCP connection isn't opened. Open ports reply with a SYN/ACK while closed ports reply with a RST/ACK.
Null scan	This is an advanced scan that may be able to pass through firewalls undetected or modified. Null scan has all flags off or not set. It only works on Unix systems. Closed ports will return a RST flag.
Windows scan	This type of scan is similar to the ACK scan and can also detect open ports.
ACK scan	This type of scan is used to map out firewall rules. ACK scan only works on Unix. The port is considered filtered by firewall rules if an ICMP destination unreachable message is received as a result of the ACK scan.

The nmap command has numerous switches to perform different types of scans. The common command switches are listed in Table 3.3.

TABLE 3.3   Common nmap command switches

nmap command switch	Scan performed
–sT	TCP connect scan
–sS	SYN scan
–sF	FIN scan
–sX	XMAS tree scan
–sN	Null scan
–sP	Ping scan
–sU	UDP scan

TABLE 3.3   Common nmap command switches *(continued)*

nmap command switch	Scan performed
-sO	Protocol scan
-sA	ACK scan
-sW	Windows scan
-sR	RPC scan
-sL	List/DNS scan
-sI	Idle scan
-Po	Don't ping
-PT	TCP ping
-PS	SYN ping
-PI	ICMP ping
-PB	TCP and ICMP ping
-PB	ICMP timestamp
-PM	ICMP netmask
-oN	Normal output
-oX	XML output
-oG	Greppable output
-oA	All output
-T Paranoid	Serial scan; 300 sec between scans
-T Sneaky	Serial scan; 15 sec between scans
-T Polite	Serial scan; .4 sec between scans
-T Normal	Parallel scan
-T Aggressive	Parallel scan, 300 sec timeout, and 1.25 sec/probe
-T Insane	Parallel scan, 75 sec timeout, and .3 sec/probe

To perform an nmap scan, at the Windows command prompt type **Nmap *IPaddress*** followed by any command switches used to perform specific type of scans. For example, to scan the host with the IP address 192.168.0.1 using a TCP connect scan type, enter this command:

```
Nmap 192.168.0.1 -sT
```

 Make sure you're familiar with the different types of nmap scans, the syntax to run nmap, and how to analyze nmap results. The syntax and switches used by the nmap command will be tested on the CEH exam.

Scan Types

As a CEH, you need to be familiar with the following scan types and uses:

SYN   A SYN or stealth scan is also called a half-open scan because it doesn't complete the TCP three-way handshake. (The TCP/IP three-way handshake will be covered in the next section.) A hacker sends a SYN packet to the target; if a SYN/ACK frame is received back, then it's assumed the target would complete the connect and the port is listening. If an RST is received back from the target, then it's assumed the port isn't active or is closed. The advantage of the SYN stealth scan is that fewer IDS systems log this as an attack or connection attempt.

XMAS   XMAS scans send a packet with the FIN, URG, and PSH flags set. If the port is open, there is no response; but if the port is closed, the target responds with a RST/ACK packet. XMAS scans work only on target systems that follow the RFC 793 implementation of TCP/IP and don't work against any version of Windows.

FIN   A FIN scan is similar to an XMAS scan but sends a packet with just the FIN flag set. FIN scans receive the same response and have the same limitations as XMAS scans.

NULL   A NULL scan is also similar to XMAS and FIN in its limitations and response, but it just sends a packet with no flags set.

IDLE   An IDLE scan uses a spoofed IP address to send a SYN packet to a target. Depending on the response, the port can be determined to be open or closed. IDLE scans determine port scan response by monitoring IP header sequence numbers.

TCP Communication Flag Types

TCP scan types are built on the *TCP three-way handshake*. TCP connections require a three-way handshake before a connection can be made and data transferred between the sender and receiver. Figure 3.2 details the steps of the TCP three-way handshake.

FIGURE 3.2   TCP three-way handshake

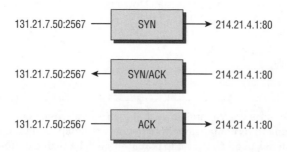

To complete the three-way handshake and make a successful connection between two hosts, the sender must send a TCP packet with the synchronize (SYN) bit set. Then, the receiving system responds with a TCP packet with the synchronize (SYN) and acknowledge (ACK) bit set to indicate the host is ready to receive data. The source system sends a final packet with the ACK bit set to indicate the connection is complete and data is ready to be sent.

Because TCP is a connection-oriented protocol, a process for establishing a connection (three-way handshake), restarting a failed connection, and finishing a connection is part of the protocol. These protocol notifications are called *flags*. TCP contains ACK, RST, SYN, URG, PSH, and FIN flags. The following list identifies the function of the TCP flags:

SYN   Synchronize. Initiates a connection between hosts.

ACK   Acknowledge. Established connection between hosts.

PSH   Push. System is forwarding buffered data.

URG   Urgent. Data in packets must be processed quickly.

FIN   Finish. No more transmissions.

RST   Reset. Resets the connection.

A hacker can attempt to bypass detection by using flags instead of completing a normal TCP connection. The TCP scan types in Table 3.4 are used by some scanning tools to elicit a response from a system by setting one or more flags.

TABLE 3.4   TCP scan types

XMAS scan	Flags sent by hacker
XMAS scan	All flags set (ACK, RST, SYN, URG, PSH, FIN)
FIN scan	FIN
NULL scan	No flags set

TABLE 3.4   TCP scan types *(continued)*

XMAS scan	Flags sent by hacker
TCP connect/full-open scan	SYN, then ACK
SYN scan / half-open scan	SYN, then RST

Hacking Tools

IPEye is a TCP port scanner that can do SYN, FIN, Null, and XMAS scans. It's a command-line tool.

IPEye probes the ports on a target system and responds with closed, reject, drop, or open. Closed means there is a computer on the other end, but it doesn't listen at the port. Reject means a firewall is rejecting the connection to the port (sending a reset back). Drop means a firewall is dropping everything to the port, or there is no computer on the other end. Open means some kind of service is listening at the port. These responses help a hacker identify what type of system is responding.

IPSecScan is a tool that can scan either a single IP address or a range of addresses looking for systems that are IPSec enabled.

NetScan Tools Pro, hping2, KingPingicmpenum, and SNMP Scanner are all scanning tools and can also be used to fingerprint the operating system (discussed later).

Icmpenum uses not only ICMP Echo packets to probe networks, but also ICMP Timestamp and ICMP Information packets. Furthermore, it supports spoofing and sniffing for reply packets. Icmpenum is great for scanning networks when the firewall blocks ICMP Echo packets but fails to block Timestamp or Information packets.

The hping2 tool is notable because it contains a host of other features besides OS fingerprinting such as TCP, User Datagram Protocol (UDP), ICMP, and raw-IP ping protocols, traceroute mode, and the ability to send files between the source and target system.

SNMP Scanner allows you to scan a range or list of hosts performing ping, DNS, and Simple Network Management Protocol (SNMP) queries.

Exercise 3.2 shows how to use AngryIP scanner to perform a port scan.

EXERCISE 3.2

Free IPTools Port Scan

To use a port scan tool to determine listening ports of active hosts:

1. Download Angry IP Scanner from www.angryip.org/w/Download.

2. Enter the IP address of the target system in the Host or IP Address field or enter a range or IP address for your lab systems and click Start to perform a conventional (full connect) scan of standard ports.

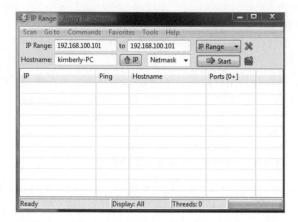

War-Dialing Techniques

War dialing is the process of dialing modem numbers to find an open modem connection that provides remote access to a network for an attack to be launched against the target system. The term *war dialing* originates from the early days of the Internet when most companies were connected to the Internet via dial-up modem connections. War dialing is included as a scanning method because it finds another network connection that may have weaker security than the main Internet connection. Many organizations set up remote-access modems that are now antiquated but have failed to remove those remote-access servers. This gives hackers an easy way into the network with much weaker security mechanisms. For example, many remote-access systems use the Password Authentication Protocol (PAP), which send passwords in cleartext, rather than newer virtual private networking (VPN) technology that encrypts passwords.

War-dialing tools work on the premise that companies don't control the dial-in ports as strictly as the firewall, and machines with modems attached are present everywhere even if those modems are no longer in use. Many servers still have modems with phone lines connected as a backup in case the primary Internet connection fails. These available modem connections can be used by a war-dialing program to gain remote access to the system and internal network.

 Real World Scenario

Using a Forgotten Modem Connection for War Dialing

I was performing a network security audit for a financial services firm a few years ago. They asked me to do a walkthrough of the site for the purposes of a physical security audit. As I was passing one of the desks in the marketing department I noticed a phone line coming out from around the desk and connecting to a wall jack. I asked about the use of modems as I was trying to ascertain the reason for the phone line cable. I was told that they used to use dial-up on some of the computers for Internet access but that two years ago they switched to a high-speed T1 connection for the entire office. As we explored further, it was revealed that the employee who used that computer still used AOL on the dial-up connection to check her personal email account. Quite surprising to everyone, when the new Internet connection was installed no one ever checked to ensure all the dial-up connections were removed. Here is a prime example of why war dialing still works in some cases.

Hacking Tools

THC-Scan, PhoneSweep, and TeleSweep are tools that identify phone numbers and can dial a target to make a connection with a computer modem. These tools generally work by using a predetermined list of common usernames and passwords in an attempt to gain access to the system. Most remote-access dial-in connections aren't secured with a password or use very rudimentary security.

Banner Grabbing and OS Fingerprinting Techniques

Banner grabbing and operating system identification—which can also be defined as *fingerprinting* the TCP/IP stack—is the fourth step in the CEH scanning methodology. The process of fingerprinting allows the hacker to identify particularly vulnerable or high-value targets on the network. Hackers are looking for the easiest way to gain access to a system or network. Banner grabbing is the process of opening a connection and reading the banner or response sent by the application. Many email, FTP, and web servers will respond to a telnet connection with the name and version of the software. This aids a hacker in fingerprinting the OS and application software. For example, a Microsoft Exchange email server would only be installed on a Windows OS.

Active stack fingerprinting is the most common form of fingerprinting. It involves sending data to a system to see how the system responds. It's based on the fact that various operating system vendors implement the TCP stack differently, and responses will differ based on the operating system. The responses are then compared to a database to determine the operating system. Active stack fingerprinting is detectable because it repeatedly attempts to connect with the same target system.

Passive stack fingerprinting is stealthier and involves examining traffic on the network to determine the operating system. It uses sniffing techniques instead of scanning techniques. Passive stack fingerprinting usually goes undetected by an IDS or other security system but is less accurate than active fingerprinting.

Drawing Network Diagrams of Vulnerable Hosts

Although it isn't a CEH exam objective, understanding the tools used in step 6 of the CEH scanning methodology—drawing a network diagram of vulnerable hosts—is a must. A number of network management tools can assist you with this step. Such tools are generally used to manage network devices but can be turned against security administrators by enterprising hackers.

SolarWinds Toolset, Queso, Harris Stat, and Cheops are network management tools that can be used for detecting operating systems, mapping network diagrams, listing services running on a network, performing generalized port scanning, and so on.

These tools diagram entire networks in a GUI interface, including routers, servers, hosts, and firewalls. Most of these tools can discover IP addresses, hostnames, services, operating systems, and version information.

Netcraft and HTTrack are tools that fingerprint an operating system. Both are used to determine the OS and web server software version numbers.

Netcraft is a website that periodically polls web servers to determine the operating system version and the web server software version. Netcraft can provide useful information the hacker can use in identifying vulnerabilities in the web server software. In addition, Netcraft has an antiphishing toolbar and web server verification tool you can use to make sure you're using the actual web server rather than a spoofed web server. Exercise 3.3 shows how to use Netcraft to identify the OS or a web server.

HTTrack arranges the original site's relative link structure. You open a page of the mirrored website in your browser, and then you can browse the site from link to link as if you were viewing it online. HTTrack can also update an existing mirrored site and resume interrupted downloads.

Use Netcraft to Identify the OS of a Web Server

1. Open a web browser to the Netcraft website, www.netcraft.com.

2. Type a website name in the What's That Site Running? field in the upper-left corner of the screen.

3. Scroll down to Hosting History to see what OS and web server software are running on the server.

Scanning Anonymously

Preparing proxy servers is the last step in the CEH scanning methodology. A *proxy server* is a computer that acts as an intermediary between the hacker and the target computer.

Using a proxy server can allow a hacker to become anonymous on the network. The hacker first makes a connection to the proxy server and then requests a connection to the target computer via the existing connection to the proxy. Essentially, the proxy requests access to the target computer, not the hacker's computer. This lets a hacker surf the Web anonymously or otherwise hide their attack.

Hacking Tools

SocksChain is a tool that gives a hacker the ability to attack through a chain of proxy servers. The main purpose of doing this is to hide the hacker's real IP address and therefore minimize the chance of detection. When a hacker works through several proxy servers in series, it's much harder to locate the hacker. Tracking the attacker's IP address through the logs of several proxy servers is complex and tedious work. If one of the proxy servers' log files is lost or incomplete, the chain is broken, and the hacker's IP address remains anonymous.

Anonymizers are services that attempt to make web surfing anonymous by utilizing a website that acts as a proxy server for the web client. The first anonymizer software tool was developed by Anonymizer.com; it was created in 1997 by Lance Cottrell. The anonymizer removes all the identifying information from a user's computers while the user surfs the Internet, thereby ensuring the privacy of the user.

To visit a website anonymously, the hacker enters the website address into the anonymizer software, and the anonymizer software makes the request to the selected site. All requests and web pages are relayed through the anonymizer site, making it difficult to track the actual requester of the web page. Use Anonymouse to web surf anonymously in Exercise 3.4.

EXERCISE 3.4

Use Anonymouse to Surf Websites Anonymously

1. Open a web browser to the `http://anonymouse.org` website and select English at the top of the page.

2. Type a website address in the Enter Website Address field and click the Surf Anonymously button.

   This works especially well if you know certain websites are blocked.

A popular method of bypassing a firewall or IDS is to tunnel a blocked protocol (such as SMTP) through an allowed protocol (such as HTTP). Almost all IDS and firewalls act as a proxy between a client's PC and the Internet and pass only the traffic defined as being allowed.

Most companies allow HTTP traffic because it's usually benign web access. However, a hacker using an HTTP tunneling tool can subvert the proxy by hiding potentially destructive protocols, such as IM or chat, within an innocent-looking protocol packet.

Hacking Tools

HTTPort, Tunneld, and BackStealth are tools to tunnel traffic through HTTP. They allow the bypassing of an HTTP proxy, which blocks certain protocols from accessing the Internet. These tools allow the following potentially dangerous software protocols to be used from behind an HTTP proxy:

- Email

- IRC

- ICQ

- News

- AIM

- FTP

A hacker can *spoof* an IP address when scanning target systems to minimize the chance of detection. One drawback of spoofing an IP address is that a TCP session can't be successfully completed.

Source routing lets an attacker specify the route that a packet takes through the Internet. This can also minimize the chance of detection by bypassing IDS and firewalls that may block or detect the attack. Source routing uses a reply address in the IP header to return the packet to a spoofed address instead of the attacker's real address. The use of source routing to bypass an IDS will be covered in more detail in Chapter 13, "Evading IDSs, Honeypots, and Firewalls."

To detect IP address spoofing, you can compare the time to live (TTL) values: the attacker's TTL will be different from the spoofed address's real TTL.

Enumeration

Enumeration occurs after scanning and is the process of gathering and compiling usernames, machine names, network resources, shares, and services. It also refers to actively querying or connecting to a target system to acquire this information.

Hackers need to be methodical in their approach to hacking. The following steps are an example of those a hacker might perform in preparation for hacking a target system:

1. Extract usernames using enumeration.

2. Gather information about the host using null sessions.

3. Perform Windows enumeration using the SuperScan tool.

4. Acquire the user accounts using the tool GetAcct.

5. Perform SNMP port scanning.

The object of enumeration is to identify a user account or system account for potential use in hacking the target system. It isn't necessary to find a system administrator account, because most account privileges can be escalated to allow the account more access than was previously granted.

The process of privilege escalation is covered in the next chapter.

Many hacking tools are designed for scanning IP networks to locate NetBIOS name information. For each responding host, the tools list IP address, NetBIOS computer name, logged-in username, and MAC address information.

On a Windows 2000 domain, the built-in tool net view can be used for NetBIOS enumeration. To enumerate NetBIOS names using the net view command, enter the following at the command prompt:

```
net view / domain
nbtstat -A IP address
```

Hacking Tools

DumpSec is a NetBIOS enumeration tool. It connects to the target system as a null user with the net use command. It then enumerates users, groups, NTFS permissions, and file ownership information.

Hyena is a tool that enumerates NetBIOS shares and additionally can exploit the null session vulnerability to connect to the target system and change the share path or edit the Registry.

The SMB Auditing Tool is a password-auditing tool for the Windows and Server Message Block (SMB) platforms. Windows uses SMB to communicate between the client and server. The SMB Auditing Tool is able to identify usernames and crack passwords on Windows systems.

The NetBIOS Auditing Tool is another NetBIOS enumeration tool. It's used to perform various security checks on remote servers running NetBIOS file sharing services.

Null Sessions

A null session occurs when you log in to a system with no username or password. NetBIOS null sessions are a vulnerability found in the Common Internet File System (CIFS) or SMB, depending on the operating system.

Microsoft Windows uses SMB, and Unix/Linux systems use CIFS.

Once a hacker has made a NetBIOS connection using a null session to a system, they can easily get a full dump of all usernames, groups, shares, permissions, policies, services, and more using the Null user account. The SMB and NetBIOS standards in Windows include APIs that return information about a system via TCP port 139.

One method of connecting a NetBIOS null session to a Windows system is to use the hidden Inter-Process Communication share (IPC$). This hidden share is accessible using the `net use` command. As mentioned earlier, the `net use` command is a built-in Windows command that connects to a share on another computer. The empty quotation marks (`""`) indicate that you want to connect with no username and no password. To make a NetBIOS null session to a system with the IP address 192.21.7.1 with the built-in anonymous user account and a null password using the `net use` command, the syntax is as follows:

```
C: \> net use \\192.21.7.1 \IPC$ "" /u: ""
```

Once the `net use` command has been successfully completed, the hacker has a channel over which to use other hacking tools and techniques.

As a CEH, you need to know how to defend against NetBIOS enumeration and null sessions. We'll discuss that in the following section.

NetBIOS Enumeration and Null Session Countermeasures

The NetBIOS null session uses specific port numbers on the target machine. Null sessions require access to TCP ports 135, 137,139, and/or 445. One countermeasure is to close these ports on the target system. This can be accomplished by disabling SMB services on individual hosts by unbinding the TCP/IP WINS client from the interface in the network connection's properties. To implement this countermeasure, perform the following steps:

1. Open the properties of the network connection.
2. Click TCP/IP and then the Properties button.
3. Click the Advanced button.
4. On the WINS tab, select Disable NetBIOS Over TCP/IP.

A security administrator can also edit the Registry directly to restrict the anonymous user from login. To implement this countermeasure, follow these steps:

1. Open regedt32 and navigate to `HKLM\SYSTEM\CurrentControlSet\LSA`.
2. Choose Edit ➪ Add Value. Enter these values:
   - Value Name: **RestrictAnonymous**
   - Data Type: **REG_WORD**
   - Value: **2**

Finally, the system can be upgraded to Windows XP and the latest Microsoft security patches, which mitigates the NetBIOS null session vulnerability from occurring.

SNMP Enumeration

SNMP enumeration is the process of using SNMP to enumerate user accounts on a target system. SNMP employs two major types of software components for communication: the SNMP agent, which is located on the networking device, and the SNMP management station, which communicates with the agent.

Almost all network infrastructure devices, such as routers and switches and including Windows systems, contain an SNMP agent to manage the system or device. The SNMP management station sends requests to agents, and the agents send back replies. The requests and replies refer to configuration variables accessible by agent software. Management stations can also send requests to set values for certain variables. Traps let the management station know that something significant has happened in the agent software, such as a reboot or an interface failure. Management Information Base (MIB) is the database of configuration variables that resides on the networking device.

SNMP has two passwords you can use to access and configure the SNMP agent from the management station. The first is called a *read community string*. This password lets you view the configuration of the device or system. The second is called the *read/write community string*; it's for changing or editing the configuration on the device. Generally, the default read community string is public and the default read/write community string is private. A common security loophole occurs when the community strings are left at the default settings: a hacker can use these default passwords to view or change the device configuration.

If you have any questions about how easy it is to locate the default passwords of devices, look at the website www.defaultpassword.com.

Hacking Tools

SNMPUtil and IP Network Browser are SNMP enumeration tools.

SNMPUtil gathers Windows user account information via SNMP in Windows systems. Some information—such as routing tables, ARP tables, IP addresses, MAC addresses, TCP and UDP open ports, user accounts, and shares—can be read from a Windows system that has SNMP enabled using the SNMPUtil tools.

IP Network Browser from the SolarWinds Toolset also uses SNMP to gather more information about a device that has an SNMP agent.

SNMP Enumeration Countermeasures

The simplest way to prevent SNMP enumeration is to remove the SNMP agent on the potential target systems or turn off the SNMP service. If shutting off SNMP isn't an option, then change the default read and read/write community names.

In addition, an administrator can implement the Group Policy security option Additional Restrictions For Anonymous Connections, which restricts SNMP connections.

 Group Policy is implemented on a Windows domain controller. Network administrators should be familiar with how to do this. It's outside the scope of this book, because many steps are involved in performing this task.

Windows 2000 DNS Zone Transfer

In a Windows 2000 domain, clients use service (SRV) records to locate Windows 2000 domain services, such as Active Directory and Kerberos. This means every Windows 2000 Active Directory domain must have a DNS server for the network to operate properly.

A simple zone transfer performed with the `nslookup` command can enumerate lots of interesting network information. The command to enumerate using the `nslookup` command is as follows:

`nslookup ls -d domainname`

Within the `nslookup` results, a hacker looks closely at the following records, because they provide additional information about the network services:

- Global Catalog service (`_gc._tcp_`)
- Domain controllers (`_ldap._tcp`)
- Kerberos authentication (`_kerberos._tcp`)

As a countermeasure, zone transfers can be blocked in the properties of the Windows DNS server.

An Active Directory database is a Lightweight Directory Access Protocol (LDAP)-based database. This allows the existing users and groups in the database to be enumerated with a simple LDAP query. The only thing required to perform this enumeration is to create an authenticated session via LDAP. A Windows 2000 LDAP client called the Active Directory Administration Tool (`ldp.exe`) connects to an Active Directory server and identifies the contents of the database. You can find `ldp.exe` on the Windows 2000 CD-ROM in the `Support\Reskit\Netmgmt\Dstool` folder.

To perform an Active Directory enumeration attack, a hacker performs the following steps:

1. Connect to any Active Directory server using `ldp.exe` on port 389. When the connection is complete, server information is displayed in the right pane.

2. On the Connection menu, choose Authenticate. Type the username, password, and domain name in the appropriate boxes. You can use the Guest account or any other domain account.

3. Once the authentication is successful, enumerate users and built-in groups by choosing the Search option from the Browse menu.

Hacking Tools

User2SID and SID2User are command-line tools that look up Windows service identifiers (SIDs from username input and vice versa).

Enum is a command-line enumeration utility. It uses null sessions and can retrieve usernames, machine names, shares, group and membership lists, passwords, and Local Security policy information. Enum is also capable of brute-force dictionary attacks on individual accounts.

UserInfo is a command-line tool that's used to gather usernames and that can also be used to create new user accounts.

GetAcct is a GUI-based tool that enumerates user accounts on a system.

SMBBF is a SMB brute-force tool that tries to determine user accounts and accounts with blank passwords.

Summary

Scanning and enumeration are the next steps in the hacking process after the information-gathering phase has been completed. Scanning and enumeration tools are most often active information-gathering tools and therefore allow the hacker to be detected. For this reason, many tools and techniques exist to minimize the opportunity for detection and reduce the chance of the hacker being identified.

It is during the scanning and enumeration phase that information about the host and target network is discovered. As a next step, the host and network information enumerated will be used to begin to hack the target system or network. The next chapter will focus on system hacking and gaining access to a target system.

Exam Essentials

Know the three types of scanning and scanning countermeasures.   Port, network, and vulnerability scanning are the three types of scanning. Implement firewalls that prevent internal systems from being scanned by blocking ping sweeps and port-scanning tools such as nmap. IDSs and IPSs can alert an administrator to a scan taking place on the network.

Know how to determine which systems are alive on the network.   Know how to use ICMP query tools to perform ping sweeps to determine which systems are responding. Ping sweeps have limitations, and some systems may not respond to the ICMP queries.

Know how to perform port scanning using nmap.   Learn the switches for performing nmap scanning using the nmap command. For example, nmap -sS performs a SYN scan.

Understand the uses and limitations of different scan types.   Make sure you're familiar with TCP connect, SYN, NULL, IDLE, FIN, and XMAS scans and when each type should be used.

Understand the process of the TCP three-way handshake.   The TCP connection process starts with a SYN packet sent to the target system. The target system responds with a SYN+ACK packet, and the source system sends back an ACK packet to the target. This completes a successful TCP connection.

Know the uses of war dialing.   War dialing is used to test dial-in remote access system security. Phone numbers are dialed randomly in an attempt to make an unsecured modem connection and gain access to the network.

Understand how to perform operating system fingerprinting using active and passive methods.   Active fingerprinting means sending a request to a system to see how it responds (banner grabbing, for example). Passive fingerprinting is examining traffic sent to and from the system to determine the operating system.

Know how to become anonymous using an anonymizer, HTTP tunneling, and IP spoofing.   Use a website anonymizer to hide the source address to make the system surfing the Web appear anonymous. HTTP tunneling and IP spoofing are two methods of hiding the physical address or protocols that a hacker may be using. They're useful in evading firewalls and obfuscating the hacker's identity or whereabouts.

Understand how to enumerate user accounts.   Enumeration involves making active connections to systems through either SMB/CIFS or NetBIOS vulnerabilities and querying the system for information.

Be aware of the type of information that can be enumerated on a system and enumeration countermeasures.   The type of information enumerated by hackers includes network resources and shares, users and groups, and applications and banners. Use a firewall to block ports 135 and 139, or patch the Registry to prevent null sessions. Turn off the SNMP services, or change the default read and read/write community names.

Understand null sessions.   Connecting to a system using a blank password is known as a null session. Null sessions are often used by hackers to connect to target systems and then run enumeration tools against the system.

Know the types of enumeration tools and how to identify vulnerable accounts.   NetBIOS and SNMP enumerations can be performed using tools such as SNMPUtil and Enum. Tools such as User2SID, SID2User, and UserInfo can be used to identify vulnerable user accounts.

Know how to perform a DNS zone transfer on Windows 2000 computers.   NSlookup can be used to perform a DNS zone transfer.

Review Questions

1. What port number does FTP use?
    - **A.** 21
    - **B.** 25
    - **C.** 23
    - **D.** 80

2. What port number does HTTPS use?
    - **A.** 443
    - **B.** 80
    - **C.** 53
    - **D.** 21

3. What is war dialing used for?
    - **A.** Testing firewall security
    - **B.** Testing remote access system security
    - **C.** Configuring a proxy filtering gateway
    - **D.** Configuring a firewall

4. Banner grabbing is an example of what?
    - **A.** Passive operating system fingerprinting
    - **B.** Active operating system fingerprinting
    - **C.** Footprinting
    - **D.** Application analysis

5. What are the three types of scanning?
    - **A.** Port, network, and vulnerability
    - **B.** Port, network, and services
    - **C.** Grey, black, and white hat
    - **D.** Server, client, and network

6. What is the main problem with using only ICMP queries for scanning?
    - **A.** The port is not always available.
    - **B.** The protocol is unreliable.
    - **C.** Systems may not respond because of a firewall.
    - **D.** Systems may not have the service running.

7. What does the TCP RST command do?

   A. Starts a TCP connection

   B. Restores the connection to a previous state

   C. Finishes a TCP connection

   D. Resets the TCP connection

8. What is the proper sequence of a TCP connection?

   A. SYN-SYN-ACK-ACK

   B. SYN-ACK-FIN

   C. SYN-SYNACK-ACK

   D. SYN-PSH-ACK

9. A packet with all flags set is which type of scan?

   A. Full Open

   B. Syn scan

   C. XMAS

   D. TCP connect

10. What is the proper command to perform an nmap SYN scan every 5 minutes?

   A. `nmap -ss - paranoid`

   B. `nmap -sS -paranoid`

   C. `nmap -sS -fast`

   D. `namp -sS -sneaky`

11. To prevent a hacker from using SMB session hijacking, which TCP and UDP ports would you block at the firewall?

   A. 167 and 137

   B. 80 and 23

   C. 139 and 445

   D. 1277 and 1270

12. Why would an attacker want to perform a scan on port 137?

   A. To locate the FTP service on the target host

   B. To check for file and print sharing on Windows systems

   C. To discover proxy servers on a network

   D. To discover a target system with the NetBIOS null session vulnerability

13. SNMP is a protocol used to manage network infrastructure devices. What is the SNMP read/write community name used for?

    A. Viewing the configuration information

    B. Changing the configuration information

    C. Monitoring the device for errors

    D. Controlling the SNMP management station

14. Why would the network security team be concerned about ports 135–139 being open on a system?

    A. SMB is enabled, and the system is susceptible to null sessions.

    B. SMB is not enabled, and the system is susceptible to null sessions.

    C. Windows RPC is enabled, and the system is susceptible to Windows DCOM remote sessions.

    D. Windows RPC is not enabled, and the system is susceptible to Windows DCOM remote sessions.

15. Which step comes after enumerating users in the CEH hacking cycle?

    A. Crack password

    B. Escalate privileges

    C. Scan

    D. Cover tracks

16. What is enumeration?

    A. Identifying active systems on the network

    B. Cracking passwords

    C. Identifying users and machine names

    D. Identifying routers and firewalls

17. What is a command-line tool used to look up a username from a SID?

    A. UsertoSID

    B. Userenum

    C. SID2User

    D. GetAcct

18. Which tool can be used to perform a DNS zone transfer on Windows?

    A. NSlookup

    B. DNSlookup

    C. Whois

    D. IPconfig

19. What is a null session?

    A. Connecting to a system with the administrator username and password

    B. Connecting to a system with the admin username and password

    C. Connecting to a system with a random username and password

    D. Connecting to a system with no username and password

20. What is a countermeasure for SNMP enumeration?

    A. Remove the SNMP agent from the device.

    B. Shut down ports 135 and 139 at the firewall.

    C. Shut down ports 80 and 443 at the firewall.

    D. Enable SNMP read-only security on the agent device.

Answers to Review Questions

1. A. FTP uses TCP port 21. This is a well-known port number and can be found in the Windows Services file.

2. A. HTTPS uses TCP port 443. This is a well-known port number and can be found in the Windows Services file.

3. B. War dialing involves placing calls to a series of numbers in hopes that a modem will answer the call. It can be used to test the security of a remote-access system.

4. A. Banner grabbing is not detectible; therefore it is considered passive OS fingerprinting.

5. A. Port, network, and vulnerability are the three types of scanning.

6. C. Systems may not respond to ICMP because they have firewall software installed that blocks the responses.

7. D. The TCP RST command resets the TCP connection.

8. A. A SYN packet is followed by a SYN-ACK packet. Then, an ACK finishes a successful TCP connection.

9. C. An XMAS scan has all flags set.

10. B. The command `nmap -sS -paranoid` performs a SYN scan every 300 seconds, or 5 minutes.

11. C. Block the ports used by NetBIOS null sessions. These are 139 and 445.

12. D. Port 137 is used for NetBIOS null sessions.

13. B. The SNMP read/write community name is the password used to make changes to the device configuration.

14. A. Ports in the 135 to 139 range indicate the system has SMB services running and is susceptible to null sessions.

15. A. Password cracking is the next step in the CEH hacking cycle after enumerating users.

16. C. Enumeration is the process of finding usernames, machine names, network shares, and services on the network.

17. C. SID2User is a command-line tool that is used to find a username from a SID.

18. A. NSlookup is a Windows tool that can be used to initiate a DNS zone transfer that sends all the DNS records to a hacker's system.

19. D. A null session involves connecting to a system with no username and password.

20. A. The best countermeasure to SNMP enumeration is to remove the SNMP agent from the device. Doing so prevents it from responding to SNMP requests.

System Hacking: Password Cracking, Escalating Privileges, and Hiding Files

---

CEH EXAM OBJECTIVES COVERED IN THIS CHAPTER:

- ✓ Understand password-cracking techniques

- ✓ Understand different types of passwords

- ✓ Identify various password-cracking tools

- ✓ Understand escalating privileges

- ✓ Understand keyloggers and other spyware technologies

- ✓ Understand how to hide files

- ✓ Understand rootkits

- ✓ Understand steganography technologies

- ✓ Understand how to cover your tracks and erase evidence

In this chapter, we'll look at the various aspects of system hacking. As you recall from Chapter 3, "Gathering Network and Host Information: Scanning and Enumeration," the system hacking cycle consists of six steps. The first step—enumeration—was discussed in the previous chapter. This chapter covers the five remaining steps:

- Cracking passwords
- Escalating privileges
- Executing applications
- Hiding files
- Covering tracks

The Simplest Way to Get a Password

Many hacking attempts start with getting a password to a target system. Passwords are the key piece of information needed to access a system, and users often select passwords that are easy to guess. Many reuse passwords or choose one that's simple—such as a pet's name—to help them remember it. Because of this human factor, most password guessing is successful if some information is known about the target. Information gathering and reconnaissance can help give away information that will help a hacker guess a user's password.

Once a password is guessed or cracked, it can be the launching point for escalating privileges, executing applications, hiding files, and covering tracks. If guessing a password fails, then passwords may be cracked manually or with automated tools such as a dictionary or brute-force method, each of which are covered later in this chapter.

Types of Passwords

Several types of passwords are used to provide access to systems. The characters that form a password can fall into any of these categories:

- Only letters
- Only numbers
- Only special characters

- Letters and numbers
- Only letters and special characters
- Only numbers and special characters
- Letters, numbers, and special characters

A strong password is less susceptible to attack by a hacker. The following rules, proposed by the EC-Council, should be applied when you're creating a password, to protect it against attacks:

- Must not contain any part of the user's account name
- Must have a minimum of eight characters
- Must contain characters from at least three of the following categories:
  - Nonalphanumeric symbols ($,:"%@!#)
  - Numbers
  - Uppercase letters
  - Lowercase letters

A hacker may use different types of attacks in order to identify a password and gain further access to a system. The types of password attacks are as follows:

Passive Online   Eavesdropping on network password exchanges. Passive online attacks include sniffing, man-in-the-middle, and replay attacks.

Active Online   Guessing the Administrator password. Active online attacks include automated password guessing.

Offline   Dictionary, hybrid, and brute-force attacks.

Nonelectronic   Shoulder surfing, keyboard sniffing, and social engineering.

We'll look at each of these attacks in more detail in the following sections.

Passive Online Attacks

A passive online attack is also known as *sniffing* the password on a wired or wireless network. A passive attack is not detectable to the end user. The password is captured during the authentication process and can then be compared against a dictionary file or word list. User account passwords are commonly *hashed* or encrypted when sent on the network to prevent unauthorized access and use. If the password is protected by encryption or hashing, special tools in the hacker's toolkit can be used to break the algorithm.

Cracking the password-hashing will be discussed later in this chapter in the "Attacks" section.

Another passive online attack is known as *man-in-the-middle* (MITM). In a MITM attack, the hacker intercepts the authentication request and forwards it to the server. By inserting a sniffer between the client and the server, the hacker is able to sniff both connections and capture passwords in the process.

A *replay attack* is also a passive online attack; it occurs when the hacker intercepts the password en route to the authentication server and then captures and resends the authentication packets for later authentication. In this manner, the hacker doesn't have to break the password or learn the password through MITM but rather captures the password and reuses the password-authentication packets later to authenticate as the client.

Active Online Attacks

The easiest way to gain administrator-level access to a system is to guess a simple password assuming the administrator used a simple password. Password guessing is an active online attack. It relies on the human factor involved in password creation and only works on weak passwords.

In Chapter 3, when we discussed the Enumeration phase of system hacking, you learned the vulnerability of NetBIOS enumeration and null sessions. Assuming that the NetBIOS TCP 139 port is open, the most effective method of breaking into a Windows NT or Windows 2000 system is password guessing. This is done by attempting to connect to an enumerated share (IPC$ or C$) and trying a username and password combination. The most commonly used Administrator account and password combinations are words like Admin, Administrator, Sysadmin, or Password, or a null password.

A hacker may first try to connect to a default Admin$, C$, or C:\Windows share. To connect to the hidden C: drive share, for example, type the following command in the Run field (Start ⇨ Run):

`\\ip_address\c$`

Automated programs can quickly generate dictionary files, word lists, or every possible combination of letters, numbers, and special characters and then attempt to log on using those credentials. Most systems prevent this type of attack by setting a maximum number of login attempts on a system before the account is locked.

In the following sections, we'll discuss how hackers can perform automated password guessing more closely, as well as countermeasures to such attacks.

Performing Automated Password Guessing

To speed up the guessing of a password, hackers use automated tools. An easy process for automating password guessing is to use the Windows shell commands based on the standard NET USE syntax. To create a simple automated password-guessing script, perform the following steps:

1. Create a simple username and password file using Windows Notepad. Automated tools such as the Dictionary Generator are available to create this word list. Save the file on the C: drive as credentials.txt.

2. Pipe this file using the FOR command:

```
C:\> FOR /F "token=1, 2*" %i in (credentials.txt)
```

3. Type **net use \\targetIP\IPC$ %i /u: %j** to use the credentials.txt file to attempt to log on to the target system's hidden share.

> Another example of how the FOR command can be used by an attacker is to wipe the contents of the hard disk with zeros using the command syntax ((i=0; i<11; i++)); do dd if=/dev/random of=/dev/hda && dd if=/dev/zero of=dev/hda done. The wipe command could also be used to perform the wiping of data from the hard disk using the command $ wipe -fik /dev/hda1.

Defending Against Password Guessing

Two options exist to defend against password guessing and password attacks. Both smart cards and biometrics add a layer of security to the insecurity that's inherent when users create their own passwords.

A user can also be authenticated and validated using *biometrics*. Biometrics use physical characteristics such as fingerprints, hand geometry scans, and retinal scans as credentials to validate users.

Both smart cards and biometrics use *two-factor authentication*, which requires two forms of identification (such as the actual smart card and a password) when validating a user. By requiring something the user physically has (a smart card, in this instance) and something the user knows (their password), security is increased, and the authentication process isn't susceptible to password attacks.

> RSA Secure ID is a two-factor authentication system that utilizes a token and a password.

Offline Attacks

Offline attacks are performed from a location other than the actual computer where the passwords reside or were used. Offline attacks usually require physical access to the computer and copying the password file from the system onto removable media. The hacker then takes the file to another computer to perform the cracking. Several types of offline password attacks exist, as you can see in Table 4.1.

TABLE 4.1   Offline attacks

Type of attack	Characteristics	Example password
Dictionary attack	Attempts to use passwords from a list of dictionary words	Administrator
Hybrid attack	Substitutes numbers of symbols for password characters	Adm1n1strator
Brute-force attack	Tries all possible combinations of letters, numbers, and special characters	Ms!tr245@F5a

A dictionary attack is the simplest and quickest type of attack. It's used to identify a password that is an actual word, which can be found in a dictionary. Most commonly, the attack uses a dictionary file of possible words, which is hashed using the same algorithm used by the authentication process. Then, the hashed dictionary words are compared with hashed passwords as the user logs on, or with passwords stored in a file on the server. The dictionary attack works only if the password is an actual dictionary word; therefore, this type of attack has some limitations. It can't be used against strong passwords containing numbers or other symbols.

A hybrid attack is the next level of attack a hacker attempts if the password can't be found using a dictionary attack. The hybrid attack starts with a dictionary file and substitutes numbers and symbols for characters in the password. For example, many users add the number 1 to the end of their password to meet strong password requirements. A hybrid attack is designed to find those types of anomalies in passwords.

The most time-consuming type of attack is a brute-force attack, which tries every possible combination of uppercase and lowercase letters, numbers, and symbols. A brute-force attack is the slowest of the three types of attacks because of the many possible combinations of characters in the password. However, brute force is effective; given enough time and processing power, all passwords can eventually be identified.

A *rainbow table* is a list of dictionary words that have already been hashed. Rainbow tables can speed up the discovery and cracking of passwords by pre-computing the hashes for common strings of characters. For example, a rainbow table can include characters from a to z or A to Z. Essentially, rainbow table tools are hash crackers. A traditional brute-force cracker will try all possible plaintext passwords one by one in order. It is time consuming to break complex passwords in this way. The idea of rainbow tables is to do all cracking-time computation in advance.

Nonelectronic Attacks

Nonelectronic—or nontechnical attacks—are attacks that do not employ any technical knowledge. This kind of attack can include social engineering, shoulder surfing, keyboard sniffing, and dumpster diving.

Social engineering is the art of interacting with people either face to face or over the telephone and getting them to give out valuable information such as passwords. Social engineering relies on people's good nature and desire to help others. Many times, a help desk is the target of a social-engineering attack because their job is to help people—and recovering or resetting passwords is a common function of the help desk. The best defense against social-engineering attacks is security-awareness training for all employees and security procedures for resetting passwords.

Social engineering was covered in more detail in Chapter 2, "Gathering Target Information: Reconnaissance, Footprinting, and Social Engineering."

Shoulder surfing involves looking over someone's shoulder as they type a password. This can be effective when the hacker is in close proximity to the user and the system. Special screens that make it difficult to see the computer screen from an angle can cut down on shoulder surfing. In addition, employee awareness and training can virtually eliminate this type of attack.

 Real World Scenario

Shoulder Surfing

Sue is a receptionist at a busy doctor's office. She was working at her computer when a flower delivery man came into the office. He told Sue he had a flower delivery for Dr. Smith. This was the doctor's name he saw on the front door of the office as he entered the waiting room.

Sue was busy that day and Dr. Smith was in with a patient, so she told the flower delivery man that he could leave the flowers on the desk and she would make sure the doctor received them. He said he needed to wait and give them directly to the person who was listed on the delivery ticket. So, Sue asked him to stay in the waiting room until Dr. Smith was available to receive the flower delivery. As Sue turned back to her computer to finish writing an email she had started, she was distracted thinking about the work she had in front of her. She quickly typed the password to unlock her Windows workstation. The flower delivery man paused for just a moment before turning to take a seat in the waiting room. As he paused, he was able to see the five-character password Sue typed to unlock her screen. It was in this manner that he was able to discern her password and continue the hacking process. The password was gathered using shoulder surfing, a form of social engineering.

Dumpster diving hackers look through the trash for information such as passwords, which may be written down on a piece of paper. Again, security awareness training on shredding important documents can prevent a hacker from gathering passwords by dumpster diving.

Cracking a Password

Manual password cracking involves attempting to log on with different passwords. The hacker follows these steps:

1. Find a valid user account (such as Administrator or Guest).
2. Create a list of possible passwords.
3. Rank the passwords from high to low probability.
4. Key in each password.
5. Try again until a successful password is found.

A hacker can also create a script file that tries each password in a list. This is still considered manual cracking, but it's time consuming and not usually effective.

A more efficient way of cracking a password is to gain access to the password file on a system. Most systems *hash* (one-way encrypt) a password for storage on a system. During the logon process, the password entered by the user is hashed using the same algorithm and then compared to the hashed passwords stored in the file. A hacker can attempt to gain access to the hashing algorithm stored on the server instead of trying to guess or otherwise identify the password. If the hacker is successful, they can decrypt the passwords stored on the server.

 Passwords are stored in the Security Accounts Manager (SAM) file on a Windows system and in a password shadow file on a Linux system.

Hacking Tools

Legion automates the password guessing in NetBIOS sessions. Legion scans multiple IP address ranges for Windows shares and also offers a manual dictionary attack tool.

NTInfoScan is a security scanner for NT 4.0. This vulnerability scanner produces an HTML-based report of security issues found on the target system and other information.

L0phtCrack is a password auditing and recovery package distributed by @stake software, which is now owned by Symantec. It performs Server Message Block (SMB) packet captures on the local network segment and captures individual login sessions. L0phtCrack contains dictionary, brute-force, and hybrid attack capabilities. Symantec has recently stopped development of the L0phtCrack tool, but it can still be found on the Internet.

LC5 is another good password cracking tool. LC5 is a suitable replacement for L0phtCrack.

John the Ripper is a command-line tool designed to crack both Unix and NT passwords. The cracked passwords are case insensitive and may not represent the real mixed-case password.

KerbCrack consists of two programs: kerbsniff and kerbcrack. The sniffer listens on the network and captures Windows 2000/XP Kerberos logins. The cracker can be used to find the passwords from the capture file using a brute-force attack or a dictionary attack.

Understanding the LAN Manager Hash

Windows 2000 uses NT LAN Manager (NTLM) hashing to secure passwords in transit on the network. Depending on the password, NTLM hashing can be weak and easy to break. For example, let's say that the password is 123456abcdef. When this password is encrypted with the NTLM algorithm, it's first converted to all uppercase: 123456ABCDEF. The password is padded with null (blank) characters to make it 14 characters long: 123456ABCDEF__. Before the password is encrypted, the 14-character string is split in half: 123456A and BCDEF__. Each string is individually encrypted, and the results are concatenated:

```
123456A = 6BF11E04AFAB197F
BCDEF__ = F1E9FFDCC75575B15
```

The hash is 6BF11E04AFAB197FF1E9FFDCC75575B15.

 The first half of the password contains alphanumeric characters; L0pht-Crack will take 24 hours to crack this part. The second half contains only letters and symbols and will take 60 seconds to crack. This is because there are many fewer combinations in the second half of the hashed password. If the password is seven characters or fewer, the second half of the hash will always be AAD3B435B51404EE.

Cracking Windows 2000 Passwords

The SAM file in Windows contains the usernames and hashed passwords. It's located in the Windows\system32\config directory. The file is locked when the operating system is running so that a hacker can't attempt to copy the file while the machine is booted to Windows.

One option for copying the SAM file is to boot to an alternate operating system such as DOS or Linux with a boot CD. Alternately, the file can be copied from the repair directory. If a system administrator uses the RDISK feature of Windows to back up the system, then a compressed copy of the SAM file called SAM._ is created in C:\windows\repair. To expand this file, use the following command at the command prompt:

C:\>expand sam._ sam

After the file is uncompressed, a dictionary, hybrid, or brute-force attack can be run against the SAM file using a tool like L0phtCrack. A similar tool to L0phtcrack is Ophcrack. Exercise 4.1 illustrates how to use Ophcrack to crack passwords.

Hacking Tools

Win32CreateLocalAdminUser is a program that creates a new user with the username and password X and adds the user to the local administrator's group. This action is part of the Metasploit Project and can be launched with the Metasploit framework on Windows.

Offline NT Password Resetter is a method of resetting the password to the administrator's account when the system isn't booted to Windows. The most common method is to boot to a Linux boot CD and then access the NTFS partition, which is no longer protected, and change the password.

EXERCISE 4.1

Use Ophcrack to Crack Passwords

1. Download and install ophcrack from http://ophcrack.sourceforge.net/.

2. Run the ophcrack program and set the number of threads under the Preferences tab to the number of cores of the computer running ophcrack plus one. If you change this value, you have to exit ophcrack and restart it in order to save the change.

    Note: This step is optional but will speed up the cracking process.

3. Click the Load button to add hashes. There are numerous ways to add the hashes:

    -   Enter the hash manually (Single Hash option)

    -   Import a text file containing hashes you created with pwdump, fgdump, or similar third-party tools (PWDUMP File option)

    -   Extract the hashes from the SYSTEM and SAM files (Encrypted SAM option)

    -   Dump the SAM from the computer ophcrack is running on (Local SAM option)

    -   Dump the SAM from a remote computer (Remote SAM option)

Note: For the Encrypted SAM option, the SAM is located under the Windows system32/config directory and can only be accessed for a Windows partition that is *not* running. For the Local SAM and Remote SAM options, you must be logged in with the administrator rights on the computer you want to dump the SAM.

4. Click the Tables button.

5. Click the enable (green and yellow) buttons.

6. Using the up and down arrows, sort the rainbow tables you are going to use. Keep in mind that storing the rainbow tables on a fast medium like a hard disk will significantly speed up the cracking process.

7. Click the Crack button to start the cracking process. You'll see the progress of the cracking process in the bottom boxes of the ophcrack window. When a password is found, it will be displayed in the NT Pwd field. You can save the results of a cracking session at any time by clicking the Save button.

Redirecting the SMB Logon to the Attacker

Another way to discover passwords on a network is to redirect the Server Message Block (SMB) logon to an attacker's computer so that the passwords are sent to the hacker. In order to do this, the hacker must sniff the NTLM responses from the authentication server and trick the victim into attempting Windows authentication with the attacker's computer. A common technique is to send the victim an email message with an embedded link to a fraudulent SMB server. When the link is clicked, the user unwittingly sends their credentials over the network.

SMBRelay   An SMB server that captures usernames and password hashes from incoming SMB traffic. SMBRelay can also perform man-in-the-middle (MITM) attacks.

SMBRelay2   Similar to SMBRelay but uses NetBIOS names instead of IP addresses to capture usernames and passwords.

pwdump2   A program that extracts the password hashes from a SAM file on a Windows system. The extracted password hashes can then be run through L0phtCrack to break the passwords.

Samdump   Another program that extracts NTLM hashed passwords from a SAM file.

C2MYAZZ   A spyware program that makes Windows clients send their passwords as cleartext. It displays usernames and their passwords as users attach to server resources.

SMB Relay MITM Attacks and Countermeasures

An SMB relay MITM attack is when the attacker sets up a fraudulent server with a relay address. When a victim client connects to the fraudulent server, the MITM server intercepts the call, hashes the password, and passes the connection to the victim server. Figure 4.1 illustrates such an attack.

FIGURE 4.1   SMB relay MITM attack

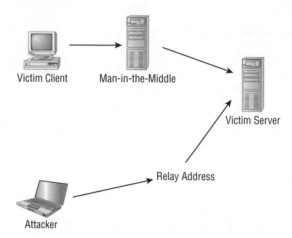

SMB relay countermeasures include configuring Windows 2000 to use SMB signing, which causes it to cryptographically sign each block of SMB communications.

Hacking Tools

SMBGrind increases the speed of L0phtCrack sessions on sniffer dumps by removing duplication and providing a way to target specific users without having to edit the dump files manually.

The SMBDie tool crashes computers running Windows 2000, XP, or NT by sending specially crafted SMB requests.

NBTdeputy can register a NetBIOS computer name on a network and respond to NetBIOS over TCP/IP (NetBT) name-query requests. It simplifies the use of SMBRelay. The relay can be referred to by computer name instead of IP address.

NetBIOS DoS Attacks

A NetBIOS denial-of-service (DoS) attack sends a NetBIOS Name Release message to the NetBIOS Name Service on a target Windows systems and forces the system to place its name in conflict so that the name can no longer be used. This essentially blocks the client from participating in the NetBIOS network and creates a network DoS for that system.

Hacking Tool

NBName can disable entire LANs and prevent machines from rejoining them. Nodes on a NetBIOS network infected by the tool think that their names are already in use by other machines.

Another way to create a more secure and memorable password is to follow a repeatable pattern, which will enable to password to be re-created when needed.

1. Start with a memorable phrase, such as

    Maryhadalittlelamb

2. Change every other character to uppercase, resulting in

    MaRyHaDaLiTtLeLaMb

3. Change a to @ and i to 1 to yield

    M@RyH@D@L1TtLeL@Mb

4. Drop every other pair to result in a secure repeatable password or

    M@H@L1LeMb

Now you have a password that meets all the requirements, yet can be "remade" if necessary.

Password-Cracking Countermeasures

The strongest passwords possible should be implemented to protect against password cracking. Systems should enforce 8–12-character alphanumeric passwords. The length of time the same password should be used is discussed in the next section.

To protect against cracking of the hashing algorithm for passwords stored on the server, you must take care to physically isolate and protect the server. The system administrator can use the SYSKEY utility in Windows to further protect hashes stored on the server's hard disk. The server logs should also be monitored for brute-force attacks on user accounts.

A system administrator can implement the following security precautions to decrease the effectiveness of a brute-force password-cracking attempt:

- Never leave a default password.

- Never use a password that can be found in a dictionary.

- Never use a password related to the hostname, domain name, or anything else that can be found with Whois.

- Never use a password related to your hobbies, pets, relatives, or date of birth.

- As a last resort, use a word that has more than 21 characters from a dictionary as a password.

 This subject is discussed further in the section "Monitoring Event Viewer Logs," later in this chapter.

In the following sections, we'll look at two measures you can take to strengthen passwords and prevent password-cracking.

Password Change Interval

Passwords should expire after a certain amount of time so that users are forced to change them. If the password interval is set too low, users will forget their current passwords; as a result, a system administrator will have to reset users' passwords frequently. On the other hand, if passwords are allowed to be used for too long, security may be compromised. The recommended password-change interval is every 30 days. In addition, most security professionals recommended that users not be allowed to reuse the last three passwords.

 You cannot completely block brute-force password attacks if the hacker switches the proxy server where the source packet is generated. A system administrator can only add security features to decrease the likelihood that brute-force password attacks will be useful.

Monitoring Event Viewer Logs

Administrators should monitor Event Viewer logs to recognize any intrusion attempts either before they take place or while they're occurring. Generally, several failed attempts are logged in the system logs before a successful intrusion or password attack. The security logs are only as good as the system administrators who monitor them.

Tools such as VisualLast aid a network administrator in deciphering and analyzing the security log files. VisualLast provides greater insight into the NT event logs so the administrator can assess the activity of the network more accurately and efficiently. The program is designed to allow network administrators to view and report individual users' logon and logoff times; these events may be searched according to time frame, which is invaluable to security analysts who are looking for intrusion details.

The event log located at `c:\\windows\system32\config\Sec.Event.Evt` contains the trace of an attacker's brute-force attempts.

Understanding Keyloggers and Other Spyware Technologies

If all other attempts to gather passwords fail, then a *keystroke logger* is the tool of choice for hackers. Keystroke loggers (keyloggers) can be implemented either using hardware or software. Hardware keyloggers are small hardware devices that connect the keyboard to the PC and save every keystroke into a file or in the memory of the hardware device. In order to install a hardware keylogger, a hacker must have physical access to the system.

Software keyloggers are pieces of stealth software that sit between the keyboard hardware and the operating system so that they can record every keystroke. Software keyloggers can be deployed on a system by Trojans or viruses.

 Using Trojans and viruses will be discussed in Chapter 5, "Installing Software on Target Systems: Spyware, Trojans, Backdoors, Viruses, and Worms."

Hacking Tools

Spector is spyware that records everything a system does on the Internet, much like a surveillance camera. Spector automatically takes hundreds of snapshots every hour of whatever is on the computer screen and saves these snapshots in a hidden location on the system's hard drive. Spector can be detected and removed with Anti-spector.

eBlaster is Internet spy software that captures incoming and outgoing emails and immediately forwards them to another email address. eBlaster can also capture both sides of an Instant Messenger conversation, perform keystroke logging, and record websites visited.

SpyAnywhere is a tool that allows you to view system activity and user actions, shut down/restart, lock down/freeze, and even browse the file system of a remote system. SpyAnywhere lets you control open programs and windows on the remote system and view Internet histories and related information.

Invisible KeyLogger Stealth (IKS) Software Logger is a high-performance virtual device driver (VxD) that runs silently at the lowest level of the Windows 95, 98, or ME operating system. All keystrokes are recorded in a binary keystroke file.

Fearless Key Logger is a Trojan that remains resident in memory to capture all user keystrokes. Captured keystrokes are stored in a log file and can be retrieved by a hacker.

E-mail Keylogger logs all emails sent and received on a target system. The emails can be viewed by sender, recipient, subject, and time/date. The email contents and any attachments are also recorded.

Escalating Privileges

Escalating privileges is the third step in the hacking cycle. *Escalating privileges* basically means adding more rights or permissions to a user account. Simply said, escalating privileges makes a regular user account into an administrator account.

Generally, administrator accounts have more stringent password requirements, and their passwords are more closely guarded. If it isn't possible to find a username and password of an account with administrator privileges, a hacker may choose to use an account with lower privileges. In this case, the hacker must then escalate that account's privileges.

This is accomplished by first gaining access using a nonadministrator user account—typically by gathering the username and password through one of the previously discussed methods—and then increasing the privileges on the account to the level of an administrator.

Hacking Tools

GetAdmin.exe is a small program that adds a user to the local administrators group. It uses a low-level NT kernel routine to allowing access to any running process. A logon to the server console is needed to execute the program. GetAdmin.exe is run from the command line or from a browser. It works only with Windows NT 4.0 Service Pack 3.

The Hk.exe utility exposes a local procedure call (LPC) flaw in Windows NT. A nonadministrator user can be escalated to the administrators group using this tool.

Once a hacker has a valid user account and password, the next step is to execute applications. Generally the hacker needs to have an account with administrator-level access in order to install programs, and that is why escalating privileges is so important. In the following sections, we'll see what hackers can do with your system once they have administrator privileges.

Executing Applications

Once a hacker has been able to access an account with administrator privileges, the next thing they do is execute applications on the target system. The purpose of executing applications may be to install a backdoor on the system, install a keystroke logger to gather confidential information, copy files, or just cause damage to the system—essentially, anything the hacker wants to do on the system.

Once the hacker is able to execute applications, the system is considered *owned* and under the control of the hacker.

Hacking Tools

PsExec is a program that connects to and executes files on remote systems. No software needs to be installed on the remote system.

Remoxec executes a program using RPC (Task Scheduler) or DCOM (Windows Management Instrumentation) services. Administrators with null or weak passwords may be exploited through Task Scheduler (1025/tcp or above) or Distributed Component Object Mode (DCOM; default 135/tcp).

Buffer Overflows

Buffer overflows are hacking attempts that exploit a flaw in an application's code. Essentially, the buffer overflow attack sends too much information to a field variable in an application, which can cause an application error. Most times, the application doesn't know what action to perform next because it's been overwritten with the overflow data. Therefore, it either executes the command in the overflow data or displays a command prompt to allow the user to enter the next command. The command prompt or shell is the key for a hacker and can be used to execute other applications.

 Buffer overflows will be discussed in greater detail in Chapter 9, "Attacking Applications: SQL Injection and Buffer Overflows."

Understanding Rootkits

A rootkit is a type of program often used to hide utilities on a compromised system. Rootkits include so-called *backdoors* to help an attacker subsequently access the system more easily. For example, the rootkit may hide an application that spawns a shell when the attacker connects to a particular network port on the system. A backdoor may also allow processes started by a nonprivileged user to execute functions normally reserved for the administrator. A rootkit is frequently used to allow the programmer of the rootkit to see and access usernames and log-in information for sites that require them.

There are several types of rootkits, including the following:

Kernel-Level Rootkits   Kernel-level rootkits add code and/or replace a portion of kernel code with modified code to help hide a backdoor on a computer system. This is often accomplished by adding new code to the kernel via a device driver or loadable module, such as loadable kernel modules in Linux or device drivers in Windows. Kernel-level rootkits are especially dangerous because they can be difficult to detect without appropriate software.

Library-Level Rootkits   Library-level rootkits commonly patch, hook, or replace system calls with versions that hide information that might allow the hacker to be identified.

Application-Level Rootkits   Application-level rootkits may replace regular application binaries with Trojanized fakes, or they may modify the behavior of existing applications using hooks, patches, injected code, or other means.

In the following sections, we'll explore the process of infecting a system with a rootkit.

Planting Rootkits on Windows 2000 and XP Machines

The Windows NT/2000 rootkit is built as a kernel-mode driver, which can be dynamically loaded at runtime. The rootkit runs with system privileges at the core of the NT kernel, so it has access to all the resources of the operating system. The rootkit can also hide processes, hide files, hide Registry entries, intercept keystrokes typed at the system console, issue a debug interrupt to cause a blue screen of death, and redirect EXE files.

The rootkit contains a kernel mode device driver called _root_.sys and a launcher program called DEPLOY.EXE. After gaining access to the target system, the attacker copies _root_.sys and DEPLOY.EXE onto the target system and executes DEPLOY.EXE. Doing so installs the rootkit device driver and starts it. The attacker later deletes DEPLOY.EXE from the target machine. The attacker can then stop and restart the rootkit at will by using the commands net stop _root_ and net start _root_. Once the rootkit is started, the file _root_.sys no longer appears in directory listings; the rootkit intercepts system calls for file listings and hides all files beginning with _root_ from display.

Rootkit Embedded TCP/IP Stack

A new feature of the Windows NT/2000 rootkit is a stateless TCP/IP stack. It works by determining the state of the connection based on the data in the incoming packet. The rootkit has a hard-coded IP address (10.0.0.166) to which it will respond. The rootkit uses raw Ethernet connections to the system's network card, so it's very powerful. The target port doesn't matter; a hacker can telnet to any port on the system. In addition, multiple people can log into the rootkit at once.

Rootkit Countermeasures

All rootkits require administrator access to the target system, so password security is critical. If you detect a rootkit, you should back up critical data and reinstall the operating system and applications from a trusted source. The administrator should also keep available a well-documented automated installation procedure and trusted restoration media.

Another countermeasure is to use the *MD5 checksum* utility. The MD5 checksum for a file is a 128-bit value, something like the file's fingerprint. (There is a small possibility of getting two identical checksums for two different files.) This algorithm is designed so that changing even one bit in the file data causes a different checksum value. This feature can be useful for comparing files and ensuring their integrity. Another good feature is the checksum's fixed length, regardless of the size of the source file.

The MD5 checksum makes sure a file hasn't changed. This can be useful in checking file integrity if a rootkit has been found on a system. Tools such as Tripwire implement MD5 checksums to identify files affected by the rootkit.

Countermeasure Tools

Tripwire is a file system integrity-checking program for Unix and Linux operating systems. In addition to one or more cryptographic checksums representing the contents of each directory and file, the Tripwire database also contains information that lets you verify access permissions and file mode settings, the username of the file owner, the date and time the file was last accessed, and the last modification made to the item.

Hiding Files

A hacker may want to hide files on a system to prevent their detection. These files may then be used to launch an attack on the system. There are two ways to hide files in Windows. The first is to use the `attrib` command. To hide a file with the `attrib` command, type the following at the command prompt:

```
attrib +h [file/directory]
```

The second way to hide a file in Windows is with NTFS alternate data streaming. NTFS file systems used by Windows NT, 2000, and XP have a feature called *alternate data streams* that allow data to be stored in hidden files linked to a normal, visible file. Streams aren't limited in size; more than one stream can be linked to a normal file.

NTFS File Streaming

NTFS file streaming allows a hidden file to be created within a legitimate file. The hidden file does not appear in a directory listing but the legitimate file does. A user would usually not suspect the legitimate file, but the hidden file can be used to store or transmit information. In Exercise 4.2, you'll learn how to hide files using NTFS file streaming.

EXERCISE 4.2

Hiding Files Using NTFS File Streaming

Note: This exercise will only work on systems using the NTFS file system.

To create and test an NTFS file stream:

1. At the command line, enter **notepad test.txt**.

2. Put some data in the file, save the file, and close Notepad. Step 1 will open Notepad.

3. At the command line, enter **dir test.txt** and note the file size.

4. At the command line, enter **notepad test.txt:hidden.txt**. Type some text into Notepad, save the file, and close it.

5. Check the file size again (it should be the same as in step 3).

6. Open test.txt. You see only the original data.

7. Enter **type test.txt:hidden.txt** at the command line. A syntax error message is displayed.

Hacking Tool

makestrm.exe is a utility that moves the data from a file to an alternate data stream linked to the original file.

NTFS Stream Countermeasures

To delete a stream file, copy the first file to a FAT partition, and then copy it back to an NTFS partition.

Streams are lost when the file is moved to a FAT partition because they're a feature of NTFS and therefore exist only on an NTFS partition.

> **Countermeasure Tool**
>
> You can use `lns.exe` to detect NTFS streams. LNS reports the existence and location of files that contain alternate data streams.

Understanding Steganography Technologies

Steganography is the process of hiding data in other types of data such as images or text files. The most popular method of hiding data in files is to utilize graphic images as hiding places. Attackers can embed any information in a graphic file using steganography. The hacker can hide directions on making a bomb, a secret bank account number, or answers to a test. Any text imaginable can be hidden in an image. In Exercise 4.3 you will use Image Hide to hide text within an image.

> **Hacking Tools**
>
> ImageHide is a steganography program that hides large amounts of text in images. Even after adding bytes of data, there is no increase in the image size. The image looks the same in a normal graphics program. It loads and saves to files and therefore is able to bypass most email sniffers.
>
> Blindside is a steganography application that hides information inside BMP (bitmap) images. It's a command-line utility.
>
> MP3Stego hides information in MP3 files during the compression process. The data is compressed, encrypted, and then hidden in the MP3 bitstream.
>
> Snow is a whitespace steganography program that conceals messages in ASCII text by appending whitespace to the end of lines. Because spaces and tabs generally aren't visible in text viewers, the message is effectively hidden from casual observers. If the built-in encryption is used, the message can't be read even if it's detected.
>
> CameraShy works with Windows and Internet Explorer and lets users share censored or sensitive information stored in an ordinary GIF image.
>
> Stealth is a filtering tool for PGP files. It strips off identifying information from the header, after which the file can be used for steganography.

EXERCISE 4.3

Hiding Data in an Image Using ImageHide

To hide data in an image using ImageHide:

1. Download and install the ImageHide program.

2. Add an image in the Image Hide program.

3. Add text in the field at the bottom of the ImageHide screen.

4. Hide the text within the image using ImageHide.

Steganography can be detected by some programs, although doing so is difficult. The first step in detection is to locate files with hidden text, which can be done by analyzing patterns in the images and changes to the color palette.

Countermeasure Tools

Stegdetect is an automated tool for detecting steganographic content in images. It's capable of detecting different steganographic methods to embed hidden information in JPEG images.

Dskprobe is a tool on the Windows 2000 installation CD. It's a low-level hard-disk scanner that can detect steganography.

Covering Your Tracks and Erasing Evidence

Once intruders have successfully gained administrator access on a system, they try to cover their tracks to prevent detection of their presence (either current or past) on the system. A hacker may also try to remove evidence of their identity or activities on the system to prevent tracing of their identity or location by authorities. To prevent detection, the hacker usually erases any error messages or security events that have been logged. Disabling auditing and clearing the event log are two methods used by a hacker to cover their tracks and avoid detection.

The first thing intruders do after gaining administrator privileges is disable auditing. Windows auditing records certain events in a log file that is stored in the Windows Event Viewer. Events can include logging into the system, an application, or an event log. An administrator can choose the level of logging implemented on a system. Hackers want to determine the level of logging implemented to see whether they need to clear events that indicate their presence on the system.

Hacking Tool

Auditpol is a tool included in the Windows NT Resource Kit for system administrators. This tool can disable or enable auditing from the Windows command line. It can also be used to determine the level of logging implemented by a system administrator.

Intruders can easily wipe out the security logs in the Windows Event Viewer. An event log that contains one or just a few events is suspicious because it usually indicates that other events have been cleared. It's still necessary to clear the event log after disabling auditing, because using the Auditpol tool places an entry in the event log indicating that auditing has been disabled. Several tools exist to clear the event log, or a hacker can do so manually in the Windows Event Viewer.

Hacking Tools

The elsave.exe utility is a simple tool for clearing the event log. It's command line based.

WinZapper is a tool that an attacker can use to erase event records selectively from the security log in Windows 2000. WinZapper also ensures that no security events are logged while the program is running.

Evidence Eliminator is a data-cleansing system for Windows PCs. It prevents unwanted data from becoming permanently hidden in the system. It cleans the Recycle Bin, Internet cache, system files, temp folders, and so on. Evidence Eliminator can also be used by a hacker to remove evidence from a system after an attack.

Summary

The actual hacking of a target system can be broken down into simple steps. Guessing or cracking passwords, escalating privileges, hiding files, and covering tracks are all parts of the hacking process. It is these steps that usually uncover the most valuable information for hackers. However, the information-gathering and scanning steps should not be forgotten as they are critical in getting the most information about a target and its weaknesses. Good information gathering can greatly improve the success and speed of the hacking steps.

Exam Essentials

Understand the importance of password security. Implementing password-change intervals, strong alphanumeric passwords, and other password security measures is critical to network security.

Know the different types of password attacks. Passive online attacks include sniffing, man-in-the-middle, and replay. Active online attacks include passive and automated password guessing. Offline attacks include dictionary, hybrid, and brute force. Nonelectronic attacks include shoulder surfing, keyboard sniffing, and social engineering.

Understand the various types of offline password attacks. Dictionary, hybrid, and brute-force attacks are all offline password attacks.

Know the ways to defend against password guessing. Smart cards and biometrics are two ways to increase security and defend against password guessing.

Understand the differences between the types of nonelectronic attacks. Social engineering, shoulder surfing, and dumpster diving are all types of nonelectronic attacks.

Know how evidence of hacking activity is eliminated by attackers. Clearing event logs and disabling auditing are methods that attackers use to cover their tracks.

Realize that hiding files are means used to sneak out sensitive information. Steganography, NTFS streaming, and the attrib command are all ways hackers can hide and steal files.

Review Questions

1. What is the process of hiding text within an image called?

    A. Steganography

    B. Encryption

    C. Spyware

    D. Keystroke logging

2. What is a rootkit?

    A. A simple tool to gain access to the root of the Windows system

    B. A Trojan that sends information to an SMB relay

    C. An invasive program that affects the system files, including the kernel and libraries

    D. A tool to perform a buffer overflow

3. Why would hackers want to cover their tracks?

    A. To prevent another person from using the programs they have installed on a target system

    B. To prevent detection or discovery

    C. To prevent hacking attempts

    D. To keep other hackers from using their tools

4. What is privilege escalation?

    A. Creating a user account with higher privileges

    B. Creating a user account with administrator privileges

    C. Creating two user accounts: one with high privileges and one with lower privileges

    D. Increasing privileges on a user account

5. What are two methods used to hide files? (Choose all that apply.)

    A. NTFS file streaming

    B. `attrib` command

    C. Steganography

    D. Encrypted File System

6. What is the recommended password-change interval?

    A. 30 days

    B. 20 days

    C. 1 day

    D. 7 days

7. What type of password attack would be most successful against the password T63k#s23A?

   A. Dictionary

   B. Hybrid

   C. Password guessing

   D. Brute force

8. Which of the following is a passive online attack?

   A. Password guessing

   B. Network sniffing

   C. Brute-force attack

   D. Dictionary attack

9. Why is it necessary to clear the event log after using the `auditpol` command to turn off logging?

   A. The `auditpol` command places an entry in the event log.

   B. The `auditpol` command doesn't stop logging until the event log has been cleared.

   C. `auditpol` relies on the event log to determine whether logging is taking place.

   D. The event log doesn't need to be cleared after running the `auditpol` command.

10. What is necessary in order to install a hardware keylogger on a target system?

   A. The IP address of the system

   B. The administrator username and password

   C. Physical access to the system

   D. Telnet access to the system

11. What is the easiest method to get a password?

   A. Brute-force cracking

   B. Guessing

   C. Dictionary attack

   D. Hybrid attack

12. Which command is used to cover tracks on a target system?

   A. `elsave`

   B. `coverit`

   C. `legion`

   D. `nmap`

13. What type of hacking application is Snow?

    A. Password cracker

    B. Privilege escalation

    C. Spyware

    D. Steganography

14. What is the first thing a hacker should do after gaining administrative access to a system?

    A. Create a new user account

    B. Change the administrator password

    C. Copy important data files

    D. Disable auditing

15. Which of the following programs is a steganography detection tool?

    A. Stegdetect

    B. Stegoalert

    C. Stegstopper

    D. Stegorama

16. Which countermeasure tool will detect NTFS streams?

    A. Windows Security Manager

    B. LNS

    C. Auditpol

    D. RPS

17. Which program is used to create NTFS streams?

    A. StreamIT

    B. `makestrm.exe`

    C. NLS

    D. Windows Explorer

18. Why is it important to clear the event log after disabling auditing?

    A. An entry is created that the administrator has logged on.

    B. An entry is created that a hacking attempt is underway.

    C. An entry is created that indicates auditing has been disabled.

    D. The system will shut down otherwise.

19. What is the most dangerous type of rootkit?

    A. Kernel level

    B. Library level

    C. System level

    D. Application level

20. What is the command to hide a file using the `attrib` command?

    A. `att +h [file/directory]`

    B. `attrib +h [file/directory]`

    C. `attrib hide [file/directory]`

    D. `hide [file/directory]`

Answers to Review Questions

1. A. Steganography is the process of hiding text within an image.

2. C. A rootkit is a program that modifies the core of the operating system: the kernel and libraries.

3. B. Hackers cover their tracks to keep from having their identity or location discovered.

4. D. Privilege escalation is a hacking method to increase privileges on a user account.

5. A, B. NTFS file streaming and the `attrib` command are two hacking techniques used to hide files.

6. A. Passwords should be changed every 30 days for the best balance of security and usability.

7. D. A brute-force attack tries every combination of letters, numbers, and symbols.

8. B. Network sniffing is a passive online attack because it can't be detected.

9. A. The event log must be cleared because the `auditpol` command places an entry in the event log indicating that logging has been disabled.

10. C. A hardware keylogger is an adapter that connects the keyboard to the PC. A hacker needs physical access to the PC in order to plug in the hardware keylogger.

11. B. The easiest way to get a password is to guess the password. For this reason it is important to create strong passwords and to not reuse passwords.

12. A. `elsave` is a command used to clear the event log and cover a hacker's tracks.

13. D. Snow is a steganography program used to hide data within the whitespace of text files.

14. D. The first thing a hacker should do after gaining administrative level access to a system is disable system auditing to prevent detection and attempt to cover tracks.

15. A. Stegdetect is a steganography detection tool.

16. B. LNS is an NTFS countermeasure tool used to detect NTFS streams.

17. B. `makestrm.exe` is a program used to make NTFS streams.

18. C. It is important to clear the event log after disabling auditing because an entry is created indicating that auditing is disabled.

19. A. A kernel-level rootkit is the most dangerous because it infects the core of the system.

20. B. `attrib +h [file/directory]` is the command used to hide a file using the `hide` attribute.

Chapter
5

Trojans, Backdoors, Viruses, and Worms

CEH EXAM OBJECTIVES COVERED IN THIS CHAPTER:

- ✓ What is a Trojan?
- ✓ What is meant by overt and covert channels?
- ✓ List the different types of Trojans
- ✓ What are the indications of a Trojan attack?
- ✓ Understand how the "Netcat" Trojan works
- ✓ What is meant by "wrapping"?
- ✓ How do reverse connecting Trojans work?
- ✓ What are the countermeasure techniques in preventing Trojans?
- ✓ Understand Trojan evading techniques
- ✓ Understand the differences between a virus and a worm
- ✓ Understand the types of viruses
- ✓ How a virus spreads and infects a system
- ✓ Understand antivirus evasion techniques
- ✓ Understand virus detection methods

Trojans and backdoors are two ways a hacker can gain access to a target system. They come in many different varieties, but they all have one thing in common: they must be installed by another program, or the user must be tricked into installing the Trojan or backdoor on their system. Trojans and backdoors are potentially harmful tools in the ethical hacker's toolkit and should be used judiciously to test the security of a system or network.

Viruses and worms can be just as destructive to systems and networks as Trojans and backdoors. In fact, many viruses carry Trojan executables and can infect a system, then create a backdoor for hackers. This chapter will discuss the similarities and differences among Trojans, backdoors, viruses, and worms. All of these types of *malicious code* or *malware* are important to ethical hackers because they are commonly used by hackers to attack and compromise systems.

Trojans and Backdoors

Trojans and backdoors are types of malware used to infect and compromise computer systems. A *Trojan* is a malicious program disguised as something benign. In many cases the Trojan appears to perform a desirable function for the user but actually allows a hacker access to the user's computer system. Trojans are often downloaded along with another program or software package. Once installed on a system, they can cause data theft and loss, as well as system crashes or slowdowns. Trojans can also be used as launching points for other attacks, such as distributed denial of service (DDoS). Many Trojans are used to manipulate files on the victim computer, manage processes, remotely run commands, intercept keystrokes, watch screen images, and restart or shut down infected hosts. Sophisticated Trojans can connect themselves to their originator or announce the Trojan infection on an Internet Relay Chat (IRC) channel.

Trojans ride on the backs of other programs and are usually installed on a system without the user's knowledge. A Trojan can be sent to a victim system in many ways, such as the following:

- An instant messenger (IM) attachment
- IRC
- An email attachment
- NetBIOS file sharing
- A downloaded Internet program

Many fake programs purporting to be legitimate software such as freeware, spyware-removal tools, system optimizers, screensavers, music, pictures, games, and videos can install a Trojan on a system just by being downloaded. Advertisements on Internet sites for free programs, music files, or video files lure a victim into installing the Trojan program; the program then has system-level access on the target system, where it can be destructive and insidious.

Table 5.1 lists some common Trojans and their default port numbers.

TABLE 5.1   Common Trojan programs

Trojan	Protocol	Port
BackOrifice	UDP	31337 or 31338
Deep Throat	UDP	2140 and 3150
NetBus	TCP	12345 and 12346
Whack-a-Mole	TCP	12361 and 12362
NetBus 2	TCP	20034
GirlFriend	TCP	21544
Master's Paradise	TCP	3129, 40421, 40422, 40423, and 40426

A *backdoor* is a program or a set of related programs that a hacker installs on a target system to allow access to the system at a later time. A backdoor can be embedded in a malicious Trojan. The objective of installing a backdoor on a system is to give hackers access into the system at a time of their choosing. The key is that the hacker knows how to get into the backdoor undetected and is able to use it to hack the system further and look for important information.

Adding a new service is the most common technique to disguise backdoors in the Windows operating system. Before the installation of a backdoor, a hacker must investigate the system to find services that are running. Again the use of good information-gathering techniques is critical to knowing what services or programs are already running on the target system. In most cases the hacker installs the backdoor, which adds a new service and gives it an inconspicuous name or, better yet, chooses a service that's never used and that is either activated manually or completely disabled.

This technique is effective because when a hacking attempt occurs the system administrator usually focuses on looking for something odd in the system, leaving all existing services unchecked. The backdoor technique is simple but efficient: the hacker can get back into the machine with the least amount of visibility in the server logs. The backdoored service lets the hacker use higher privileges—in most cases, as a System account.

Remote Access Trojans (RATs) are a class of backdoors used to enable remote control over a compromised machine. They provide apparently useful functions to the user and, at the same time, open a network port on the victim computer. Once the RAT is started, it behaves as an executable file, interacting with certain Registry keys responsible for starting processes and sometimes creating its own system services. Unlike common backdoors, RATs hook themselves into the victim operating system and always come packaged with two files: the client file and the server file. The server is installed in the infected machine, and the client is used by the intruder to control the compromised system.

RATs allow a hacker to take control of the target system at any time. In fact one of the indications that a system has been exploited is unusual behavior on the system, such as the mouse moving on its own or pop-up windows appearing on an idle system.

A Word of Caution about Practicing with Trojans

I intentionally left any step-by-step exercises out of this section on Trojans and backdoors because I do not want to advocate anyone installing them on production systems and experiencing loss of data. However, the best way to learn how to use these tools and their capabilities is to install them and test them out. So here is my recommendation to learn ethical hacking skills using Trojans and backdoors.

Take an older computer that you do not have any intention of using again, or buy a second hard drive for your laptop (this is what I did). Install the Windows XP operating system with no service packs or updates enabled. Do not install any virus scanning or firewall. The next step is to really go crazy installing all the Trojans, rootkits, and backdoors tools listed in this chapter. This will give you the freedom to learn and test the tools without being blocked by a virus scan or personal firewall trying to protect your computer. Once you are finished, you can either reinstall Windows or just switch out the hard drive for your production drive.

A final suggestion if you are looking for a small, inexpensive computer to use as a test machine is to purchase an inexpensive netbook that runs Windows XP and use it to install and test tools.

Overt and Covert Channels

An *overt channel* is the normal and legitimate way that programs communicate within a computer system or network. A *covert channel* uses programs or communications paths in ways that were not intended.

Trojans can use covert channels to communicate. Some client Trojans use covert channels to send instructions to the server component on the compromised system. This sometimes makes Trojan communication difficult to decipher and understand. An unsuspecting intrusion detection system (IDS) sniffing the transmission between the Trojan client and server would not flag it as anything unusual. By using the covert channel, the Trojan can communicate or "phone home" undetected, and the hacker can send commands to the client component undetected.

 Real World Scenario

Using a Covert Channel

Jeremiah Denton, a prisoner of war during the Vietnam War, used a covert channel to communicate without his captors' knowledge. Denton was interviewed by a Japanese TV reporter, and eventually a videotape of the interview made its way to the United States. As American intelligence agents viewed the tape, one of them noticed Denton was blinking in an unusual manner. They discovered he was blinking letters in Morse code. The letters were T-O-R-T-U-R-E, and Denton was blinking them over and over. This is a real-world example of how a covert channel can be used to send a communication message undetected.

Another example of using a computer to convey information via a covert channel is the use a characteristic of a file to deliver information rather that the file itself. A computer-based example of a covert channel is in the creation of a seemingly innocent computer file 16 bytes in size. The file can contain any data as that is not the important information. The file can then be emailed to another person. Again, it seems innocent enough but the real communication is of the number 16. The file size is the important data, not the contents of the file.

Some covert channels rely on a technique called *tunneling*, which lets one protocol be carried over another protocol. Internet Control Message Protocol (ICMP) tunneling is a method of using ICMP echo-request and echo-reply to carry any payload an attacker may wish to use, in an attempt to stealthily access or control a compromised system. The `ping` command is a generally accepted troubleshooting tool, and it uses the ICMP protocol. For that reason, many router, switches, firewalls, and other packet filtering devices allow the ICMP protocol to be passed through the device. Therefore, ICMP is an excellent choice of tunneling protocols.

> **Hacking Tool**
>
> Loki is a hacking tool that provides shell access over ICMP, making it much more difficult to detect than TCP- or UDP-based backdoors. As far as the network is concerned, a series of ICMP packets are being sent across the network. However, the hacker is really sending commands from the Loki client and executing them on the server.

Types of Trojans

Trojans can be created and used to perform different attacks. Here are some of the most common types of Trojans:

Remote Access Trojans (RATs)   Used to gain remote access to a system.

Data-Sending Trojans   Used to find data on a system and deliver data to a hacker.

Destructive Trojans   Used to delete or corrupt files on a system.

Denial-of-Service Trojans   Used to launch a denial-of-service attack.

Proxy Trojans   Used to tunnel traffic or launch hacking attacks via other systems.

FTP Trojans   Used to create an FTP server in order to copy files onto a system.

Security Software Disabler Trojans   Used to stop antivirus software.

How Reverse-Connecting Trojans Work

Reverse-connecting Trojans let an attacker access a machine on the internal network from the outside. The hacker can install a simple Trojan program on a system on the internal network, such as the reverse WWW shell server. On a regular basis (usually every 60 seconds), the internal server tries to access the external master system to pick up commands. If the attacker has typed something into the master system, this command is retrieved and executed on the internal system. The reverse WWW shell server uses standard HTTP. It's dangerous because it's difficult to detect: it looks like a client is browsing the Web from the internal network.

> **Hacking Tools**
>
> TROJ_QAZ is a Trojan that renames the application notepad.exe file to note.com and then copies itself as notepad.exe to the Windows folder. This will cause the Trojan to be launched every time a user runs Notepad. It has a backdoor that a remote user or hacker can use to connect to and control the computer using port 7597. TROJ_QAZ also infects the Registry so that it is loaded every time Windows is started.

Tini is a small and simple backdoor Trojan for Windows operating systems. It listens on port 7777 and gives a hacker a remote command prompt on the target system. To connect to a Tini server, the hacker telnets to port 7777.

Donald Dick is a backdoor Trojan for Windows OSs that allows a hacker full access to a system over the Internet. The hacker can read, write, delete, or run any program on the system. Donald Dick also includes a keylogger and a Registry parser, and can perform functions such as opening or closing the CD-ROM tray. The attacker uses the client to send commands to the victim listening on a predefined port. Donald Dick uses default port 23476 or 23477.

NetBus is a Windows GUI Trojan program and is similar in functionality to Donald Dick. It adds the Registry key HKEY_CURRENT_USER\NetBus Server and modifies the HKEY_CURRENT_USER\NetBus Server\General\TCPPort key. If NetBus is configured to start automatically, it adds a Registry entry called NetBus Server Pro in HKEY_LOCAL_MACHINE\Software\Microsoft\Windows\CurrentVersion\RunServices.

SubSeven is a Trojan that can be configured to notify a hacker when the infected computer connects to the Internet and can tell the hacker information about the system. This notification can be done over an IRC network, by ICQ, or by email. SubSeven can cause a system to slow down, and generates error messages on the infected system.

Back Orifice 2000 is a remote administration tool that an attacker can use to control a system across a TCP/IP connection using a GUI interface. Back Orifice doesn't appear in the task list or list of processes, and it copies itself into the Registry to run every time the computer is started. The filename that it runs is configurable before it's installed. Back Orifice modifies the HKEY_LOCAL_MACHINE\SOFTWARE\Microsoft\Windows\CurrentVersion\RunServices Registry key. BackOrifice plug-ins add features to the BackOrifice program. Plug-ins include cryptographically strong Triple DES encryption, a remote desktop with optional mouse and keyboard control, drag-and-drop encrypted file transfers, Explorer-like file system browsing, graphical remote Registry editing, reliable UDP and ICMP communications protocols, and stealth capabilities that are achieved by using ICMP instead of TCP and UDP.

BoSniffer appears to be a fix for Back Orifice but is actually a Back Orifice server with the SpeakEasy plug-in installed. If BoSniffer.exe, the BoSniffer executable, is run on a target system, it attempts to log on to a predetermined IRC server on channel #BO_OWNED with a random username. It then proceeds to announce its IP address and a custom message every few minutes so that the hacker community can use this system as a zombie for future attacks.

ComputerSpy Key Logger is a program that a hacker can use to record computer activities on a computer, such as websites visited; logins and passwords for ICQ, MSN, AOL, AIM, and Yahoo! Messenger or webmail; current applications that are running or executed; Internet chats; and email. The program can even take snapshots of the entire Windows desktop at set intervals.

Beast is a Trojan that runs in the memory allocated for the `WinLogon.exe` service. Once installed, the program inserts itself into Windows Explorer or Internet Explorer. One of Beast's most distinct features is that it's an all-in-one Trojan, meaning the client, the server, and the server editor are stored in the same application.

CyberSpy is a telnet Trojan that copies itself into the Windows system directory and registers itself in the system Registry so that it starts each time an infected system is rebooted. Once this is done, it sends a notice via email or ICQ and then begins to listen to a previously specified TCP/IP port.

Subroot is a remote administration Trojan that a hacker can use to connect to a victim system on TCP port 1700.

LetMeRule! is a remote access Trojan that can be configured to listen on any port on a target system. It includes a command prompt that an attacker uses to control the target system. It can delete all files in a specific director, execute files at the remote host, or view and modify the Registry.

Firekiller 2000 disables antivirus programs and software firewalls. For instance, if Norton AntiVirus is in auto scan mode in the Taskbar, and AtGuard Firewall is activated, the program stops both on execution and makes the installations of both unusable on the hard drive. They must then be reinstalled to restore their functionality. Firekiller 2000 works with all major protection software, including AtGuard, Norton AntiVirus, and McAfee Antivirus.

The Hard Drive Killer Pro programs offer the ability to fully and permanently destroy all data on any given DOS or Windows system. The program, once executed, deletes files and infects and reboots the system within a few seconds. After rebooting, all hard drives attached to the system are formatted in an unrecoverable manner within only one to two seconds, regardless of the size of the hard drive.

How the Netcat Trojan Works

Netcat is a Trojan that uses a command-line interface to open TCP or UDP ports on a target system. A hacker can then telnet to those open ports and gain shell access to the target system. Exercise 5.1 shows you how to use Netcat.

For the CEH exam, it's important to know how to use Netcat. Make sure you download the Netcat tool and practice the commands before attempting the exam.

EXERCISE 5.1

Using Netcat

Download a version of Netcat for your system. There are many versions of Netcat for all Windows OSs. Also, Netcat was originally developed for the Unix system and is available in many Linux distributions, including BackTrack.

```
C:\WINDOWS\System32\cmd.exe                                                _ □ ×

C:\>nc.exe -h
[v1.11 NT www.vulnwatch.org/netcat/]
connect to somewhere:  nc [-options] hostname port[s] [ports] ...
listen for inbound:    nc -l -p port [options] [hostname] [port]
options:
        -d                  detach from console, background mode

        -e prog             inbound program to exec [dangerous!!]
        -g gateway          source-routing hop point[s], up to 8
        -G num              source-routing pointer: 4, 8, 12, ...
        -h                  this cruft
        -i secs             delay interval for lines sent, ports scanned
        -l                  listen mode, for inbound connects
        -L                  listen harder, re-listen on socket close
        -n                  numeric-only IP addresses, no DNS
        -o file             hex dump of traffic
        -p port             local port number
        -r                  randomize local and remote ports
        -s addr             local source address
        -t                  answer TELNET negotiation
        -u                  UDP mode
        -v                  verbose [use twice to be more verbose]
        -w secs             timeout for connects and final net reads
        -z                  zero-I/O mode [used for scanning]
port numbers can be individual or ranges: m-n [inclusive]

C:\>
```

Netcat needs to run on both a client and the server. The server side of the connection in enabled by the -l attribute and is used to create a listener port. For example, use the following command to enable the Netcat listener on the server:

```
nc -L -p 123 -t -e cmd.exe
```

On the Netcat client, run the following command to connect to the Netcat listener on the server:

```
nc <ip address of the server> <listening port on the server>
```

The client should then have a command prompt shell open from the server.

Unusual system behavior is usually an indication of a Trojan attack. Actions such as programs starting and running without the user's initiation; CD-ROM drawers opening or closing; wallpaper, background, or screen saver settings changing by themselves; the screen display flipping upside down; and a browser program opening strange or unexpected websites are all indications of a Trojan attack. Any action that is suspicious or not initiated by the user can be an indication of a Trojan attack.

Real World Scenario

Indications of a Virus or Trojan Infection

Carrie was using her computer at work and noticed that her computer seemed to be running slowly. When she tried to open files in Microsoft Word, her system would give an error message and then she was unable to use certain functions in the program. She had not received any new email messages in the last 24 hours; she usually received 50 or so messages per day, so this seemed a bit unusual. Lastly, a client of hers had said he received duplicate emails from her last week, which seemed odd.

So, Carrie called John, the company network administrator, and asked him to look at her computer to determine what was causing the computer slowdown and other issues with Microsoft Outlook. John looked at Carrie's computer and noticed that the virus definitions were 6 months old. The antivirus program kept popping up with windows indicating that the virus definitions were out of date, but Carrie just ignored them and kept closing the pop-up windows. John updated the antivirus definitions and ran a full system scan. The antivirus program determined that the system had been infected with 114 viruses and Trojans. The antivirus program was able to clean the infections and restore the computer to its previous uninfected state. John was testing Microsoft Outlook to ensure that it was indeed working when he noticed several emails from online horoscope services, entertainment websites, and online gaming websites. John removed several questionable programs from her computer. Apparently, Carrie did not realize that these types of downloads could cause harm to her computer.

Network software to push virus updates to all workstations, network controls to prevent installation of unauthorized software, and user security awareness training could have prevented this incident from occurring.

Wrappers are software packages that can be used to deliver a Trojan. The wrapper binds a legitimate file to the Trojan file. Both the legitimate software and the Trojan are combined into a single executable file and installed when the program is run.

Generally, games or other animated installations are used as wrappers because they entertain the user while the Trojan in being installed. This way, the user doesn't notice the slower processing that occurs while the Trojan is being installed on the system—the user only sees the legitimate application being installed.

Hacking Tools

Graffiti is an animated game that can be wrapped with a Trojan. It entertains the user with an animated game while the Trojan is being installed in the background.

Silk Rope 2000 is a wrapper that combines the BackOrifice server and any other specified application.

ELiTeWrap is an advanced EXE wrapper for Windows used for installing and running programs. ELiTeWrap can create a setup program to extract files to a directory and execute programs or batch files that display help menus or copy files on to the target system.

Icon Converter Plus is a conversion program that translates icons between various formats. An attacker can use this type of application to disguise malicious code or a Trojan so that users are tricked into executing it, thinking it is a legitimate application.

Trojan Construction Kit and Trojan Makers

Several Trojan-generator tools enable hackers to create their own Trojans. Such toolkits help hackers construct Trojans that can be customized. These tools can be dangerous and can backfire if not executed properly. New Trojans created by hackers usually have the added benefit of passing undetected through virus-scanning and Trojan-scanning tools because they don't match any known signatures.

Some of the Trojan kits available in the wild are Senna Spy Generator, the Trojan Horse Construction Kit v2.0, Progenic Mail Trojan Construction Kit, and Pandora's Box.

Trojan Countermeasures

Most commercial antivirus program have anti-Trojan capabilities as well as spyware detection and removal functionality. These tools can automatically scan hard drives on startup to detect backdoor and Trojan programs before they can cause damage. Once a system is infected, it's more difficult to clean, but you can do so with commercially available tools.

Although several commercially antivirus or Trojan removal tools are available, my personal recommendation is Norton Internet Security (Figure 5.1). Norton Internet Security includes a personal firewall, intrusion detection system, antivirus, antispyware, antiphishing, and email scanning. Norton Internet Security will clean most Trojans from a system as well.

FIGURE 5.1   Norton Internet Security

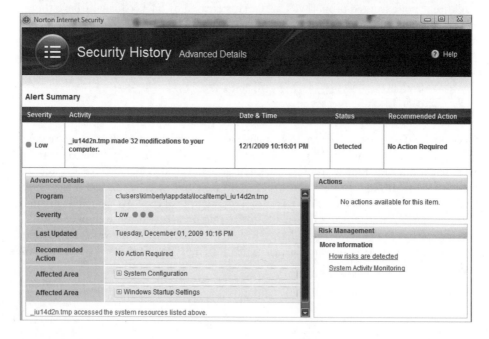

The security software works by having known signatures of malware, such as Trojans and viruses. The repair for the malware is made through the use of definitions of the malware. When installing and using any personal security software or antivirus and anti-Trojan software, you must make sure that the software has all the current definitions. To ensure the latest patches and fixes are available, you should connect the system to the Internet so the software can continually update the malware definitions and fixes.

It's important to use commercial applications to clean a system instead of freeware tools, because many freeware removal tools can further infect the system. In addition, a lot of commercial security software includes an intrusion detection component that will perform port monitoring and can identify ports that have been opened or files that have changed.

The key to preventing Trojans and backdoors from being installed on a system is to educate users not to install applications downloaded from the Internet or open email attachments from parties they don't know. Many system administrators don't give users the system permissions necessary to install programs on their system for that very reason. Proper use of Internet technologies should be included in regular employee security awareness training.

Port-Monitoring and Trojan-Detection Tools

Fport reports all open TCP/IP and UDP ports and maps them to the owning application. You can use fport to quickly identify unknown open ports and their associated applications.

TCPView is a Windows program that shows detailed listings of all TCP and UDP endpoints on the system, including the local and remote addresses and state of TCP connections. When TCPView runs, it enumerates all active TCP and UDP endpoints, resolving all IP addresses to their domain name versions.

PrcView is a process viewer utility that displays detailed information about processes running under Windows. PrcView comes with a command-line version you can use to write scripts that check whether a process is running and, if so, kill it.

Inzider is a useful tool that lists processes in the Windows system and the ports on which each one listens. Inzider may pick up some Trojans. For instance, BackOrifice injects itself into other processes, so it isn't visible in the Task Manager as a separate process, but it does have an open port that it listens on.

Tripwire verifies system integrity. It automatically calculates cryptographic hashes of all key system files or any file that is to be monitored for modifications. The Tripwire software works by creating a baseline snapshot of the system. It periodically scans those files, recalculates the information, and sees whether any of the information has changed. If there is a change, the software raises an alarm.

Dsniff is a collection of tools used for network auditing and penetration testing. Dsniff, filesnarf, mailsnarf, msgsnarf, urlsnarf, and WebSpy passively monitor a network for interesting data such as passwords, email, and file transfers. Arpspoof, dnsspoof, and macof facilitate the interception of network traffic normally unavailable to an attacker due to Layer 2 switching. Sshmitm and webmitm implement active man-in-the-middle attacks against redirected Secure Shell (SSH) and HTTP Over SSL (HTTPS) sessions by exploiting weak bindings in ad hoc Public Key Infrastructure (PKI). These tools will be discussed in further detail in Chapter 6, "Gathering Data from Networks: Sniffers."

Checking a System with System File Verification

Windows 2003 includes a feature called Windows File Protection (WFP) that prevents the replacement of protected files. WFP checks the file integrity when an attempt is made to overwrite a SYS, DLL, OCX, TTF, or EXE file. This ensures that only Microsoft-verified files are used to replace system files.

Another tool, sigverif, checks to see what files Microsoft has digitally signed on a system. In Exercise 5.2, we will use this tool.

EXERCISE 5.2

Signature Verification

We will run sigverif, a signature verification checker, and compare the results to the currently running processes in Task Manager:

1. Press Ctrl+Alt+Del and select Start Task Manager.

2. Click the Processes tab. Note any unusual processes and the amount of CPU time they are using. Any processes using a consistently high percentage of CPU time may indicate a virus or Trojan infection.

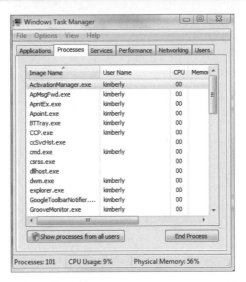

3. Click the Performance tab in Task Manager to view the current CPU usage.

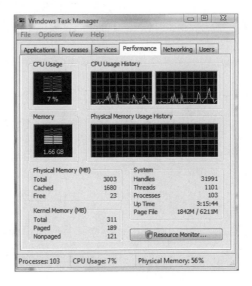

4. Click Start ➢ Run.

5. Type **sigverif**, and click Start.

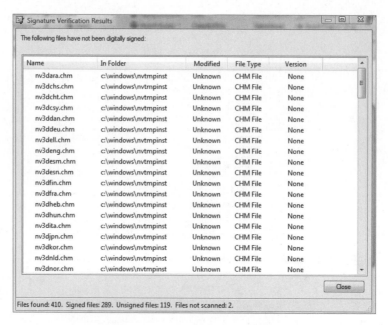

6. In the sigverif program, choose Advanced to see the signature verification report.

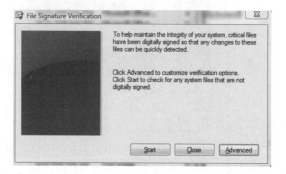

EXERCISE 5.2 *(continued)*

7. Click the View Log button to see the report.

```
SIGVERIF - Notepad
File  Edit  Format  View  Help
*******************************

Microsoft Signature Verification

Log file generated on 12/8/2009 at 9:30 AM
OS Platform:  Windows (x86), Version:  6.0, Build: 6002, CSDVersion:  Service Pack 2
Scan Results:  Total Files: 410, Signed: 289, Unsigned: 119, Not Scanned: 2

File                      Modified      Version        Status          Catalog          Signed By
------------------        ------------  -----------    ------------    -----------      -------------------
[c:\program files\apoint]
apinst.dll                2/20/2008     2:6.0          Signed          apfiltr.cat      Microsoft Windows
Hardware Compatibility Publisher
apmsgfwd.exe              2/20/2008     2:6.0          Signed          apfiltr.cat      Microsoft Windows
Hardware Compatibility Publisher
apntex.exe                2/20/2008     2:6.0          Signed          apfiltr.cat      Microsoft Windows
Hardware Compatibility Publisher
apoint.dll                2/20/2008     2:6.0          Signed          apfiltr.cat      Microsoft Windows
Hardware Compatibility Publisher
apoint.exe                2/20/2008     2:6.0          Signed          apfiltr.cat      Microsoft Windows
Hardware Compatibility Publisher
apointcs.chm              2/20/2008     2:6.0          Signed          apfiltr.cat      Microsoft Windows
Hardware Compatibility Publisher
apointct.chm              2/20/2008     2:6.0          Signed          apfiltr.cat      Microsoft Windows
Hardware Compatibility Publisher
apointfr.chm              2/20/2008     2:6.0          Signed          apfiltr.cat      Microsoft Windows
Hardware Compatibility Publisher
apointgr.chm              2/20/2008     2:6.0          Signed          apfiltr.cat      Microsoft Windows
Hardware Compatibility Publisher
apointit.chm              2/20/2008     2:6.0          Signed          apfiltr.cat      Microsoft Windows
Hardware Compatibility Publisher
apointjp.chm              2/20/2008     2:6.0          Signed          apfiltr.cat      Microsoft Windows
Hardware Compatibility Publisher
```

System File Checker is another command line–based tool used to check whether a Trojan program has replaced files. If System File Checker detects that a file has been overwritten, it retrieves a known good file from the Windows\system32\dllcache folder and overwrites the unverified file. The command to run the System File Checker is sfc/scannow.

Viruses and Worms

Viruses and worms can be used to infect a system and modify a system to allow a hacker to gain access. Many viruses and worms carry Trojans and backdoors. In this way, a virus or worm is a carrier and allows malicious code such as Trojans and backdoors to be transferred from system to system much in the way that contact between people allows germs to spread.

A *virus* and a *worm* are similar in that they're both forms of malicious software (*malware*). A virus infects another executable and uses this carrier program to spread itself. The virus code is injected into the previously benign program and is spread when the program is run. Examples of virus carrier programs are macros, games, email attachments, Visual Basic scripts, and animations.

A worm is similar to a virus in many ways but does not need a carrier program. A worm can self-replicate and move from infected host to another host. A worm spreads from system to system automatically, but a virus needs another program in order to spread. Viruses and worms both execute without the knowledge or desire of the end user.

Types of Viruses

Viruses are classified according to two factors: what they infect and how they infect. A virus can infect the following components of a system:

- System sectors
- Files
- Macros (such as Microsoft Word macros)
- Companion files (supporting system files like DLL and INI files)
- Disk clusters
- Batch files (BAT files)
- Source code

A virus infects through interaction with an outside system. Viruses need to be carried by another executable program. By attaching itself to the benign executable a virus can spread fairly quickly as users or the system runs the executable. Viruses are categorized according to their infection technique, as follows:

Polymorphic Viruses   These viruses encrypt the code in a different way with each infection and can change to different forms to try to evade detection.

Stealth Viruses   These viruses hide the normal virus characteristics, such as modifying the original time and date stamp of the file so as to prevent the virus from being noticed as a new file on the system.

Fast and Slow Infectors   These viruses can evade detection by infecting very quickly or very slowly. This can sometimes allow the program to infect a system without detection by an antivirus program.

Sparse Infectors   These viruses infect only a few systems or applications.

Armored Viruses   These viruses are encrypted to prevent detection.

Multipartite Viruses   These advanced viruses create multiple infections.

Cavity (Space-Filler) Viruses   These viruses attach to empty areas of files.

Tunneling Viruses   These viruses are sent via a different protocol or encrypted to prevent detection or allow it to pass through a firewall.

Camouflage Viruses   These viruses appear to be another program.

NTFS and Active Directory Viruses   These viruses specifically attack the NT file system or Active Directory on Windows systems.

An attacker can write a custom script or virus that won't be detected by antivirus programs. Because virus detection and removal is based on a signature of the program, a hacker just needs to change the signature or look of the virus to prevent detection. The virus signature or definition is the way an antivirus program is able to determine if a system is infected by a virus. Until the virus is detected and antivirus companies have a chance to update virus definitions, the virus goes undetected. Additional time may elapse before a user updates the antivirus program, allowing the system to be vulnerable to an infection. This allows an attacker to evade antivirus detection and removal for a period of time. A critical countermeasure to virus infection is to maintain up-to-date virus definitions in an antivirus program.

One of the most longstanding viruses was the Melissa virus, which spread through Microsoft Word Macros. Melissa infected many users by attaching to the Word doc and then when the file was copied or emailed, the virus spread along with the file.

Virus Hoaxes are emails sent to users usually with a warning about a virus attack. The Virus Hoax emails usually make outlandish claims about the damage that will be caused by a virus and then offer to download a remediation patch from well-known companies such as Microsoft or Norton. Other Hoaxes recommend users delete certain critical systems files in order to remove the virus. Of course, should a user follow these recommendations they will most certainly have negative consequences. Some of the most common virus hoaxes are shown in Table 5.1:

TABLE 5.1   Common Virus Hoaxes

Name	Executable	Description
Antichrist	(none)	This is a hoax that warned about a supposed virus discovered by Microsoft and McAfee named "Antichrist", telling the user that it is installed via an email with the subject line: "SURPRISE?!!!!!!!!!!" after which it destroys the zeroth sector of the hard disk, rendering it unusable.
Budweiser Frogs	BUDSAVER.EXE	Supposedly would erase the user's hard drive and steal the user's screen name and password.
Goodtimes virus	(none)	Warnings about a computer virus named "Good Times" began being passed around among Internet users in 1994. The Goodtimes virus was supposedly transmitted via an email bearing the subject header "Good Times" or "Goodtimes," hence the virus's name, and the warning recommended deleting any such email unread. The virus described in the warnings did not exist, but the warnings themselves, were, in effect, virus-like.

TABLE 5.1 Common Virus Hoaxes *(continued)*

Name	Executable	Description
Invitation attachment (computer virus hoax)	Allright now/ I'm just sayin	The invitation virus hoax involved an email spam in 2006 that advised computer users to delete an email, with any type of attachment that stated "invitation" because it was a computer virus.
Jdbgmgr.exe	bear.a	The jdbgmgr.exe virus hoax involved an email spam in 2002 that advised computer users to delete a file named jdbgmgr.exe because it was a computer virus. jdbgmgr.exe, which had a little teddy bear-like icon (The Microsoft Bear), was actually a valid Microsoft Windows file, the Debugger Registrar for Java (also known as Java Debug Manager, hence jdbgmgr).
Life is beautiful	Life is wonderful	The hoax was spread through the Internet around January 2001 in Brazil. It told of a virus attached to an email, which was spread around the Internet. The attached file was supposedly called "Life is beautiful.pps" or "La vita è bella.pps".
Olympic Torch	Postcard or Postcard from Hallmark	Olympic Torch is a computer virus hoax sent out by email. The hoax emails first appeared in February 2006. The "virus" referred to by the email does not actually exist. The hoax email warns recipients of a recent outbreak of "Olympic Torch" viruses, contained in emails titled "Invitation," which erase the hard disk of the user's computer when opened.
SULFNBK.EXE Warning	none	SULFNBK.EXE (short for Setup Utility for Long File Name Backup) is an internal component of the Microsoft Windows operating system (in Windows 98 and Windows Me) for restoring long file names. The component became famous in the early 2000s as the subject of an email hoax. The hoax claimed that SULFNBK.EXE was a virus, and contained instructions to locate and delete the file. While the instructions worked, they were needless and (in some rare cases, for example, when the long file names are damaged and need to be restored) can cause disruptions, as SULFNBK.EXE is not a virus, but instead an operating system component.

To find out whether an email regarding a virus is legitimate, review the list of virus hoaxes on the website home.mcafee.com/virusinfo.

Virus Detection Methods

The following techniques are used to detect viruses:

- Scanning
- Integrity checking with checksums
- Interception based on a virus signature

The process of virus detection and removal is as follows:

1. Detect the attack as a virus. Not all anomalous behavior can be attributed to a virus.

2. Trace processes using utilities such as handle.exe, listdlls.exe, fport.exe, netstat.exe, and pslist.exe, and map commonalities between affected systems.

3. Detect the virus payload by looking for altered, replaced, or deleted files. New files, changed file attributes, or shared library files should be checked.

4. Acquire the infection vector and isolate it. Then, update your antivirus definitions and rescan all systems.

In Exercise 5.3, we will create a test virus.

EXERCISE 5.3

Creating a Test Virus

A test virus can be created by typing the following code in Notepad and saving the file as EICAR.COM. Your antivirus program should respond when you attempt to open, run, or copy it.

X5O!P%@AP[4\PZX54(P^)7CC)7}$EICAR-STANDARD-ANTIVIRUS-TEST-FILE!$H+H*

Worms can be prevented from infecting systems in much the same way as viruses. Worms can be more difficult to stop because they spread on their own, meaning they do not need user intervention to install and continue to propagate the malware. Worms can be detected with the use of antimalware software that contains definitions for worms. Worms, most importantly, need to be stopped from spreading. In order to do this, an administrator may need to take systems off line. The best practice for cleaning worms off networked systems is to first remove the computer from the network and then run the security software to clean the worm.

Summary

Trojans, backdoors, viruses, and worms are all forms of malware used to infect systems and either cause data damage or infect the system so a hacker can gain further access to a system. The types of viruses, ways they infect, and how they are used are exam objectives for the CEH exam.

The best way to prevent malware from infecting systems is to ensure Internet security software is installed and up-to-date with virus and Trojans signatures and definitions. Additionally, malware can be avoided with security awareness training of users to prevent them from opening and running any files they are not familiar with or can verify.

Exam Essentials

Understand the definition of a Trojan.   Trojans are malicious pieces of code that are carried by software to a target system.

Understand what a covert channel is.   A covert channel uses communications in a way that was not intended. ICMP tunneling, reverse WWW shell, and man-in-the-middle attacks are common covert channels.

Understand the definition of a backdoor.   A backdoor is usually a component of a Trojan. It's used to maintain access after the initial system weakness has been discovered and removed. It usually takes the form of a port being opened on a compromised system.

Understand what a Trojan is and how it works.   Trojans are used primarily to gain and retain access on the target system. A Trojan often resides deep in the system and makes Registry changes that allow it to meet its purpose as a remote administration tool.

Know the best Trojan countermeasures.   Awareness and preventive measures are the best defenses against Trojans.

Understand how a virus is different from a worm.   Viruses must attach themselves to other programs, whereas worms spread automatically.

Understand the different types of viruses.   Polymorphic, stealth, fast infectors, slow infectors, sparse infectors, armored, multipartite, cavity, tunneling, camouflage, NTFS, and AD viruses are all types of viruses.

Review Questions

1. What is a wrapper?

   A. A Trojaned system

   B. A program used to combine a Trojan and legitimate software into a single executable

   C. A program used to combine a Trojan and a backdoor into a single executable

   D. A way of accessing a Trojaned system

2. What is the difference between a backdoor and a Trojan?

   A. A Trojan usually provides a backdoor for a hacker.

   B. A backdoor must be installed first.

   C. A Trojan is not a way to access a system.

   D. A backdoor is provided only through a virus, not through a Trojan.

3. What port does Tini use by default?

   A. 12345

   B. 71

   C. 7777

   D. 666

4. Which is the best Trojan and backdoor countermeasure?

   A. Scan the hard drive on network connection, and educate users not to install unknown software.

   B. Implement a network firewall.

   C. Implement personal firewall software.

   D. Educate systems administrators about the risks of using systems without firewalls.

   E. Scan the hard drive on startup.

5. How do you remove a Trojan from a system?

   A. Search the Internet for freeware removal tools.

   B. Purchase commercially available tools to remove the Trojan.

   C. Reboot the system.

   D. Uninstall and reinstall all applications.

6. What is ICMP tunneling?

   A. Tunneling ICMP messages through HTTP

   B. Tunneling another protocol through ICMP

   C. An overt channel

   D. Sending ICMP commands using a different protocol

7. What is reverse WWW shell?

   A. Connecting to a website using a tunnel

   B. A Trojan that connects from the server to the client using HTTP

   C. A Trojan that issues commands to the client using HTTP

   D. Connecting through a firewall

8. What is a covert channel?

   A. Using a communications channel in a way that was not intended

   B. Tunneling software

   C. A Trojan removal tool

   D. Using a communications channel in the original, intended way

9. What is the purpose of system file verification?

   A. To find system files

   B. To determine whether system files have been changed or modified

   C. To find out if a backdoor has been installed

   D. To remove a Trojan

10. Which of the following is an example of a covert channel?

   A. Reverse WWW shell

   B. Firewalking

   C. SNMP enumeration

   D. Steganography

11. What is the difference between a virus and a worm?

   A. A virus can infect the boot sector but a worm cannot.

   B. A worm spreads by itself but a virus must attach to an email.

   C. A worm spreads by itself but a virus must attach to another program.

   D. A virus is written in C++ but a worm is written in shell code.

12. What type of virus modifies itself to avoid detection?

   A. Stealth virus

   B. Polymorphic virus

   C. Multipartite virus

   D. Armored virus

13. Which virus spreads through Word macros?

    A. Melissa

    B. Slammer

    C. Sobig

    D. Blaster

14. Which worm affects SQL servers?

    A. Sobig

    B. SQL Blaster

    C. SQL Slammer

    D. Melissa

15. Which of the following describes armored viruses?

    A. Hidden

    B. Tunneled

    C. Encrypted

    D. Stealth

16. What are the three methods used to detect a virus?

    A. Scanning

    B. Integrity checking

    C. Virus signature comparison

    D. Firewall rules

    E. IDS anomaly detection

    F. Sniffing

17. What components of a system do viruses infect? (Choose all that apply.)

    A. Files

    B. System sectors

    C. Memory

    D. CPU

    E. DLL files

18. Which of the following are the best indications of a virus attack? (Choose all that apply.)

    A. Any anomalous behavior

    B. Unusual program opening or closing

    C. Strange pop-up messages

    D. Normal system operations as most viruses run in the background

19. A virus that can cause multiple infections is known as what type of virus?

    A. Multipartite

    B. Stealth

    C. Camouflage

    D. Multi-infection

20. Which of the following is a way to evade an antivirus program?

    A. Write a custom virus script.

    B. Write a custom virus signature.

    C. Write a custom virus evasion program.

    D. Write a custom virus detection program.

Answers to Review Questions

1. B. A wrapper is software used to combine a Trojan and legitimate software into a single executable so that the Trojan is installed during the installation of the other software. After a Trojan has been installed, a system is considered "Trojaned." A backdoor is a way of accessing a Trojaned system and can be part of the behavior of a Trojan.

2. A. A Trojan infects a system first and usually includes a backdoor for later access. The backdoor is not installed independently, but is part of a Trojan. A Trojan is one way a hacker can access a system.

3. C. Tini uses port 7777 by default. Doom uses port 666.

4. A. The best prevention is to scan the hard drive for known Trojans on network connections and backdoors and to educate users not to install any unknown software. Scanning the hard drive at startup is a good method for detecting a Trojan, but will not prevent its installation. User education is an important component of security but will not always and consistently prevent a Trojan attack.

5. B. To remove a Trojan, you should use commercial tools. Many freeware tools contain Trojans or other malware. Rebooting the system alone will not remove a Trojan from the system. Uninstalling and reinstalling applications will not remove a Trojan as it infects the OS.

6. B. ICMP tunneling involves sending what appear to be ICMP commands but really are Trojan communications. An overt channel sends data via a normal communication path such as via email. Sending or tunneling ICMP within another protocol such as HTTP is not considered ICMP tunneling.

7. B. Reverse WWW shell is a connection from a Trojan server component on the compromised system to the Trojan client on the hacker's system. Connecting to a website using tunneling or through a firewall is not considered a reverse WWW shell.

8. A. A covert channel is the use of a protocol or communications channel in a nontraditional way. Tunneling software is one way of using a covert channel but does not necessarily define all covert channels. Using a communications channel in the original intended way is considered an overt channel.

9. B. System file verification tracks changes made to system files and ensures that a Trojan has not overwritten a critical system file. System files and backdoors are not located using system file verification. To remove a Trojan, you should use commercial removal tools.

10. A. Reverse WWW shell is an example of a covert channel. Firewalking is enumerating a firewall for firewall rules, allowed traffic, and open ports. Steganography is hiding information in text or graphics. SNMP enumeration is used to identify SNMP MIB settings on networking devices.

11. **C.** A worm can replicate itself automatically, but a virus must attach to another program. Viruses are not always spread via email but can also be attached to other programs or installed directly by tricking the user. Both viruses and worms can infect the boot sector. The programming language is not used to categorize malware as either viruses or worms.

12. **B.** A polymorphic virus modifies itself to evade detection. Stealth viruses hide the normal virus characteristics to prevent detection. Multipartite viruses are viruses that create multiple infections or infect multiple files or programs. Armored viruses use encryption to evade detection.

13. **A.** Melissa is a virus that spreads via Word macros. Slammer and Blaster are actually worm infections, not viruses. Sobig is another type of virus.

14. **C.** SQL Slammer is a worm that attacks SQL servers. Melissa affects Word files through the use of macros. There is no such worm as SQL Blaster.

15. **C.** Armored viruses are encrypted. They are not by nature tunneled and do not change characteristics, as do stealth viruses. Also, armored viruses are not hidden in any other way.

16. **A, B, C.** Scanning, integrity checking, and virus signature comparison are three ways to detect a virus infection. Firewalls, IDS anomaly detection, and sniffing all work at lower layers of the OSI model and are not able to detect viruses.

17. **A, B, E.** A virus can affect files, system sectors, and DLL files. Memory and CPU cannot be infected by viruses.

18. **B, C.** Trojans, backdoors, spyware, and other malicious software can cause a system to not act normally. Any indications of programs opening or closing without user intervention, unresponsive programs, unusual error messages, or pop-ups *could* indicate any type of malware has infected the system. But not all anomalous behavior can be attributed to a virus.

19. **A.** A multipartite virus can cause multiple infections. Stealth viruses hide the normal virus characteristics to prevent detection. Camouflage and multi-infection are not categories of viruses.

20. **A.** A custom virus script can be used to evade detection because the script will not match a virus signature.

Chapter
6

Gathering Data from Networks: Sniffers

CEH EXAM OBJECTIVES COVERED IN THIS CHAPTER:

- ✓ Understand the protocol susceptible to sniffing
- ✓ Understand active and passive sniffing
- ✓ Understand ARP poisoning
- ✓ Understand ethereal capture and display filters
- ✓ Understand MAC flooding
- ✓ Understand DNS spoofing techniques
- ✓ Describe sniffing countermeasures

A *sniffer* is a packet-capturing or frame-capturing tool. It basically captures and displays the data as it is being transmitted from host to host on the network. Generally a sniffer intercepts traffic on the network and displays it in either a command-line or GUI format for a hacker to view. Most sniffers display both the Layer 2 (frame) or Layer 3 (packet) headers and the data payload. Some sophisticated sniffers interpret the packets and can reassemble the packet stream into the original data, such as an email or a document.

Sniffers are used to capture traffic sent between two systems, but they can also provide a lot of other information. Depending on how the sniffer is used and the security measures in place, a hacker can use a sniffer to discover usernames, passwords, and other confidential information transmitted on the network. Several hacking attacks and various hacking tools require the use of a sniffer to obtain important information sent from the target system. This chapter will describe how sniffers work and identify the most common sniffer hacking tools.

The term *packet* refers to the data at Layer 3, or the Network layer, of the OSI model, whereas *frame* refers to data at Layer 2, or the Data Link layer. Frames contain MAC addresses, and packets contain IP addresses.

Understanding Host-to-Host Communication

All Host-to-Host network communications is based upon the TCP/IP Data Communications Model. The TCP/IP Model is a 4 layer model. The TCP/IP Model maps to the older OSI model with 7 layers of data communication. Most applications use the TCP/IP suite for host-to-host data communications. See Figure 6-1.

In normal network operations, the application layer data is encapsulated and a header containing address information is added to the beginning of the data. An IP header containing source and destination IP address are added to the data as well as a MAC header containing source and destination MAC addresses. IP addresses are used to route traffic to the appropriate IP network, and the MAC addresses ensure the data is sent to the correct host on the destination IP network. In this manner, traffic is sent from source host to destination host across the Internet and delivery to the correct host is ensured. The postal system works much the same way. Mail is routed to the appropriate area using the zip code, and then the mail is delivered within the zip code to the street and house number. The IP address is similar to the zip code to deliver mail to the regional area, and the street and house numbers are like the MAC address of that exact station on the network.

FIGURE 6.1 TCP/IP Model

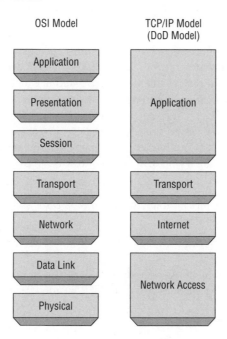

The address system ensures accurate delivery to the receiver. In normal network operations, a host should not receive data intended for another host as the data packet should only be received by the intended receiver. Simply said, the data should only be received by the station with the correct IP and MAC address. However, we know that sniffers do receive data not intended for them.

🌐 Real World Scenario

What Does Mail Delivery Have to Do with Hacking?

In the real world, sometimes mail is not delivered to the intended receiver. I'm sure you have all opened your mailbox to discover an envelope addressed to your neighbor or someone who used to live at your address. This happens on a fairly regular basis at my house. Most people will just leave the mail in the box for the postal carrier to redeliver or physically take the envelope to a neighbor. This same type of situation can occur in computer networking, where application layer data does not reach its intended recipient because of a delivery error or other network fault.

Another cause of mail not being received by the intended recipient is someone is performing reconnaissance and watching your mailbox. Let's assume you are not home and the postal carrier delivers your mail to the mailbox. Someone watching the mailbox from down the street or a nearby building could wait for the mail to be delivered to the mailbox, and they go take the mail or just a particular envelope out of the box. This would be especially effective if the hacker performed some reconnaissance and knew what time each day the mail was delivered. The hacker could then examine and read the information in the envelope, and if they were trying to cover their tracks simply reseal the envelope and put it back in the mailbox.

Sniffing data on a network occurs in much the same way. Data is intercepted, read, and either sent on to the intended recipient or just discarded.

In addition to understanding network addresses, it is also important to understand the format of the TCP Header. Figure 6.2 shows the TCP Header format.

FIGURE 6.2   TCP Header Format

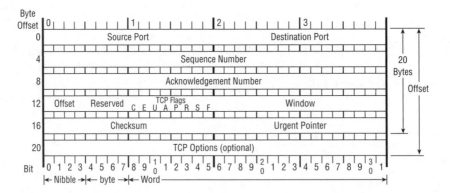

The TCP Header is comprised of the following fields:

Source Port: 16 bits   The source port number.

Destination Port: 16 bits   The destination port number.

Sequence Number: 32 bits   The sequence number of the first data octet in this segment (except when SYN is present). If SYN is present the sequence number is the initial sequence number (ISN) and the first data octet is ISN+1.

Acknowledgment Number: 32 bits   If the ACK control bit is set this field contains the value of the next sequence number the sender of the segment is expecting to receive.

Data Offset: 4 bits   The number of 32 bit words in the TCP Header. This indicates where the data begins.

Reserved: 6 bits   Reserved for future use. Must be zero.

Control Bits: 6 bits

- URG: Urgent Pointer field significant
- ACK: Acknowledgment field significant
- PSH: Push Function
- RST: Reset the connection
- SYN: Synchronize sequence numbers
- FIN: No more data from sender

Window: 16 bits   The number of data octets beginning with the one indicated in the acknowledgment field which the sender of this segment is willing to accept.

Checksum: 16 bits   The checksum field is a computation of all fields to ensure all data was received and the data was not modified in transit.

Urgent Pointer: 16 bits   This field communicates the current value of the urgent pointer as a positive offset from the sequence number in this segment. The urgent pointer points to the sequence number of the octet following the urgent data. This field is only be interpreted in segments with the URG control bit set.

Options: variable   Options may occupy space at the end of the TCP header and are a multiple of 8 bits in length.

When referring to the length of the fields in the TCP Header, 8 bits comprises a single byte. A Nibble is less than a byte and a Word is more than a byte.

In the next section we will explore how a hacking tool manipulates normal network operations in order to capture traffic on a host that is not the intended receiver.

How a Sniffer Works

Sniffer software works by capturing packets not destined for the sniffer system's MAC address but rather for a target's destination MAC address. This is known as *promiscuous mode*. Normally, a system on the network reads and responds only to traffic sent directly to its MAC address. However, many hacking tools change the system's NIC to promiscuous mode. In promiscuous mode, a NIC reads all traffic and sends it to the sniffer for processing. Promiscuous mode is enabled on a network card with the installation of special driver software. Many of the hacking tools for sniffing include a promiscuous-mode driver to facilitate this process. Not all Windows drivers support promiscuous mode, so when using hacking tools ensure that the driver will support the necessary mode.

Any protocols that don't encrypt data are susceptible to sniffing. Protocols such as HTTP, POP3, Simple Network Management Protocol (SNMP), and FTP are most commonly captured using a sniffer and viewed by a hacker to gather valuable information such as usernames and passwords.

There are two different types of sniffing: passive and active. *Passive sniffing* involves listening and capturing traffic, and is useful in a network connected by hubs; *active sniffing* involves launching an Address Resolution Protocol (ARP) spoofing or traffic-flooding attack against a switch in order to capture traffic. As the names indicate, active sniffing is detectable but passive sniffing is not detectable.

In networks that use hubs or wireless media to connect systems, all hosts on the network can see all traffic; therefore, a passive packet sniffer can capture traffic going to and from all hosts connected via the hub. A switched network operates differently. The switch looks at the data sent to it and tries to forward packets to their intended recipients based on MAC address. The switch maintains a MAC table of all the systems and the port numbers to which they're connected. This enables the switch to segment the network traffic and send traffic only to the correct destination MAC addresses. A switch network has greatly improved throughput and is more secure than a shared network connected via hubs.

Another way to sniff data through a switch is to use a span port or port mirroring to enable all data sent to a physical switch port to be duplicated to another port. In many cases, span ports are used by network administrators to monitor traffic for legitimate purposes.

Sniffing Countermeasures

The best security defense against a sniffer on the network is encryption. Although encryption won't prevent sniffing, it renders any data captured during the sniffing attack useless because hackers can't interpret the information. Encryption such as AES and RC4 or RC5 can be utilized in VPN technologies and is commonly used to prevent sniffing on a network.

Countermeasure Tools

NetIntercept is a spam and virus firewall. It has advanced filtering options and can learn and adapt as it identifies new spam. It also intercepts and quarantines the latest email viruses and Trojans, preventing a Trojan from being installed and possibly installing a sniffer.

Sniffdet is a set of tests for remote sniffer detection in TCP/IP network environments. Sniffdet implements various tests for the detection of machines running in promiscuous mode or with a sniffer.

WinTCPKill is a TCP connection termination tool for Windows. The tool requires the ability to use a sniffer to sniff incoming and outgoing traffic of the target. In a switched network, WinTCPKill can use an ARP cache-poisoning tool that performs ARP spoofing.

Bypassing the Limitations of Switches

Because of the way Ethernet switches operate, it is more difficult to gather useful information when sniffing on a switched network. Since most modern networks have been upgraded from hub to switches, it takes a little more effort to sniff on a switched network. One of the ways to do that is to trick the switch into sending the data to the hackers' computer using ARP poisoning.

How ARP Works

ARP allows the network to translate IP addresses into MAC addresses. When one host using TCP/IP on a LAN tries to contact another, it needs the MAC address or hardware address of the host it's trying to reach. It first looks in its ARP cache to see if it already has the MAC address; if it doesn't, it broadcasts an ARP request asking, "Who has the IP address I'm looking for?" If the host that has that IP address hears the ARP query, it responds with its own MAC address, and a conversation can begin using TCP/IP.

ARP poisoning is a technique that's used to attack an Ethernet network and that may let an attacker sniff data frames on a switched LAN or stop the traffic altogether. ARP poisoning utilizes ARP spoofing, where the purpose is to send fake, or spoofed, ARP messages to an Ethernet LAN. These frames contain false MAC addresses that confuse network devices such as network switches. As a result, frames intended for one machine can be mistakenly sent to another (allowing the packets to be sniffed) or to an unreachable host (a denial-of-service, or DoS, attack). ARP spoofing can also be used in a man-in-the-middle attack, in which all traffic is forwarded through a host by means of ARP spoofing and analyzed for passwords and other information.

ARP Spoofing and Poisoning Countermeasures

To prevent ARP spoofing, permanently add the MAC address of the gateway to the ARP cache on a system. You can do this on a Windows system by using the ARP -s command at the command line and appending the gateway's IP and MAC addresses. Doing so prevents a hacker from overwriting the ARP cache to perform ARP spoofing on the system but can be difficult to manage in a large environment because of the number of systems. In an enterprise environment, port-based security can be enabled on a switch to allow only one MAC address per switch port.

In Exercise 6.1 you will use Wireshark to sniff traffic.

EXERCISE 6.1

Use Wireshark to Sniff Traffic

1. Download and install the latest stable version of Wireshark from www.wireshark.org.

2. Click on the Capture menu and then select interfaces.

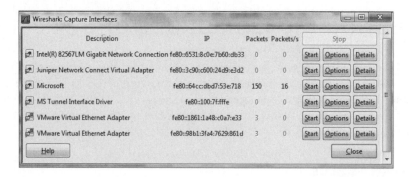

3. Click the Start button next to the interface that shows packets being sent and received. If you have multiple interfaces with packet activity, choose one of them— preferably the interface with the most activity.

4. Click on a packet to analyze that single packet. The detailed headers will be displayed beneath the packet capture screen.

5. Expand each header (IP, TCP) of a packet and identify the address information.

This exercise will provide much more network traffic if performed on a hub rather than a switch. A wireless network can be used, as a wireless LAN is a shared network segment similar to how a hub operates.

Hacking Tools

Wireshark is a freeware sniffer that can capture packets from a wired or wireless LAN connection. The software was previously called Ethereal. Wireshark is a common and popular program because it is free, but it has some drawbacks. An untrained user may find it difficult to write filters in Wireshark to capture only certain types of traffic.

Snort is an intrusion detection system (IDS) that also has sniffer capabilities. It can be used to detect a variety of attacks and probes, such as buffer overflows, stealth port scans, Common Gateway Interface (CGI) attacks, Server Message Block (SMB) probes, and OS fingerprinting attempts.

WinDump is the Windows version of tcpdump, the command-line network analyzer for Unix. WinDump is fully compatible with tcpdump and can be used to watch, diagnose, and save to disk network traffic according to various rules.

EtherPeek is a great sniffer for wired networks with extensive filtering and TCP/IP conversation tracking capabilities. The latest version of EtherPeek has been renamed OmniPeek.

WinSniffer is an efficient password sniffer. It monitors incoming and outgoing network traffic and decodes FTP, POP3, HTTP, ICQ, Simple Mail Transfer Protocol (SMTP), telnet, Internet Message Access Protocol (IMAP), and Network News Transfer Protocol (NNTP) usernames and passwords.

Iris is an advanced data- and network-traffic analyzer that collects, stores, organizes, and reports all data traffic on a network. Unlike other network sniffers, Iris is able to reconstruct network traffic, such as graphics, documents, and emails including attachments.

Wireshark Filters

Wireshark is a freeware sniffer that can capture packets from a wired or wireless LAN connection. It is a very powerful tool which can provide network and upper layer protocol data captured on a network. Like a lot of other network programs, Wireshark uses the pcap network library to capture packets.

Wireshark was called Ethereal until 2006 when the main developer decided to change its name because of copyright reasons with the Ethereal name, which was registered by the company he decided to leave in 2006.

In Exercise 6.1 you installed and began capturing packets using Wireshark. To narrow down the amount of information gathered by Wireshark, you can use filters. These filters limit the amount of information captured or displayed.

Here are some examples of Wireshark filters:

ip.dst eq www.eccouncil.org   This sets the filter to capture only packets destined for the web server www.eccouncil.org.

ip.src == 192.168.1.1   This sets the filter to capture only packets coming from the host 192.168.1.1.

eth.dst eq ff:ff:ff:ff:ff:ff   This sets the filter to capture only Layer 2 broadcast packets.

host 172.18.5.4   This sets the filter to capture only traffic to or from IP address 172.18.5.4.

net 192.168.0.0/24   This sets the filter to capture traffic to or from a range of IP addresses.

port 80   This sets the filter to capture traffic to destination port 80 (HTTP).

port 80 and tcp[((tcp[12:1] & 0xf0) >> 2):4] = 0x47455420   This sets the filter to capture HTTP GET requests. The filter looks for the bytes "G", "E", "T", and " " (hex values 47, 45, 54, and 20) just after the TCP header. "tcp[12:1] & 0xf0) >> 2" figures out the TCP header length.

Exercise 6.2 shows you how to write filters in Wireshark.

EXERCISE 6.2

Create a Wireshark filter to capture only traffic to or from an IP address

1. Open Wireshark.

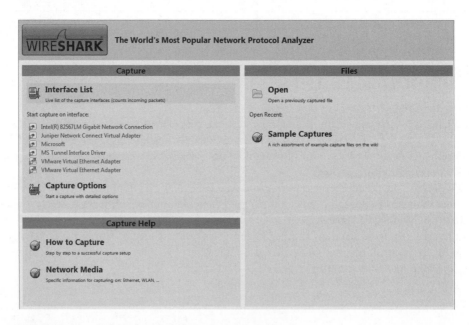

2. Click the active Network Interface to capture traffic.

3. Click Capture, then select filters.

4. Click the new button to create a new filter.

5. Name the new filter in the filter name field.

6. Type **host IPaddress** in the filter string field.

7. Click OK.

8. Select the capture menu and click start to begin the capture.

Repeat the above steps to create filters using the following strings:

net 192.168.0.0/24   To capture traffic to or from a range of IP addresses.

src net 192.168.0.0/24   To capture traffic from a range of IP addresses.

dst net 192.168.0.0/24   To capture traffic to a range of IP addresses.

port 53   To capture only DNS (port 53) traffic.

host www.example.com and not (port 80 or port 25)   To capture non-HTTP and non-SMTP traffic on your server.

port not 53 and not arp   To capture all except ARP and DNS traffic.

tcp portrange 1501-1549   To capture traffic within a range of ports.

not broadcast and not multicast   Capture only unicast traffic. Useful to get rid of noise on the network if you only want to see traffic to and from your machine.

EXERCISE 6.2 *(continued)*

Practice writing filters in Wireshark that capture only one type of protocol traffic or traffic from a specific source IP or MAC address. Use your PC's IP or MAC address to test that the filter is working.

It's important to understand how to create these filters before you attempt the CEH exam.

Understanding MAC Flooding and DNS Spoofing

A packet sniffer on a switched network can't capture all traffic as it can on a hub network; instead, it captures traffic either coming from or going to the system. It's necessary to use an additional tool to capture all traffic on a switched network. There are essentially two ways to perform active sniffing and make the switch send traffic to the system running the sniffer:

ARP Spoofing   This method involves using the MAC address of the network gateway and consequently receiving all traffic intended for the gateway on the sniffer system. A hacker can also *flood* a switch with so much traffic that it stops operating as a switch and instead reverts to acting as a hub, sending all traffic to all ports. This active sniffing attack allows the system with the sniffer to capture all traffic on the network.

 Many switches have been patched or redesigned to not be susceptible to the flooding vulnerability.

DNS Spoofing (or DNS Poisoning)   This is a technique that tricks a DNS server into believing it has received authentic information when in reality it hasn't. Once the DNS server has been poisoned, the information is generally cached for a while, spreading the effect of the attack to the users of the server. When a user requests a certain website URL, the address is looked up on a DNS server to find the corresponding IP address. If the DNS server has been compromised, the user is redirected to a website other than the one that was requested, such as a fake website.

To perform a DNS attack, the attacker exploits a flaw in the DNS server software that can make it accept incorrect information. If the server doesn't correctly validate DNS responses to ensure that they come from an authoritative source, the server ends up caching the incorrect entries locally and serving them to users that make subsequent requests.

This technique can be used to replace arbitrary content for a set of victims with content of an attacker's choosing. For example, an attacker poisons the IP address's DNS entries for a target website on a given DNS server, replacing them with the IP address of a server the hacker controls. The hacker then creates fake entries for files on this server with names matching those on the target server. These files may contain malicious content, such as a worm or a virus. A user whose computer has referenced the poisoned DNS server is tricked into thinking the content comes from the target server and unknowingly downloads malicious content.

The types of DNS spoofing techniques are as follows:

Intranet Spoofing   Acting as a device on the same internal network

Internet Spoofing   Acting as a device on the Internet

Proxy Server DNS Poisoning   Modifying the DNS entries on a proxy server so the user is redirected to a different host system

DNS Cache Poisoning   Modifying the DNS entries on any system so the user is redirected to a different host

---

Hacking Tools

EtherFlood is used to flood an Ethernet switch with traffic to make it revert to a hub. By doing this, a hacker is able to capture all traffic on the network rather than just traffic going to and from their system, as would be the case with a switch.

Dsniff is a collection of Unix-executable tools designed to perform network auditing as well as network penetration. The following tools are contained in dsniff: filesnarf, mailsnarf, msgsnarf, urlsnarf, and webspy. These tools passively monitor a vulnerable shared network (such as a LAN where the sniffer sits behind any exterior firewall) for interesting data (passwords, email, files, and so on).

Sshmitm and webmitm implement active man-in-the-middle attacks against redirected Secure Shell (SSH) and HTTPS sessions.

Arpspoof, dnsspoof, and macof work on the interception of switched network traffic that is usually unavailable to a sniffer program because of switching. To get around the Layer 2 packet-switching issue, dsniff spoofs the network into thinking that it's a gateway that data must pass through to get outside the network.

IP Restrictions Scanner (IRS) is used to find the IP restrictions that have been set for a particular service on a host. It combines ARP poisoning with a TCP stealth or half-scan technique and exhaustively tests all possible spoofed TCP connections to the selected port of the target. IRS can find servers and network devices like routers and switches and identify access-control features like access control lists (ACLs), IP filters, and firewall rules.

sTerm is a telnet client with a unique feature: it can establish a bidirectional telnet session to a target host, without ever sending the real IP and MAC addresses in any packet. Using ARP poisoning, MAC spoofing, and IP spoofing techniques, sTerm can effectively bypass ACLs, firewall rules, and IP restrictions on servers and network devices.

Cain & Abel is a multipurpose hacking tool for Windows. It allows easy recovery of various kinds of passwords by sniffing the network; cracking encrypted passwords using dictionary or brute-force attacks; recording Voice over IP, or VoIP, conversations; decoding scrambled passwords; revealing password boxes; uncovering cached passwords; and analyzing routing protocols. The latest version contains a lot of new features like ARP Poison Routing (APR), which enables sniffing on switched LANs and man-in-the-middle attacks. The sniffer in this version can also analyze encrypted protocols such as SSH-1 and HTTPS, and it contains filters to capture credentials from a wide range of authentication mechanisms.

Packet Crafter is a tool used to create custom TCP/IP/UDP packets. The tool can change the source address of a packet to do IP spoofing and can control IP flags (such as checksums) and TCP flags (such as the state flags, sequence numbers, and ack numbers).

SMAC is a tool used to change the MAC address of a system. It lets a hacker spoof a MAC address when performing an attack.

MAC Changer is a tool used to spoof a MAC address on Unix. It can be used to set the network interface to a specific MAC address, set the MAC randomly, set a MAC of another vendor, set another MAC of the same vendor, set a MAC of the same kind, or display a vendor MAC list to choose from.

WinDNSSpoof is a simple DNS ID spoofing tool for Windows. To use it on a switched network, you must be able to sniff traffic of the computer being attacked. Therefore, it may need to be used in conjunction with an ARP spoofing or flooding tool.

Distributed DNS Flooder sends a large number of queries to create a DoS attack, disabling DNS. If DNS daemon software logs incorrect queries, the impact of this attack is amplified.

Summary

Sniffing is an invaluable tool in the CEH's toolkit. Sniffing can be used to gather information passively and capture valuable data such as passwords. The advantage of sniffing is that it can be performed passively and is virtually undetectable when used in a passive mode. More aggressive methods of sniffing, such as ARP poisoning and DNS spoofing, can be used if passive sniffing does not yield the information the CEH is looking to gather. Just be forewarned that these active methods can be detected and alert security personnel to an attack on the network.

Exam Essentials

Understand how a sniffer works.   A sniffer operates in promiscuous mode, meaning it captures all traffic regardless of the destination MAC specified in the frame.

Understand the differences between sniffing in a shared network connected via hubs and a switched network.   All traffic is broadcast by a hub, but it's segmented by a switch. To sniff on a switched network, either flooding or ARP spoofing tools must be used.

Know the difference between packets and frames.   Packets are created at Layer 3 of the OSI model, and frames are created at Layer 2.

Understand how the Address Resolution Protocol (ARP) works.   ARP is used to find a MAC address from a known IP address by broadcasting the request on the network.

Know the difference between active and passive sniffing.   Active sniffing is used to trick the switch into acting like a hub so that it forwards traffic to the attacker. Passive sniffing captures packets that are already being broadcast on a shared network.

Review Questions

1. What is sniffing?
   A. Sending corrupted data on the network to trick a system
   B. Capturing and deciphering traffic on a network
   C. Corrupting the ARP cache on a target system
   D. Performing a password-cracking attack

2. What is a countermeasure to passive sniffing?
   A. Implementing a switched network
   B. Implementing a shared network
   C. ARP spoofing
   D. Port-based security

3. What type of device connects systems on a shared network?
   A. Routers
   B. Gateways
   C. Hubs
   D. Switches

4. Which of the following is a countermeasure to ARP spoofing?
   A. Port-based security
   B. WinTCPkill
   C. Wireshark
   D. MAC-based security

5. What is dsniff?
   A. A MAC spoofing tool
   B. An IP address spoofing tool
   C. A collection of hacking tools
   D. A sniffer

6. At what layer of the OSI model is data formatted into packets?
   A. Layer 1
   B. Layer 2
   C. Layer 3
   D. Layer 4

7. What is snort?

   A. An IDS and packet sniffer

   B. Only an IDS

   C. Only a packet sniffer

   D. Only a frame sniffer

8. What mode must a network card operate in to perform sniffing?

   A. Shared

   B. Unencrypted

   C. Open

   D. Promiscuous

9. The best defense against any type of sniffing is _____.

   A. Encryption

   B. A switched network

   C. Port-based security

   D. A good security training program

10. For what type of traffic can WinSniffer capture passwords? (Choose all that apply.)

   A. POP3

   B. SMTP

   C. HTTP

   D. HTTPS

11. Which of the following software tools can perform sniffing? (Choose all that apply.)

   A. Dsniff

   B. Wireshark

   C. NetBSD

   D. Netcraft

12. At what layer of the OSI model is data formatted into frames?

   A. Layer 1

   B. Layer 2

   C. Layer 3

   D. Layer 4

13. In which type of header are MAC addresses located?

   A. Layer 1

   B. Layer 2

   C. Layer 3

   D. Layer 7

14. In which type of header are IP addresses located?

   A. Layer 1

   B. Layer 2

   C. Layer 3

   D. Layer 7

15. In which header do port numbers appear?

   A. IP

   B. MAC

   C. Data Link

   D. Transport

16. What is the proper Wireshark filter to capture traffic only sent from IP address 131.1.4.7?

   A. `ip.src == 131.1.4.7`

   B. `ip.address.src == 131.1.4.7`

   C. `ip.source.address == 131.1.4.7`

   D. `src.ip == 131.1.4.7`

17. Which Wireshark filter will only capture traffic to `www.google.com`?

   A. `ip.dst = www.google.com`

   B. `ip.dst eq www.google.com`

   C. `ip.dst == www.google.com`

   D. `http.dst == www.google.com`

18. Passwords are found in which layer of the OSI model?

   A. Application

   B. IP

   C. Data Link

   D. Physical

19. Wireshark was previously known as _____.

   A. Packet Sniffer

   B. Ethereal

   C. EtherPeek

   D. SniffIT

20. Cain & Abel can perform which of the following functions? (Choose all that apply.)

   A. Sniffing

   B. Packet generation

   C. Password cracking

   D. ARP poisoning

Answers to Review Questions

1. B. Sniffing is the process of capturing and analyzing data on a network.

2. A. By implementing a switched network, passive sniffing attacks are prevented.

3. C. A network connected via hubs is called a shared network.

4. A. Port-based security implemented on a switch prevents ARP spoofing.

5. C. Dsniff is a group of hacking tools.

6. C. Packets are created and used to carry data at Layer 3.

7. A. Snort is both an intrusion detection system (IDS) and a sniffer.

8. D. A network card must operate in promiscuous mode in order to capture traffic destined for a different MAC address than its own.

9. A. Encryption renders the information captured in a sniffer useless to a hacker.

10. A, B, C. WinSniffer can capture passwords for POP3, SMTP, and HTTP traffic.

11. A, B. Dsniff and Wireshark are sniffer software tools.

12. B. Data is formatted into frames at Layer 2.

13. B. MAC addresses are added in the Layer 2 header.

14. C. IP addresses are added in the Layer 3 header.

15. D. Port numbers are in the Transport layer.

16. A. `ip.src == 131.1.4.7` will capture traffic sent from IP address 131.1.4.7.

17. B. `ip.dst eq www.google.com` is the filter that will capture traffic with the destination www.google.com.

18. A. Most passwords such as HTTP, FTP, and telnet passwords are found at the Application layer of the OSI model.

19. B. Wireshark was previously called Ethereal.

20. A, C, D. Cain & Abel can perform sniffing, password cracking, and ARP poisoning.

Chapter

7

Denial of Service and Session Hijacking

CEH EXAM OBJECTIVES COVERED IN THIS CHAPTER:

- ✓ Understand the types of DoS attacks

- ✓ Understand how a DDoS attack works

- ✓ Understand how BOTs/BOTNETs work

- ✓ What is a "smurf" attack?

- ✓ What is "SYN" flooding?

- ✓ Describe the DoS/DDoS countermeasures

- ✓ Understand spoofing vs. hijacking

- ✓ List the types of session hijacking

- ✓ Understand sequence prediction

- ✓ What are the steps in performing session hijacking?

- ✓ Describe how you would prevent session hijacking

During a denial-of-service (DoS) attack, a hacker renders a system unusable or significantly slows the system by overloading resources or preventing legitimate users from accessing the system. These attacks can be perpetrated against an individual system or an entire network and are usually successful in their attempts. The hacking attack is one of availability, meaning legitimate users no longer have access to the network.

Session hijacking is a hacking method that creates a temporary DoS for an end user when an attacker takes over the session. Session hijacking is used by hackers to take over a current session after the user has established an authenticated session. Session hijacking can also be used to perpetrate a man-in-the-middle attack when the hacker steps between the server and legitimate client and intercepts all traffic.

This chapter explains DoS attacks, distributed denial-of-service (DDoS) attacks, and the elements of session hijacking, such as spoofing methods, the TCP three-way handshake, sequence-number prediction, and how hackers use tools for session hijacking. In addition, the countermeasures for DoS and session hijacking are discussed at the end of this chapter.

Denial of Service

A DoS attack is an attempt by a hacker to flood a user's or an organization's system. As a CEH, you need to be familiar with the types of DoS attacks and should understand how DoS and DDoS attacks work. You should also be familiar with robots (BOTs) and robot networks (BOTNETs), as well as smurf attacks and SYN flooding. Finally, as a CEH, you need to be familiar with various DoS and DDoS countermeasures.

There are two main categories of DoS attacks:

- Attacks sent by a single system to a single target (simple DoS)
- Attacks sent by many systems to a single target (distributed denial of service, or DDoS)

The goal of DoS isn't to gain unauthorized access to machines or data, but to prevent legitimate users of a service from using it. A DoS attack may do the following:

- Flood a network with traffic, thereby preventing legitimate network traffic.
- Disrupt connections between two machines, thereby preventing access to a service.
- Prevent a particular individual from accessing a service.
- Disrupt service to a specific system or person.

Different tools use different types of traffic to flood a victim, but the result is the same: a service on the system or the entire system is unavailable to a user because it's kept busy trying to respond to an exorbitant number of requests.

 Real World Scenario

A Denial of Service Attack

On the evening of May 28, 2008, the company I was working for (alfasystems.com) suddenly dropped off the Internet. Their web servers were no longer accessible from the Internet.

Within a minute of the start of the attack, it was clear to the Alpha Systems engineers that they were experiencing a "packet flooding" attack of some sort. After looking at the log files of their Cisco router, it showed that both of their two T1 trunk interfaces to the Internet were receiving some sort of traffic at their maximum 1.54 megabit rate, while their outbound traffic had fallen to nearly zero. They were drowning in a flood of malicious traffic and valid traffic was unable to get out. Alpha Systems was the victim of a denial-of-service attack, more commonly referred to as a DoS. The engineers knew they had to do something quickly to stop the attack and get the web servers back up and accessible for their customers. But no one really knew what to do as this had never happened to the systems before. Then someone thought of the packet filtering capabilities of the router.

Luckily, because this DoS attack was prone to filtering, Alpha Systems was able to weed out the bad packets and return their service to almost normal operation. In two minutes Alpha Systems engineers applied "brute force" filters to their routers, shutting down all UDP and ICMP traffic, and alfaystems.com instantly popped back onto the Internet.

It was finally determined that their server had been attacked by 474 security-compromised Windows PCs containing remote-control attack "zombies," in a classic DoS attack generated by the coordinated efforts of these hundreds of individual PCs.

A DoS attack is usually an attack of last resort. It's considered an unsophisticated attack because it doesn't gain the hacker access to any information but rather annoys the target and interrupts their service. DoS attacks can be destructive and have a substantial impact when sent from multiple systems at the same time (DDoS attacks).

Hacking Tools

Ping of Death is an attack that can cause a system to lock up by sending multiple IP packets, which will be too large for the receiving system when reassembled. Ping of Death can cause a DoS to clients trying to access the server that has been a victim of the attack.

SSPing is a program that sends several large fragmented, Internet Control Message Protocol (ICMP) data packets to a target system. This will cause the computer receiving the data packets to freeze when it tries to reassemble the fragments.

A LAND attack sends a packet to a system where the source IP is set to match the target system's IP address. As a result, the system attempts to reply to itself, causing the system to create a loop—which will tie up system resources and eventually may crash the OS.

CPUHog is a DoS attack tool that uses up the CPU resources on a target system, making it unavailable to the user.

WinNuke is a program that looks for a target system with port 139 open, and sends junk IP traffic to the system on that port. This attack is also known as an out-of-bounds (OOB) attack and causes the IP stack to become overloaded—eventually the system crashes.

Jolt2 is a DoS tool that sends a large number of fragmented IP packets to a Windows target. This ties up system resources and eventually locks up the system. Jolt2 isn't Windows specific; many Cisco routers and other gateways may be vulnerable to the Jolt2 attack.

Bubonic is a DoS tool that works by sending TCP packets with random settings, in order to increase the load of the target machine so that it eventually crashes.

Targa is a program that can be used to run eight different DoS attacks. The attacker has the option to either launch individual attacks or try all of the attacks until one is successful.

RPC Locator is a service that, if unpatched, has a vulnerability to overflows. Details on patching a system to prevent RPC vulnerabilities will be covered later in the chapter. The RPC Locator service in Windows allows distributed applications to run on the network. It is susceptible to DoS attacks, and many of the tools that perform DoS attacks exploit this vulnerability.

Because DoS attacks are so powerful and can cripple a production system or network, this chapter does not include any DoS tool exercises. If you want to test the tools listed here, ensure that you are not using them on a production network or system. The DoS tools could render the target systems unusable.

DDoS attacks can be perpetrated by BOTs and BOTNETs, which are compromised systems that an attacker uses to launch the attack against the end victim. The system or network that has been compromised is a secondary victim, whereas the DoS and DDoS attacks flood the primary victim or target.

How DDoS Attacks Work

DDoS is an advanced version of the DoS attack. Like DoS, DDoS tries to deny access to services running on a system by sending packets to the destination system in a way that the destination system can't handle. The key of a DDoS attack is that it relays attacks from many different hosts (which must first be compromised), rather than from a single host like DoS. DDoS is a large-scale, coordinated attack on a victim system.

Hacking Tools

Trinoo is a tool that sends User Datagram Protocol (UDP) traffic to create a DDoS attack. The Trinoo master is a system used to launch a DoS attack against one or more target systems. The master instructs agent processes (called daemons) on previously compromised systems (secondary victims) to attack one or more IP addresses. This attack occurs for a specified period of time. The Trinoo agent or daemon is installed on a system that suffers from a buffer overflow vulnerability. WinTrinoo is a Windows version of Trinoo and has the same functionality as Trinoo.

Shaft is a derivative of the Trinoo tool that uses UDP communication between masters and agents. Shaft provides statistics on the flood attack that attackers can use to know when the victim system is shut down; Shaft provides UDP, ICMP, and TCP flooding attack options.

Tribal Flood Network (TFN) allows an attacker to use both bandwidth-depletion and resource-depletion attacks. TFN does UDP and ICMP flooding as well as TCP SYN and smurf attacks. TFN2K is based on TFN, with features designed specifically to make TFN2K traffic difficult to recognize and filter. It remotely executes commands, hides the source of the attack using IP address spoofing, and uses multiple transport protocols (including UDP, TCP, and ICMP).

Stacheldraht is similar to TFN and includes ICMP flood, UDP flood, and TCP SYN attack options. It also provides a secure telnet connection (using symmetric key encryption) between the attacker and the agent systems (secondary victims). This prevents system administrators from intercepting and identifying this traffic.

Mstream uses spoofed TCP packets with the ACK flag set to attack a target. It consists of a handler and an agent portion, but access to the handler is password protected.

The services under attack are those of the primary victim; the compromised systems used to launch the attack are secondary victims. These compromised systems, which send the DDoS to the primary victim, are sometimes called *zombies* or *BOTs*. They're usually compromised through another attack and then used to launch an attack on the primary victim at a certain time or under certain conditions. It can be difficult to track the source of the attacks because they originate from several IP addresses.

Normally, DDoS consists of three parts:

- Master/handler
- Slave/secondary victim/zombie/agent/BOT/BOTNET
- Victim/primary victim

The *master* is the attack launcher. A *slave* is a host that is compromised by and controlled by the master. The *victim* is the target system. The master directs the slaves to launch the attack on the victim system. See Figure 7.1.

FIGURE 7.1   Master and Slaves in a DDoS Attack

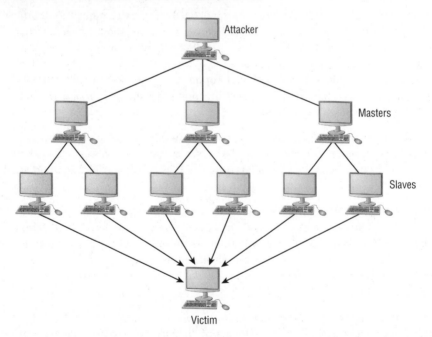

DDoS is done in two phases. In the intrusion phase, the hacker compromises weak systems in different networks around the world and installs DDoS tools on those compromised slave systems. In the DDoS attack phase, the slave systems are triggered to cause them to attack the primary victim. See Figure 7.2.

FIGURE 7.2   Bots or Zombie systems

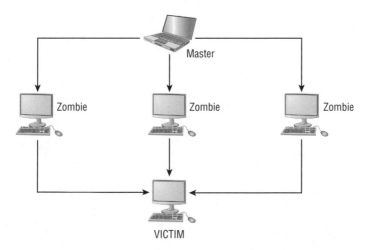

How BOTs/BOTNETs Work

A BOT is short for *web robot* and is an automated software program that behaves intelligently. Spammers often use BOTs to automate the posting of spam messages on newsgroups or the sending of emails. BOTs can also be used as remote attack tools. Most often, BOTs are web software agents that interface with web pages. For example, web crawlers (spiders) are web robots that gather web page information.

The most dangerous BOTs are those that covertly install themselves on users' computers for malicious purposes.

Some BOTs communicate with other users of Internet-based services via instant messaging, Internet Relay Chat (IRC), or another web interface. These BOTs allow IRQ users to ask questions in plain English and then formulate a proper response. Such BOTs can often handle many tasks, including reporting weather; providing zip code information; listing sports scores; converting units of measure, such as currency; and so on.

A BOTNET is a group of BOT systems. BOTNETs serve various purposes, including DDoS attacks; creation or misuse of Simple Mail Transfer Protocol (SMTP) mail relays for spam; Internet marketing fraud; and the theft of application serial numbers, login IDs, and financial information such as credit card numbers. Generally a BOTNET refers to a group of compromised systems running a BOT for the purpose of launching a coordinated DDoS attack. See Figure 7.3.

FIGURE 7.3   Anatomy of a Distributed DoS Attack

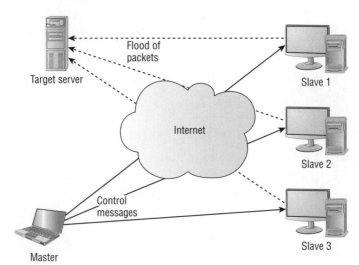

Smurf and SYN Flood Attacks

A *smurf* attack sends a large amount of ICMP Echo (ping) traffic to a broadcast IP address with the spoofed source address of a victim. Each secondary victim's host on that IP network replies to the ICMP Echo request with an Echo reply, multiplying the traffic by the number of hosts responding. On a multiaccess broadcast network, hundreds of machines might reply to each packet. This creates a magnified DoS attack of ping replies, flooding the primary victim. IRC servers are the primary victim of smurf attacks on the Internet.

A *SYN flood* attack sends TCP connection requests faster than a machine can process them. The attacker creates a random source address for each packet and sets the SYN flag to request a new connection to the server from the spoofed IP address. The victim responds to the spoofed IP address and then waits for the TCP confirmation that never arrives. Consequently, the victim's connection table fills up waiting for replies; after the table is full, all new connections are ignored. Legitimate users are ignored as well and can't access the server.

A SYN flood attack can be detected through the use of the `netstat` command. An example of the `netstat` output from a system under a SYN flood is shown in Figure 7.4.

Here are some of the methods used to prevent SYN flood attacks:

SYN Cookies   SYN cookies ensure the server does not allocate system resources until a successful three-way handshake has been completed.

RST Cookies   Essentially the server responds to the client SYN frame with an incorrect SYN ACK. The client should then generate an RST packet telling the server that something is wrong. At this point, the server knows the client is valid and will now accept incoming connections from that client normally.

Micro Blocks   Micro blocks prevent SYN floods by allocating only a small space in memory for the connection record. In some cases, this memory allocation is as small as 16 bytes.

Stack Tweaking   This method involves changing the TCP/IP stack to prevent SYN floods. Techniques of stack tweaking include selectively dropping incoming connections or reducing the timeout when the stack will free up the memory allocated for a connection.

FIGURE 7.4   netstat output under a SYN flood attack

```
# netstat -n -p TCP

tcp       0       0 10.100.0.200:21          237.177.154.8:25882      SYN_RECV
tcp       0       0 10.100.0.200:21          236.15.133.204:2577      SYN_RECV
tcp       0       0 10.100.0.200:21          127.160.6.129:51748      SYN_RECV
tcp       0       0 10.100.0.200:21          230.220.13.25:47393      SYN_RECV
tcp       0       0 10.100.0.200:21          227.200.204.182:60427    SYN_RECV
tcp       0       0 10.100.0.200:21          232.115.18.38:278        SYN_RECV
tcp       0       0 10.100.0.200:21          229.116.95.96:5122       SYN_RECV
tcp       0       0 10.100.0.200:21          236.219.139.207:49162    SYN_RECV
tcp       0       0 10.100.0.200:21          238.100.72.228:37899     SYN_RECV
```

In Exercise 7.1, you will learn how to prevent SYN flood attacks on Windows 2000 servers.

EXERCISE 7.1

Preventing SYN Flood Attacks on Windows 2000 Servers

1. Run the Windows Registry editor by clicking Start ➢ Run and typing **Regedit**.

2. Navigate to the HKLM\SYSTEM\CurrentControlSet\Services\Tcpip\Parameters Registry key.

3. Add the SynAttackProtect=2 DWORD value to the Registry key.

4. Close the regedit program.

This change will allow the operating system to handle more SYN requests. When the value of SynAttackProtect is 2, Windows delays the creation of a socket until the three-way handshake is completed. This change will effectively prevent SYN flood attacks from tying up resources on a Windows server.

DoS/DDoS Countermeasures

There are several ways to detect, halt, or prevent DoS attacks. The following are common security features:

Network-Ingress Filtering   All network access providers should implement network-ingress filtering to stop any downstream networks from injecting packets with faked or spoofed addresses into the Internet. Although this doesn't stop an attack from occurring, it does make it much easier to track down the source of the attack and terminate the attack quickly. Most IDS, firewalls, and routers provide network-ingress filtering capabilities.

Rate-Limiting Network Traffic   A number of routers on the market today have features that let you limit the amount of bandwidth some types of traffic can consume. This is sometimes referred to as *traffic shaping.*

Intrusion Detection Systems   Use an intrusion detection system (IDS) to detect attackers who are communicating with slave, master, or agent machines. Doing so lets you know whether a machine in your network is being used to launch a known attack but probably won't detect new variations of these attacks or the tools that implement them. Most IDS vendors have signatures to detect Trinoo, TFN, or Stacheldraht network traffic.

Automated Network-Tracing Tools   Tracing streams of packets with spoofed addresses through the network is a time-consuming task that requires the cooperation of all networks carrying the traffic and that must be completed while the attack is in progress.

Host-Auditing and Network-Auditing Tools   File-scanning tools are available that attempt to detect the existence of known DDoS tool client and server binaries in a system. Network-scanning tools attempt to detect the presence of DDoS agents running on hosts on your network.

DoS Scanning Tools

Find_ddos is a tool that scans a local system that likely contains a DDoS program. It can detect several known DoS attack tools.

SARA gathers information about remote hosts and networks by examining network services. This includes information about the network information services as well as potential security flaws, such as incorrectly set up or configured network services, well-known bugs in the system or network utilities system software vulnerabilities listed in the Common Vulnerabilities and Exposures (CVE) database, and weak policy decisions.

RID is a free scanning tool that detects the presence of Trinoo, TFN, or Stacheldraht clients.

Zombie Zapper instructs zombie routines to go to sleep, thus stopping their attack. You can use the same commands an attacker would use to stop the attack.

Session Hijacking

Session hijacking is when a hacker takes control of a user session after the user has successfully authenticated with a server. Session hijacking involves an attack identifying the current session IDs of a client/server communication and taking over the client's session. Session hijacking is made possible by tools that perform sequence-number prediction. The details of sequence-number prediction will be discussed later in this chapter in the sequence prediction section.

Spoofing attacks are different from hijacking attacks. In a spoofing attack, the hacker performs sniffing and listens to traffic as it's passed along the network from sender to receiver. The hacker then uses the information gathered to spoof or uses an address of a legitimate system. Hijacking involves actively taking another user offline to perform the attack. The attacker relies on the legitimate user to make a connection and authenticate. After that, the attacker takes over the session, and the valid user's session is disconnected.

Session hijacking involves the following three steps to perpetuate an attack:

Tracking the Session   The hacker identifies an open session and predicts the sequence number of the next packet.

Desynchronizing the Connection   The hacker sends the valid user's system a TCP reset (RST) or finish (FIN) packet to cause them to close their session.

Injecting the Attacker's Packet   The hacker sends the server a TCP packet with the predicted sequence number, and the server accepts it as the valid user's next packet.

Hackers can use two types of session hijacking: active and passive. The primary difference between active and passive hijacking is the hacker's level of involvement in the session. In an active attack, an attacker finds an active session and takes over the session by using tools that predict the next sequence number used in the TCP session.

In a passive attack, an attacker hijacks a session and then watches and records all the traffic that is being sent by the legitimate user. Passive session hijacking is really no more than sniffing. It gathers information such as passwords and then uses that information to authenticate as a separate session.

TCP Concepts: Three-Way Handshake

Two of the key features of TCP are reliability and ordered delivery of packets. To accomplish these goals, TCP uses acknowledgment (ACK) packets and sequence numbers. Manipulating these numbers is the basis for TCP session hijacking. To understand session hijacking, let's review the TCP three-way handshake described in earlier chapters:

1. The valid user initiates a connection with the server. This is accomplished by the valid user sending a packet to the server with the SYN bit set and the user's initial sequence number (ISN).

2. The server receives this packet and sends back a packet with the SYN bit set and an ISN for the server, plus the ACK bit set identifying the user's ISN incremented by a value of 1.

3. The valid user acknowledges the server by returning a packet with the ACK bit set and incrementing the server's ISN by 1.

This connection can be closed from either side due to a timeout or upon receipt of a package with the FIN or RST flag set.

Upon receipt of a packet with the RST flag set, the receiving system closes the connection, and any incoming packets for the session are discarded. If the FIN flag is set in a packet, the receiving system goes through the process of closing the connection, and any packets received while closing the connection are still processed. Sending a packet with the FIN or RST flag set is the most common method hijackers use to close the client's session with the server and take over the session by acting as the client.

Sequence Prediction

TCP is a connection-oriented protocol, responsible for reassembling streams of packets into their original intended order. Every packet has to be assigned a unique session number that enables the receiving machine to reassemble the stream of packets into their original and intended order; this unique number is known as a *sequence number.* If the packets arrive out of order, as happens regularly over the Internet, then the SN is used to stream the packets correctly. As just illustrated, the system initiating a TCP session transmits a packet with the SYN bit set. This is called a *synchronize packet* and includes the client's ISN. The ISN is a pseudo-randomly generated number with over 4 billion possible combinations, yet it is statistically possible for it to repeat.

When the ACK packet is sent, each machine uses the SN from the packet being acknowledged, plus an increment. This not only properly confirms receipt of a specific packet, but also tells the sender the next expected TCP packet SN. Within the three-way handshake, the increment value is 1. In normal data communications, the increment value equals the size of the data in bytes (for example, if you transmit 45 bytes of data, the ACK responds using the incoming packet's SN plus 45).

Figure 7.5 illustrates the sequence numbers and acknowledgments used during the TCP three-way handshake.

FIGURE 7.5   Sequence numbers and acknowledgment during the TCP three-way handshake

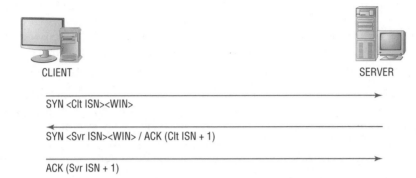

CLIENT   SERVER

SYN <Clt ISN><WIN>

SYN <Svr ISN><WIN> / ACK (Clt ISN + 1)

ACK (Svr ISN + 1)

Hacking tools used to perform session hijacking do sequence number prediction. To successfully perform a TCP sequence prediction attack, the hacker must sniff the traffic between two systems. Next, the hacker or the hacking tool must successfully guess the SN or locate an ISN to calculate the next sequence number. This process can be more difficult than it sounds, because packets travel very fast.

When the hacker is unable to sniff the connection, it becomes much more difficult to guess the next SN. For this reason, most session-hijacking tools include features to permit sniffing the packets to determine the SNs.

Hackers generate packets using a spoofed IP address of the system that had a session with the target system. The hacking tools issue packets with the SNs that the target system is expecting. But the hacker's packets must arrive before the packets from the trusted system whose connection is being hijacked. This is accomplished by flooding the trusted system with packets or sending an RST packet to the trusted system so that it is unavailable to send packets to the target system.

Hacking Tools

Juggernaut is a network sniffer that can be used to hijack TCP sessions. It runs on Linux operating systems and can be used to watch for all network traffic, or it can be given a keyword such as a password to look for. The program shows all active network connections, and the attacker can then choose a session to hijack.

Hunt is a program that can be used to sniff and hijack active sessions on a network. Hunt performs connection management, Address Resolution Protocol (ARP) spoofing, resetting of connections, monitoring of connections, Media Access Control (MAC) address discovery, and sniffing of TCP traffic.

TTYWatcher is a session-hijacking utility that allows the hijacker to return the stolen session to the valid user as though it was never hijacked. TTYWatcher is only for Sun Solaris systems.

IP Watcher is a session-hijacking tool that lets an attacker monitor connections and take over a session. This program can monitor all connections on a network, allowing the attacker to watch an exact copy of a session in real time.

T-Sight is a session-monitoring and -hijacking tool for Windows that can assist when an attempt at a network break-in or compromise occurs. With T-Sight, a system administrator can monitor all network connections in real time and observe any suspicious activity that takes place. T-Sight can also hijack any TCP session on the network. For security reasons, En Garde Systems licenses this software only to predetermined IP addresses.

The Remote TCP Session Reset Utility displays current TCP session and connection information such as IP addresses and port numbers. The utility is primarily used to reset TCP sessions.

Dangers Posed by Session Hijacking

TCP session hijacking is a dangerous attack: most systems are vulnerable to it, because they use TCP/IP as their primary communication protocol. Newer operating systems have attempted to secure themselves from session hijacking by using pseudo-random number generators to calculate the ISN, making the sequence number harder to guess. However, this security measure is ineffective if the attacker is able to sniff packets, which gives all the information required to perform this attack.

The following are reasons why it's important for a CEH to be aware of session hijacking:

- Most computers are vulnerable.
- Few countermeasures are available to adequately protect against it.
- Session hijacking attacks are simple to launch.
- Hijacking is dangerous because of the information that can be gathered during the attack.

Preventing Session Hijacking

To defend against session hijack attacks, a network should employ several defenses. The most effective protection is encryption, such as Internet Protocol Security (IPSec). This also defends against any other attack vectors that depend on sniffing. Attackers may be able to passively monitor your connection, but they won't be able to interpret the encrypted data. Other countermeasures include using encrypted applications such as Secure Shell (SSH, an encrypted telnet) and Secure Sockets Layer (SSL, for HTTPS traffic).

You can help prevent session hijacking by reducing the potential methods of gaining access to your network—for example, by eliminating remote access to internal systems. If the network has remote users who need to connect to carry out their duties, then use virtual private networks (VPNs) that have been secured with tunneling protocols and encryption (Layer 3 Tunneling Protocol [L3TP]/Point-to-Point Tunneling Protocol [PPTP] and IPSec).

The use of multiple safety nets is always the best countermeasure to any potential threat. Employing any one countermeasure may not be enough, but using them together to secure your enterprise will make the attack success rate minimal for anyone but the most professional and dedicated attacker. The following is a checklist of countermeasures that should be employed to prevent session hijacking:

- Use encryption.
- Use a secure protocol.
- Limit incoming connections.
- Minimize remote access.
- Have strong authentication.
- Educate your employees.
- Maintain different username and passwords for different accounts.
- Use Ethernet switches rather than hubs to prevent session hijacking attacks.

Summary

Denial-of-service attacks are used to render a system or network unusable and are considered attacks against the availability of the user data. When other hacking attempts fail, a hacker may resort to DoS attacks as a way of attacking the system. Even though data may not be acquired by a hacker using DoS, the hacker can prevent legitimate users from accessing the data. DoS attacks and especially DDoS attacks are difficult to countermeasure. The best option is to attempt to prevent the attacks by using traffic filtering at the firewall or an IDS.

Session hijacking is used by a hacker to intercept a user's connection and place themselves between the legitimate user and the server. Session hijacking involves predicting sequence numbers and intercepting the legitimate TCP/IP data and replacing it with the hacker's attack exploit. Session hijacking is a dangerous attack used to gather valuable user data, and most systems that run a TCP/IP stack are susceptible to session hijacking.

Exam Essentials

Know the purpose of DoS and DDoS attacks. The purpose of a DoS attack is to send so much traffic to a target system that users are prevented from accessing the system. A distributed denial-of-service (DDoS) attack is a coordinated attack by many systems sent to one target, whereas DoS involves a single system attacking the target.

Know how to prevent DoS attacks. Network traffic filtering, IDS, and auditing tools are all ways to detect and prevent DoS attacks.

Know the two phases of DDoS. During the first phase, systems are compromised and DDoS tools are installed, making the systems zombies or slaves; this is called the intrusion phase. The second phase involves launching an attack against the victim system.

Know what a zombie, slave, and master are in a DDoS attack. A zombie or slave is a system that has been compromised by a hacker and can be commanded to participate in the sending of a DDoS attack to a target system. The master is the controlling system in a DDoS attack scenario. It tells the zombies when to launch the attack.

Understand session hijacking and spoofing. Session hijacking involves taking over another user's session after they have authenticated in order to gain access to a system. Spoofing involves artificial identification of a packet's source address, where that address is often deduced from sniffed network traffic, whereas hijacking refers to a compromised session— normally one in which the attacker takes the user offline and uses their session.

Understand the difference between active and passive session hijacking and some of the tools used. Active session hijacking is the more common of the two types and involves taking over another user's session and desynchronizing the valid user's connection. Passive hijacking monitors the session and allows a hacker to gather confidential information via sniffing packets. Juggernaut, Hunt, TTYWatcher, IP Watcher, T-Sight, and the TCP Reset utility are all session-hijacking tools.

Understand the importance of sequence numbers in a session-hijacking attack. It's necessary to either guess or locate sequence numbers in order to initiate a session-hijacking attack. Sequence numbers are used to order packets and permit a receiving station to reassemble data correctly.

Understand the dangers and countermeasures of session hijacking. Most computers are vulnerable to session-hijacking attacks, and available countermeasures aren't always successful. Confidential and important information, such as passwords, account information, and credit card numbers, can be obtained through session-hijacking attacks. Use encryption, strong authentication, and secure protocols; limit incoming connections; minimize remote access connections; educate employees; and maintain unique usernames and passwords for different accounts.

Review Questions

1. Which is a method to prevent denial-of-service attacks?

   A. Static routing

   B. Traffic filtering

   C. Firewall rules

   D. Personal firewall

2. What is a zombie?

   A. A compromised system used to launch a DDoS attack

   B. The hacker's computer

   C. The victim of a DDoS attack

   D. A compromised system that is the target of a DDoS attack

3. The Trinoo tool uses what protocol to perform a DoS attack?

   A. TCP

   B. IP

   C. UDP

   D. HTTP

4. What is the first phase of a DDoS attack?

   A. Intrusion

   B. Attack

   C. DoS

   D. Finding a target system

5. Which tool can run eight different types of DoS attacks?

   A. Ping of Death

   B. Trinoo

   C. Targa

   D. TFN2K

6. What is a smurf attack?

   A. Sending a large amount of ICMP traffic with a spoofed source address

   B. Sending a large amount of TCP traffic with a spoofed source address

   C. Sending a large number of TCP connection requests with a spoofed source address

   D. Sending a large number of TCP connection requests

7. What is a LAND attack? (Choose all that apply.)

   A. Sending oversized ICMP packets

   B. Sending packets to a victim with a source address set to the victim's IP address

   C. Sending packets to a victim with a destination address set to the victim's IP address

   D. Sending a packet with the same source and destination address

8. What is the Ping of Death?

   A. Sending packets that, when reassembled, are too large for the system to understand

   B. Sending very large packets that cause a buffer overflow

   C. Sending packets very quickly to fill up the receiving buffer

   D. Sending a TCP packet with the fragment offset out of bounds

9. How does a denial-of-service attack work? (Choose all that apply.)

   A. Cracks passwords, causing the system to crash

   B. Imitates a valid user

   C. Prevents a legitimate user from using a system or service

   D. Attempts to break the authentication method

10. What is the goal of a DoS attack?

   A. To capture files from a remote system

   B. To incapacitate a system or network

   C. To exploit a weakness in the TCP/IP stack

   D. To execute a Trojan using the hidden shares

11. Which of the following tools is only for Sun Solaris systems?

   A. Juggernaut

   B. T-Sight

   C. IP Watcher

   D. TTYWatcher

12. What is a sequence number?

   A. A number that indicates where a packet falls in the data stream

   B. A way of sending information from the sending to the receiving station

   C. A number that the hacker randomly chooses in order to hijack a session

   D. A number used in reconstructing a UDP session

13. What type of information can be obtained during a session-hijacking attack? (Choose all that apply.)

A. Passwords

B. Credit card numbers

C. Confidential data

D. Authentication information

14. Which of the following is essential information to a hacker performing a session-hijacking attack?

A. Session ID

B. Session number

C. Sequence number

D. Source IP address

15. Which of the following is a session-hijacking tool that runs on Linux operating systems?

A. Juggernaut

B. Hunt

C. TTYWatcher

D. TCP Reset Utility

16. Which of the following is the best countermeasure to session hijacking?

A. Port filtering firewall

B. Encryption

C. Session monitoring

D. Strong passwords

17. Which of the following best describes sniffing?

A. Gathering packets to locate IP addresses in order to initiate a session-hijacking attack

B. Analyzing packets in order to locate the sequence number to start a session hijack

C. Monitoring TCP sessions in order to initiate a session-hijacking attack

D. Locating a host susceptible to a session-hijack attack

18. What is session hijacking?

A. Monitoring UDP sessions

B. Monitoring TCP sessions

C. Taking over UDP sessions

D. Taking over TCP sessions

19. What types of packets are sent to the victim of a session-hijacking attack to cause them to close their end of the connection?

    A. FIN and ACK

    B. SYN or ACK

    C. SYN and ACK

    D. FIN or RST

20. What is an ISN?

    A. Initiation session number

    B. Initial sequence number

    C. Initial session number

    D. Indication sequence number

Answers to Review Questions

1. B. Traffic filtering is a method to prevent DoS attacks. Static routing will not prevent DoS attacks as it does not perform any traffic filtering or blocking. Firewall rules and personal firewalls will not stop traffic associated with a DoS attack but will help detect an attack.

2. A. A zombie is a compromised system used to launch a DDoS attack.

3. C. Trinoo uses UDP to flood the target system with data.

4. A. The intrusion phase compromises and recruits zombie systems to use in the coordinated attack phase.

5. C. Targa is able to send eight different types of DoS attacks.

6. A. A smurf attack sends a large number of ICMP request frames with a spoofed address of the victim system.

7. A, B. A LAND attack sends packets to a system with that system as the source address, causing the system to try to reply to itself.

8. A. The Ping of Death attack sends packets that, when reassembled, are too large and cause the system to crash or lock up.

9. C. A DoS attack works by preventing legitimate users from accessing the system.

10. B. The goal of a DoS attack is to overload a system and cause it to stop responding.

11. D. TTY Watcher is used to perform session hijacking on Sun Solaris systems.

12. A. A sequence number indicates where the packet is located in the data stream so the receiving station can reassemble the data.

13. A, B, C. Passwords, credit card numbers, and other confidential data can be gathered in a session-hijacking attack. Authentication information isn't accessible because session hijacking occurs after the user has authenticated.

14. C. In order to perform a session-hijacking attack, the hacker must know the sequence number to use in the next packet so the server will accept the packet.

15. A. Juggernaut runs on Linux operating systems.

16. B. Encryption makes any information the hacker gathers during a session-hijacking attempt unreadable.

17. B. Sniffing is usually used to locate the sequence number, which is necessary for a session hijack.

18. D. The most common form of session hijacking is the process of taking over a TCP session.

19. D. FIN (finish) and RST (reset) packets are sent to the victim to desynchronize their connection and cause them to close the existing connection.

20. B. ISN is the initial sequence number that is sent by the host and is the starting point for the sequence numbers used in later packets.

Chapter

8

Web Hacking: Google, Web Servers, Web Application Vulnerabilities, and Web-Based Password Cracking Techniques

---

CEH EXAM OBJECTIVES COVERED IN THIS CHAPTER:

- ✓ List the types of web server vulnerabilities
- ✓ Understand the attacks against web servers
- ✓ Understand IIS Unicode exploits
- ✓ Understand patch-management techniques
- ✓ Understand Web Application Scanner
- ✓ What is the Metasploit Framework?
- ✓ Describe web server hardening methods
- ✓ Understand how web applications work
- ✓ Objectives of web application hacking
- ✓ Anatomy of an attack
- ✓ Web application threats
- ✓ Understand Google hacking
- ✓ Understand web application countermeasures

✓ List the authentication types

✓ What is a password cracker?

✓ How does a password cracker work?

✓ Understand password attacks—classification

✓ Understand password-cracking countermeasures

This chapter introduces the essentials of hacking web servers and exploiting web server and web application vulnerabilities. Web-based password-cracking techniques are also covered.

Web servers and web applications have a very high potential to be compromised. The primary reason for this is that the systems that run web server software must be publicly available on the Internet. The web server cannot be completely isolated and to some degree must be available to legitimate users. Once a web server has been compromised, the system can provide hackers with another door into the network. Not only the web server software but also applications that run on the web server are open to attack and can be exploited. Due to their function, web servers are more accessible than other systems and less protected, so they're easier to exploit.

The target information on a web server usually resides in a database on the web server; this database is accessed via a web application. For this reason, web servers and web applications go hand in hand. Compromising the web server is usually done to gain access to the underlying data in the web application.

How Web Servers Work

Web servers use Hypertext Transfer Protocol (HTTP) and Hypertext Transfer Protocol Secure (HTTPS) to allow web-based clients to connect to them and view and download files. HTTP is an Application-layer protocol in the TCP/IP stack. HTTP and HTTPS are the primary protocols used by web clients accessing web pages residing on web servers on the Internet. Hypertext Markup Language (HTML) is the language used to create web pages and allows those pages to be rendered in web browser software on web clients.

The HTTP protocol operates as shown in Figure 8.1.

FIGURE 8.1 HTTP protocol components

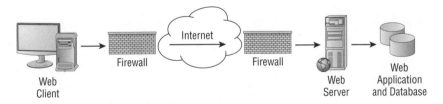

1. The web client initially opens a connection to the web server IP address using TCP port 80.

2. The web server waits for a GET request from the client requesting the home page for the website.

3. The web server responds with the HTML code for the web server home page.

4. The client processes the HTML code and the web client's browser software renders the page on the client device.

Understanding how web servers work—and consequently how they are hacked—is an important part of your job as a CEH. This includes knowing their vulnerabilities, as well as understanding the types of attacks a hacker may use. In addition, you should know when to use patch-management techniques and understand the methods used to harden web servers.

We'll look at all these topics in the following sections.

Types of Web Server Vulnerabilities

Web servers, like other systems, can be compromised by a hacker. The following vulnerabilities are most commonly exploited in web servers:

Misconfiguration of the Web Server Software   A common issue with using Microsoft's Internet Information Server (IIS) as a web server is the use of the default website. The permissions on the default website are open, meaning the default settings leave the site open to attack. For example, all users in the everyone group have full control to all the files in the default website directory. It is critical to edit and restrict permissions once IIS is installed on the server as the default system user, IUSR_COMPUTERNAME, is a member of the everyone group. Consequently, anyone accessing the default website will be able to access all files in the default website folder and will have dangerous permissions such as Execute and Full Control to the files. See Exercise 8.1 to learn how to disable the default website in IIS.

Operating System or Application Bugs, or Flaws in Programming Code   All programs, including the OS and web server applications, should be patched or updated on a regular basis. For Windows systems, this includes security patches, hotfixes, and Windows Updates. All of these patches can be automated or manually applied to the systems once they have been tested.

Vulnerable Default Installation   Operating system and web server software settings should not be left at their defaults when installed, and should be updated on a continuous basis.

Hackers exploit these vulnerabilities to gain access to the web server. Because web servers are usually located in a demilitarized zone (DMZ)—which is a publicly accessible area between two packet filtering devices and can be easily accessed by the organization's client systems—an exploit of a web server offers a hacker easier access to internal systems or databases.

EXERCISE 8.1

Disabling the Default Website in Internet Information Server

To disable the default website in IIS and add a new site, follow these steps:

1. Open IIS on your Windows Server or virtual machine (VM).

2. Select Web Sites in the left pane.

3. Right-click the default website in the right pane and select Stop from the context menu. The default website is now stopped.

4. To create a new site, right-click Web Sites in the left pane and select New ➢ Web Site.

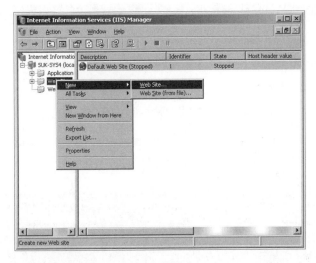

5. The Web Site Creation Wizard launches. Within the wizard will be a screen to change permission on the website directory.

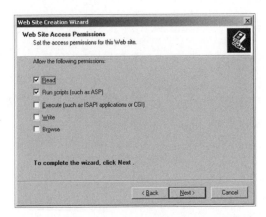

Website cloaking is the ability of a web server to display different types of web pages based on the user's IP address.

In many cases, it is useful to gather all or a portion of the files that make up a website. One option is to right-click any web page and select View Source from the context menu. This command will open up a new window with the source code for the page. You can then save the text file as a document on the local machine. This approach works, but it isn't a practical way of copying all the files for a target website. An easy-to-use program called BlackWidow can make the process of copying website files much easier. Exercise 8.2 shows you how to use the BlackWidow program to copy an entire website or a portion of the site.

EXERCISE 8.2

Using BlackWidow to Copy a Website

1. Download and install the BlackWidow application from www.softbytelabs.com.

2. Open the BlackWidow program.

3. Enter a target website address in the BlackWidow address bar:

4. Click the Scan button on the BlackWidow toolbar.

5. Click the Structure tab.

EXERCISE 8.2 *(continued)*

6. Browse the website folder structure. Right-click a file or folder and choose Copy
    Selected Files to copy the website files to your computer.

Attacking a Web Server

Web servers typically listen on TCP port 80 (HTTP) and TCP port 443 (HTTPS). Because
those ports must be open and available to web clients, any firewalls or packet filtering devices
between the web client and web server must pass traffic destined for those ports. Web application software sits on top of the web server software and allows access to additional ports.

One of the initial information-gathering steps targeting web servers is *banner grabbing*.
Banner grabbing is an attempt to gather information about a web server such as the OS and
web server software and version. Exercise 8.3 shows you how to use banner grabbing.

EXERCISE 8.3

Banner Grabbing

1. At the command prompt on your Windows PC, type

`telnet <IPaddress> 80`

> The IP address is the address of the web server target. Also, the URL can be used
> instead of the IP address.

2. Next, in the telnet window type

`HEAD/HTTP/1.0`

> Then press Enter.

The web server banner will then be returned. The banner will look something like the following:

```
Server: Microsoft-IIS/5.0
Date: Fri, 14 Aug 2009 1:14:42 GMT
Content-Length:340
Content-Type: text/html
```

The banner grabbing result will usually identify the web server type and version. This information is important because exploits against this web server type and version can be identified. The next step after banner grabbing would be to attack the web server or attack a web application and gain access to data on the server.

A benign but visible type of attack against web servers is defacement. Hackers deface websites for sheer joy and an opportunity to enhance their reputations rather than gathering any useful data. *Defacing* a website means the hacker exploits a vulnerability in the OS or web server software and then alters the website files to show that the site has been hacked. Often the hacker displays their hacker name on the website's home page.

Common website attacks that enable a hacker to deface a website include the following:

- Capturing administrator credentials through man-in-the-middle attacks
- Revealing an administrator password through a brute-force attack
- Using a DNS attack to redirect users to a different web server
- Compromising an FTP or email server
- Exploiting web application bugs that result in a vulnerability
- Misconfiguring web shares
- Taking advantage of weak permissions
- Rerouting a client after a firewall or router attack
- Using SQL injection attacks (if the SQL server and web server are the same system)
- Using telnet or Secure Shell (SSH) intrusion
- Carrying out URL poisoning, which redirects the user to a different URL
- Using web server extension or remote service intrusion
- Intercepting the communication between the client and the server and changing the cookie to make the server believe that there is a user with higher privileges (applies to cookie-enabled security)

Exercise 8.4 walks you through using the Metasploit Framework to exploit a web server vulnerability.

WARNING

It is important that the machine or VM have all antivirus and firewall programs completely shut down prior to installing Metasploit. Otherwise, the antivirus or firewall can block some components of Metasploit, causing it not to function or open properly. As we mentioned in the lab setup guide in the Introduction to this book, you should never install Metasploit on a production machine. Use either a VM or lab test machine to run this software.

EXERCISE 8.4

Using Metasploit to Exploit a Web Server Vulnerability

1. Download and install Metasploit 3.2 on your Windows XP or Vista computer or VM
    (www.metasploit.com).

2. Choose all the default options when installing Metasploit.

3. Select the Online Update option in the Metasploit 3 folder under Programs.

4. After the online update has completed, open the Metasploit GUI file in the Metasploit 3
    folder.

5. Expand the Windows folder under Exploits and then expand the IIS folder.

6. Double-click the ms03_007_ntdll_webdav exploit. The MSF Assistant Wizard launches.

7. Click the Forward button to move to the next screen of the wizard.

8. Select Windows/Exec from the Payload drop-down list, and then click Forward.

9. Type the IP address of the target IIS web server in the RHOST field. *This server should be an unpatched version of Windows 2000 for this particular payload to work. If that is not the case, choose a different payload to which the server is vulnerable.*

10. Type **sol.exe** in the CMD field. This is the executable that will be run on the remote target host. sol.exe is the solitaire game, which should be on all Windows operating systems. The payload is what will be delivered to the target system. In this case, it is similar to typing **sol.exe** at the command prompt of the IIS server. Obviously this executable is benign, but this exercise illustrates how a more dangerous executable, such as a virus or Trojan, could be run on a target system.

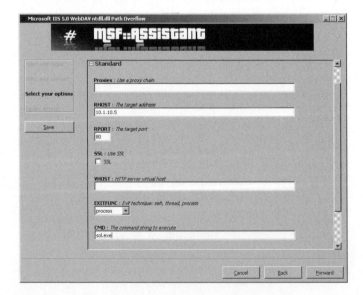

11. Click the Forward button to move to the next screen of the wizard.

12. Click the Apply button. The exploit will appear under Jobs until it is delivered to the target system.

13. Confirm in the Windows IIS Server VM or on the IIS PC that the Solitaire program is running. If the program is not running, confirm that Solitaire is installed on the IIS server and try the Metasploit exploit again.

Hacking Internet Information Server

Windows IIS is one of the most popular web server software products. Because of the popularity and number of web servers running IIS, many attacks can be launched against IIS servers. The three most common attacks against IIS are as follows:

- Directory traversal

- Source disclosure

- Buffer overflow

A *directory-traversal attack* is based on the premise that web clients are limited to specific directories within the Windows files system. The initial directory access by web clients is known as the *root directory* on a web server. This root directory typically stores the home page usually known as Default or Index, as well as other HTML documents for the web server. Subdirectories of the root directory contain other types of files; for example, scripts may contain dynamic scripting files for the web server. The web server should allow users to access only these specific directories and subdirectories of root. However, a directory-traversal attack permits access to other directories within the file system.

Windows 2000 systems running IIS are susceptible to a directory-traversal attack, also known as the Unicode exploit. The vulnerability in IIS that allows for the directory traversal/Unicode exploit occurs only in unpatched Windows 2000 systems and affects CGI scripts and Internet Server Application Programming Interface (ISAPI) extensions such as .asp. The vulnerability exists because the IIS parser was not properly interpreting Unicode, thus giving hackers system-level access.

Essentially, Unicode converts characters of any language to a universal hex code specification. However, the Unicode is interpreted twice, and the parser only scans the resulting request once (following the first interpretation). Hackers could therefore sneak file requests through IIS. For example, utilizing %c0% af instead of a slash in a relative pathname exploits the IIS vulnerability. In some cases, the request lets the hacker gain access to files that they otherwise shouldn't be able to see. The Unicode directory traversal vulnerability allows a hacker to add, change, or delete files, or upload and run code on the server. The ability to add or run files on the system enables a hacker to install a Trojan or backdoor on the system.

The IIS Unicode exploit is an outdated vulnerability and is presented in this text as a proof of concept—that is, proof that the vulnerability exists and can be exploited.

Buffer overflow attacks are not unique to web servers and can also be launched against other types of systems. A buffer overflow involves sending more data, usually in the form of a text string, than the web server is capable of handling. The primary entry point for buffer overflows is a web form on the web server. Buffer overflows and countermeasures will be covered in detail in the next chapter.

Source disclosure attacks occur when the source code of a server application can be gathered. Source disclosure attacks can lead to a hacker identifying the application type, programming language, and other application-specific information. All this information can allow a potential hacker to identify security holes and potential exploits that can be delivered to the web server. Again, most of a hacker's time is spent gathering information about a target in order to identify the best point of entry for an exploit.

Putting It All Together Using Source Disclosure Attacks

An example of performing a source disclosure attack would be to run BlackWidow against a web server and copy all the files to a local directory. In reviewing the source files from BlackWidow, you can obtain the name of the server, the IP address, and the version. Additional information-gathering tools such as Netcraft can aid in the discovery of the OS, web server software type, and version. Additional information may be gathered regarding the JavaScript (.js files) or Active Server Pages (.asp files) that reside on the server. Based on the web server applications and vulnerabilities, Metasploit can be used to deliver a payload to the server. Depending on the patch level and vulnerability, the payload can be fairly benign or serious enough to cause the hacker to gain access to valuable data. The best countermeasure to the source disclosure attack and other types of attacks is to patch the OS, web server, and all server applications to the most current level and maintain an active patch-management program.

A CEH must be aware of all the information-gathering techniques to identify potential vulnerabilities in web servers and web applications. The reason this knowledge is so important for the CEH is so that they can defend against the same attacks and implement countermeasures to prevent attacks.

Patch-Management Techniques

Patch management plays a critical role in preventing and mitigating the risk of attack against web servers and web applications. *Patch management* is the process of updating appropriate patches and hotfixes required by a system vendor. Proper patch management involves choosing how patches are to be installed and verified, and testing those patches on a non-production network prior to installation.

You should maintain a log of all patches applied to each system. To make patch installation easier, you can use automated patch-management systems provided by PatchLink, St. Bernard Software, Microsoft, and other software vendors to assess your systems and decide which patches to deploy.

 Real World Scenario

First Week on the Job as a Web Administrator

As a newly hired network administrator for a small company of 40 employees, it was my responsibility to review the configuration and patches for a small network with two servers. The company used IIS 5.0 on a Windows 2000 server that had been serving the corporate website to clients for three years. The servers had been installed and configured by a consulting company three years prior to my joining the staff. The website content was updated regularly by the marketing assistant, but no other update had been made to the server.

So, I embarked upon updating and performing patch management on the web server. The company had no firewall protecting the Internet connection, and the Windows Server OS had not had any patches or hotfixes applied to it since installation. The IIS web server software was also out of date. All of this presented a huge security risk to the organization, and patch management was the highest priority to protect the web server and applications running on it.

As I applied security patches and hotfixes, to first the OS and then IIS, I found that malware, such as the Code Red worm and numerous viruses, had already attacked the system. It took several days of applying patches and hotfixes and updating virus definitions before the web server was brought up-to-date. Luckily for the small company, I was able to bring the OS and web server software up-to-date and implement a system for patch management before the network was damaged or a serious security breach occurred.

Hacking Tools

N-Stalker Web Application Security Scanner allows you to assess a web application for a large number of vulnerabilities, including cross-site scripting, SQL injection, buffer overflow, and parameter-tampering attacks.

The Metasploit Framework is a freeware tool used to test or hack operating systems or web server software. Exploits can be used as plug-ins, and testing can be performed from a Windows or Unix platform. Metasploit was originally a command-line utility, but it now has a web browser interface. Using Metasploit, hackers can write their own exploits as well as utilize standard exploits.

CORE IMPACT and SAINT Vulnerability Scanner are commercial exploit tools used to test and compromise operating systems and web server software.

Web Server Hardening Methods

A web server administrator can do many things to *harden* a server (increase its security). The following are ways to increase the security of the web server:

- Rename the administrator account, and use a strong password. To rename the administrator account in Windows, open the User Manager, right-click the Administrator account, and select Rename.

- Disable default websites and FTP sites. The process to disable default websites was described earlier in this chapter: right-click the default website in IIS Manager and choose Stop. The same process works for the default FTP site.

- Remove unused applications from the server, such as WebDAV. Unnecessary applications can be removed on a server by using Add/Remove Programs in the Windows Control Panel.

- Disable directory browsing in the web server's configuration settings.

- Add a legal notice to the site to make potential attackers aware of the implications of hacking the site.

- Apply the most current patches, hotfixes, and service packs to the operating system and web server software.

- Perform bounds checking on input for web forms and query strings to prevent buffer overflow or malicious input attacks.

- Disable remote administration.

- Use a script to map unused file extensions to a 404 ("File not found") error message.

- Enable auditing and logging.

- Use a firewall between the web server and the Internet and allow only necessary ports (such as 80 and 443) through the firewall.

- Replace the GET method with the POST method when sending data to a web server.

Web Application Vulnerabilities

In addition to understanding how a hacker can exploit a web server, it's important for a CEH to be familiar with web application vulnerabilities. In this section, we'll discuss how web applications work, as well as the objectives of web application hacking. We'll also examine the anatomy of a web application attack and some actual web application threats. Finally, we'll look at Google hacking and countermeasures you should be familiar with.

Web applications are programs that reside on a web server to give the user functionality beyond just a website. Database queries, webmail, discussion groups, and blogs are all examples of web applications.

A web application uses a client/server architecture, with a web browser as the client and the web server acting as the application server. JavaScript is a popular way to implement web applications. Because web applications are widely implemented, any user with a web browser can interact with most site utilities.

The purpose of hacking a web application is to gain confidential data. Web applications are critical to the security of a system because they usually connect to a database that contains information such as identities with credit card numbers and passwords. Web application vulnerabilities increase the threat that hackers will exploit the operating system and web server or web application software. Web applications are essentially another door into a system and can be exploited to compromise the system.

Hacking web applications is similar to hacking other systems. Hackers follow a five-step process: they scan a network, gather information, test different attack scenarios, and finally plan and launch an attack. The steps are listed in Figure 8.2.

FIGURE 8.2   The stages of a web application attack

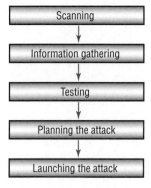

Web Application Threats and Countermeasures

Many web application threats exist on a web server. The following are the most common threats and their countermeasures:

Cross-Site Scripting   A parameter entered into a web form is processed by the web application. The correct combination of variables can result in arbitrary command execution. Countermeasure: Validate cookies, query strings, form fields, and hidden fields.

> A countermeasure to cross-site scripting is to replace left and right angle bracket characters (< and >) with < and > using server scripts. A countermeasure to SSL attacks is to install a proxy server and terminate SSL at the proxy or install a hardware SSL accelerator and terminate SSL at this layer.

SQL Injection   Inserting SQL commands into the URL gets the database server to dump, alter, delete, or create information in the database. SQL injection is covered in detail in Chapter 9, "Attacking Applications: SQL Injection and Buffer Overflows." Countermeasure: Validate user variables.

Command Injection   The hacker inserts programming commands into a web form. Countermeasure: Use language-specific libraries for the programming language.

Cookie Poisoning and Snooping   The hacker corrupts or steals cookies. Countermeasures: Don't store passwords in a cookie; implement cookie timeouts; and authenticate cookies.

Buffer Overflow   Huge amounts of data are sent to a web application through a web form to execute commands. Buffer overflows is covered in detail in Chapter 9. Countermeasures: Validate user input length; perform bounds checking.

Authentication Hijacking   The hacker steals a session once a user has authenticated. Countermeasure: Use SSL to encrypt traffic.

Directory Traversal/Unicode   The hacker browses through the folders on a system via a web browser or Windows Explorer. Countermeasures: Define access rights to private folders on the web server; apply patches and hotfixes.

Hacking Tools

Instant Source allows a hacker to see and edit HTML source code. It can be used directly from within the web browser.

Wget is a command-line tool that a hacker can use to download an entire website, complete with all the files. The hacker can view the source code offline and test certain attacks prior to launching them against the real web server.

WebSleuth uses spidering technology to index an entire website. For example, WebSleuth can pull all the email addresses from different pages of a website.

BlackWidow can scan and map all the pages of a website to create a profile of the site.

SiteScope maps out the connections within a web application and aids in the deconstruction of the program.

WSDigger is a web services testing tool that contains sample attack plug-ins for SQL injection, cross-site scripting, and other web attacks.

Burp is a Windows-based automated attack tool for web applications. It can also be used to guess passwords on web applications and perform man-in-the-middle attacks.

Google Hacking

Google hacking refers to using Google's powerful search engine to locate high-value targets or to search for valuable information such as passwords.

Many tools, such as `http://johnny.ihackstuff.com` and Acunetix Web Vulnerability Scanner, contain a list of Google hacking terms organized in a database, to make searching easier (see Exercise 8.5). For example, you can enter the term *password* or *medical records* in the Google search engine and see what information is available. Many times, Google can pull information directly out of private databases or documents.

EXERCISE 8.5

Using Acunetix Web Vulnerability Scanner

1. Download and install Acunetix Web Vulnerability Scanner from www.acunetix.com.

2. Open the web scanner and select File ➢ New Scan to open the Scan Wizard:

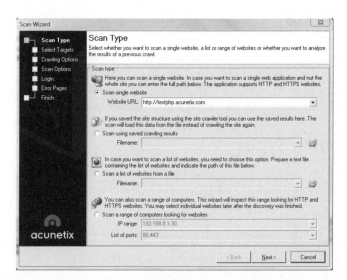

3. Follow the wizard prompts; accept the default values for the initial scan.

4. View the scan report once the scan is complete. Notice the web server and application vulnerabilities in the scan report.

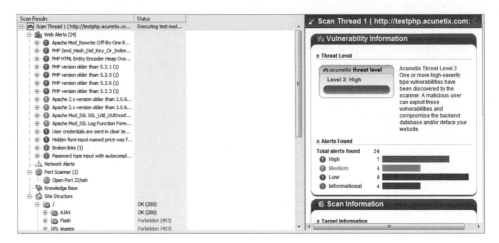

5. Create another scan using the wizard and target your lab web server or web server VM. View and analyze the scan report for your lab web server.

Web-Based Password-Cracking Techniques

As a CEH, you need to be familiar with the techniques hackers use to crack web-based passwords. This includes being able to list the various authentication types, knowing what a password cracker is, identifying the classifications of password-cracking techniques, and knowing the available countermeasures. We'll look at each in the following sections.

Authentication Types

Web servers and web applications support multiple authentication types. The most common is HTTP authentication. There are two types of HTTP authentication: basic and digest. Basic

HTTP authentication sends the username and password in cleartext, whereas digest authentication hashes the credentials and uses a challenge-response model for authentication.

In addition, web servers and web applications support the following types of authentication:

NTLM Authentication   This type uses Internet Explorer and IIS web servers, making NTLM more suitable for internal authentication on an intranet that uses Microsoft operating systems. Windows 2000 and 2003 servers utilize Kerberos authentication for a more secure option.

Certificate-Based Authentication   This type uses an x.509 certificate for public/private key technology.

Token-Based Authentication   A token, such as SecurID, is a hardware device that displays an authentication code for 60 seconds; a user uses this code to log into a network.

Biometric Authentication   This type uses a physical characteristic such as fingerprint, eye iris, or handprint to authenticate the user.

Password Attacks and Password Cracking

The three types of password attacks are as follows:

Dictionary   Uses passwords that can be found in a dictionary

Brute-Force   Guesses complex passwords that use letters, numbers, and special characters

Hybrid   Uses dictionary words with a number or special character as a substitute for a letter

A *password cracker* is a program designed to decrypt passwords or disable password protection. Password crackers rely on dictionary searches (attacks) or brute-force methods to crack passwords.

The first step in a dictionary attack is to generate a list of potential passwords that can be found in a dictionary. The hacker usually creates this list with a dictionary generator program or dictionaries that can be downloaded from the Internet. Next, the list of dictionary words is hashed or encrypted. This hash list is compared against the hashed password the hacker is trying to crack. The hacker can get the hashed password by sniffing it from a wired or wireless network or directly from the Security Accounts Manager (SAM) or shadow password files on the hard drive of a system. Finally, the program displays the unencrypted version of the password. Dictionary password crackers can only discover passwords that are dictionary words.

If the user has implemented a strong password, then brute-force password cracking can be implemented. Brute-force password crackers try every possible combination of letters, numbers, and special characters, which takes much longer than a dictionary attack because of the number of permutations. Exercise 8.6 walks you through using a password cracker called Brutus.

EXERCISE 8.6

Using a Password Cracker

1. Download and install Brutus from www.hoobie.net.

2. Open Brutus and type the web server address in the target field.

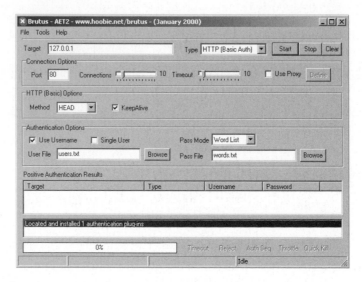

3. Click the Start button and view passwords in the positive authentication results field at the bottom of the screen.

> **Hacking Tool**
>
> Webcracker is a tool that uses a word list to attempt to log on to a web server. It looks for the "HTTP 302 object moved" response to make guesses on the password. From this response, the tool can determine the authentication type in use and attempt to log on to the system.

The best password-cracking countermeasure is to implement strong passwords that are at least eight characters long (the old standard was six) and that include alphanumeric characters. Usernames and passwords should be different, because many usernames are transmitted in cleartext. Complex passwords that require uppercase, lowercase, and numbers or special characters are harder to crack. You should also implement a strong authentication mechanism such as Kerberos or tokens to protect passwords in transit.

Summary

Web servers and web application attacks are always of highest concern with the increasing use of the Internet. Web servers and the Internet are used by customers to research companies, make online purchases, access databases at banks and investment firms, and perform numerous other database searches. As this use rises, the potential target information becomes increasingly valuable. Credit card numbers, personal information, and Social Security numbers are the golden target for hackers, and all this information is stored in web application databases.

Web server and web application hacking are the methods hackers use to attempt to breach web server security and deliver exploits that will yield valuable information. A CEH needs to be well versed in identifying potential vulnerabilities and countermeasures to prevent web server attacks.

Exam Essentials

Know the types of web server vulnerabilities.   Misconfiguration, operating system or application bugs and flaws, default installation of operating system and web server software, lack of patch management, and lack of proper security policies and procedures are all web server vulnerabilities.

Know common web application threats.   Cross-site scripting, SQL and command injection, cookie poisoning and snooping, buffer overflow, authentication hijacking, and directory traversal are all common web application threats.

Understand Google hacking.   Google hacking involves using the Google search engine to locate passwords, credit card numbers, medical records, or other confidential information.

Understand patch-management techniques.   Patch management is important for ensuring a system is up-to-date on the latest security fixes. A process for testing, applying, and logging patches to a system should be defined and followed.

Know the various authentication mechanisms for web servers.   HTTP basic and digest authentication, NTLM, tokens, biometrics, and certificates are all methods of authenticating to a web server.

Understand how password crackers work.   Password crackers use a hashed dictionary file to crack a password.

Know the types of password attacks.   Dictionary, hybrid, and brute force are the three types of password attacks.

Review Questions

1. Which of the following are types of HTTP web authentication? (Choose all that apply.)
   A. Digest
   B. Basic
   C. Windows
   D. Kerberos

2. Which of the following is a countermeasure for a buffer overflow attack?
   A. Input field length validation
   B. Encryption
   C. Firewall
   D. Use of web forms

3. A hardware device that displays a login that changes every 60 seconds is known as a/an
   _____.
   A. Login finder
   B. Authentication server
   C. Biometric authentication
   D. Token

4. Which is a common web server vulnerability?
   A. Limited user accounts
   B. Default installation
   C. Open shares
   D. No directory access

5. A password of P@SSWORD can be cracked using which type of attack?
   A. Brute force
   B. Hybrid
   C. Dictionary
   D. Zero day exploit

6. Which of the following is a countermeasure for authentication hijacking?
   A. Authentication logging
   B. Kerberos
   C. SSL
   D. Active Directory

7. Why is a web server more commonly attacked than other systems?

   A. A web server is always accessible.

   B. Attacking a web server does not require much hacking ability.

   C. Web servers are usually placed in a secure DMZ.

   D. Web servers are simple to exploit.

8. A client/server program that resides on a web server is called a/an _____.

   A. Internet program

   B. Web application

   C. Patch

   D. Configuration file

9. Which is a countermeasure to a directory-traversal attack?

   A. Enforce permissions to folders.

   B. Allow everyone access to the default page only.

   C. Allow only registered users to access the home page of a website.

   D. Make all users log in to access folders.

10. What is it called when a hacker inserts programming commands into a web form?

   A. Form tampering

   B. Command injection

   C. Buffer overflow

   D. Web form attack

11. Which of the following commands would start to execute a banner grab against a web server?

   A. `telnet www.yahoo.com 80`

   B. `telnet HTTP www.yahoo.com`

   C. `http://www.yahoo.com:80`

   D. `HEAD www.yahoo.com`

12. Which of the following exploits can be used against Microsoft Internet Information (IIS) Server? (Choose all that apply.)

   A. IPP printer overflow attack

   B. ISAPI DLL buffer overflow attack

   C. Long URL attack

   D. Proxy buffer overflow attack

13. Where does the most valuable target information reside on a web server?

   A. Web server home directory

   B. Web application system files

   C. Web application database

   D. NTHOME directory

14. Which of the following hacking tools performs directory-traversal attacks on IIS?

   A. RPC DCOM

   B. IIScrack.dll

   C. WebInspect

15. Which program can be used to download entire websites?

   A. WebSleuth

   B. WSDigger

   C. Wget

   D. BlackWidow

16. Web servers support which of the following authentication credentials? (Choose all that apply.)

   A. Certificates

   B. Tokens

   C. Biometrics

   D. Kerberos

17. Which tool can be used to pull all email addresses from a website?

   A. WebSleuth

   B. WSDigger

   C. Wget

   D. BlackWidow

18. What does SiteScope do?

   A. Maps out connections in web applications

   B. Views the HTML source for all web pages in a site

   C. Gathers email address from websites

   D. Tests exploits against web applications

19. What are the three primary types of attacks against IIS servers?

   A. Directory traversal

   B. Buffer overflows

   C. Authentication attacks

   D. Source disclosure attacks

20. Which of the following is a common website attack that allows a hacker to deface a website? (Choose all that apply)

   A. Using a DNS attack to redirect users to a different web server

   B. Revealing an administrator password through a brute-force attack

   C. Using a directory-traversal attack

   D. Using a buffer overflow attack via a web form

Answers to Review Questions

1. A, B. Digest and basic are the types of HTTP web authentication.

2. A. Validating the field length and performing bounds checking are countermeasures for a buffer overflow attack.

3. D. A token is a hardware device containing a screen that displays a discrete set of numbers used for login and authentication.

4. B. Default installation is a common web server vulnerability.

5. B. A hybrid attack substitutes numbers and special characters for letters.

6. C. SSL is a countermeasure for authentication hijacking.

7. A. A web server is always accessible, so a hacker can hack it more easily than less-available systems.

8. B. Web applications are client/server programs that reside on a web server.

9. A. A countermeasure to a directory-traversal attack is to enforce permissions to folders.

10. B. Command injection involves a hacker entering programming commands into a web form in order to get the web server to execute the commands.

11. A. To make an initial connection to the web server, use telnet to port 80.

12. A, B. IPP printer overflow and ISAPI DLL buffer overflow attacks are types of buffer overflow attacks that can be used to exploit IIS Server.

13. C. The most valuable target data, such as passwords, credit card numbers, and personal information, reside in the database of a web application.

14. D. `IISExploit.exe` is a tool used to perform automated directory-traversal attacks on IIS.

15. C. Wget is a command-line tool that can be used to download an entire website with all the source files.

16. A, B, C. Certificates, tokens. and biometrics are all credentials that can authenticate users to web servers and web applications. Kerberos is a type of security system used to protect user authentication credentials.

17. A. WebSleuth can be used to index a website and specifically pull email addresses from all the pages of a website.

18. A. SiteScope maps out the connections within a web application and aids in the deconstruction of the program.

19. A, B, D. The three most common attacks against IIS are directory traversal, buffer overflows, and source disclosure.

20. A, B. Using a DNS attack to redirect users to a different web server and revealing an administrator password through a brute-force attack are two methods of defacing a website.

Chapter

9

Attacking Applications: SQL Injection and Buffer Overflows

CEH EXAM OBJECTIVES COVERED IN THIS CHAPTER:

✓ What is SQL injection?

✓ Understand the steps to conduct SQL injection

✓ Understand SQL Server vulnerabilities

✓ Describe SQL injection countermeasures

✓ Overview of stack-based buffer overflows

✓ Identify the different types of buffer overflows and methods of detection

✓ Overview of buffer overflow mutation techniques

SQL injection and buffer overflows are hacking techniques used to exploit weaknesses in applications. When programs are written, some parameters used in the creation of the application code can leave weaknesses in the program. SQL injection and buffer overflows are covered in the same chapter because they both are methods used to attack application and are generally caused by programming flaws. Generally, the purpose of SQL injection is to convince the application to run SQL code that was not intended.

SQL injection is a hacking method used to attack SQL databases, whereas buffer overflows can exist in many different types of applications. SQL injection and buffer overflows are similar exploits in that they're both usually delivered via a user input field. The input field is where a user may enter a username and password on a website, add data to a URL, or perform a search for a keyword in another application. The SQL injection vulnerability is caused primarily by unverified or unsanitized user input via these fields.

Both SQL Server injection and buffer overflow vulnerabilities are caused by the same issue: invalid parameters that are not verified by the application. If programmers don't take the time to validate the variables a user can enter into a variable field, the results can be serious and unpredictable. Sophisticated hackers can exploit this vulnerability, causing an execution fault and shutdown of the system or application, or a command shell to be executed for the hacker.

SQL injection and buffer overflow countermeasures are designed to utilize secure programming methods. By changing the variables used by the application code, weaknesses in applications can be greatly minimized. This chapter will detail how to perform a SQL injection and a buffer overflow attack and explore the best countermeasures to prevent the attack.

SQL Injection

As a CEH, it's important for you to be able to define SQL injection and understand the steps a hacker takes to conduct a SQL injection attack. In addition, you should know SQL Server vulnerabilities, as well as countermeasures to SQL injection attacks.

SQL injection occurs when an application processes user-provided data to create a SQL statement without first validating the input. The user input is then submitted to a web application database server for execution. When successfully exploited, SQL injection can give an attacker access to database content or allow the hacker to remotely execute system commands. In the worst-case scenario, the hacker can take control of the server that is hosting the database. This exploit can give a hacker access to a remote shell into the server file system. The impact of a SQL injection attacks depends on where the vulnerability is in the code, how easy it is to exploit the vulnerability, and what level of access the application has to the database. Theoretically, SQL injection can occur in any type of application, but it is most commonly associated with web applications because they are most often attacked. As previously discussed in Chapter 8, "Web Hacking: GOOGLE, Web Servers, Web Application Vulnerabilities, and Web-Based Password Cracking Techniques," web applications are easy targets because by their very nature they are open to being accessed from the Internet. You should have a basic understanding of how databases work and how SQL commands are used to access the information in the databases prior to attempting the CEH exam.

During a web application SQL injection attack, malicious code is inserted into a web form field or the website's code to make a system execute a command shell or other arbitrary commands. Just as a legitimate user enters queries and additions to the SQL database via a web form, the hacker can insert commands to the SQL Server through the same web form field. For example, an arbitrary command from a hacker might open a command prompt or display a table from the database. A database table may contain personal information such as credit card numbers, social security numbers, or passwords. SQL Servers are very common database servers and used by many organizations to store confidential data. This makes a SQL Server a high-value target and therefore a system that is very attractive to hackers.

 Real World Scenario

Determining SQL Injection Vulnerabilities

While performing a black-hat penetration test on a corporate network, a security tester, Tom, found a custom application on one of the publicly accessible web servers. Since this was a black-hat test, Tom did not have access to the source code to see how the program had been created. But after performing some information gathering, he was able to determine that the server was running Microsoft Internet Information Server 6 along with ASP.NET, and this suggested that the database was Microsoft's SQL Server.

The login page of the web application had a username, a password field, and a forgotten password link, which ended up being the easiest way into the system. A forgotten password link works by looking in the user database for the user's email address and sending an email containing the password to that address.

So to determine if the forgotten password link was vulnerable to SQL injection, Tom entered a single quote as part of the data in the forgotten password field. The purpose was to see if the application would construct a SQL string literally without sanitizing the user input. When submitting the form with a quote in the email address, he received a 500 error (server failure), and this suggested that the user input was being parsed literally.

The underlying SQL code of the form probably looked something like this:

```
SELECT fieldlist
  FROM table
  WHERE field = '$EMAIL';
```

Tom typed his email address followed by a single quote in the forgotten email link field. The SQL parser of the web application found the extra quote mark and aborted with a syntax error. When Tom received this error message, he was able to determine that the user input was not being sanitized properly and that the application could be exploited. In this case, he did not need to continue and exploit the application since the error message was proof enough that the application was vulnerable to a SQL injection attack. As a result of this penetration test, the client was able to fix the SQL Server vulnerability.

Finding a SQL Injection Vulnerability

Before launching a SQL injection attack, the hacker determines whether the configuration of the database and related tables and variables is vulnerable. The steps to determine the SQL Server's vulnerability are as follows:

1. Using your web browser, search for a website that uses a login page or other database input or query fields (such as an "I forgot my password" form). Look for web pages that display the POST or GET HTML commands by checking the site's source code.

2. Test the SQL Server using single quotes (' '). Doing so indicates whether the user input variable is sanitized or interpreted literally by the server. If the server responds with an error message that says *use 'a'='a'* (or something similar), then it's most likely susceptible to a SQL injection attack.

3. Use the SELECT command to retrieve data from the database or the INSERT command to add information to the database.

Here are some examples of variable field text you can use on a web form to test for SQL vulnerabilities:

- Blah' or 1=1--
- Login:blah' or 1=1--
- Password::blah' or 1=1--
- http://search/index.asp?id=blah' or 1=1--

These commands and similar variations may allow a user to bypass a login depending on the structure of the database. When entered in a form field, the commands may return many rows in a table or even an entire database table because the SQL Server is interpreting the terms literally. The double dashes near the end of the command tell SQL to ignore the rest of the command as a comment.

Here are some examples of how to use SQL commands to take control:
To get a directory listing, type the following in a form field:

```
Blah';exec master..xp_cmdshell "dir c:\*.* /s >c:\directory.txt"--
```

To create a file, type the following in a form field:

```
Blah';exec master..xp_cmdshell "echo hacker-was-here > c:\hacker.txt"--
```

To ping an IP address, type the following in a form field:

```
Blah';exec master..xp_cmdshell "ping 192.168.1.1"--
```

The Purpose of SQL Injection

SQL injection attacks are used by hackers to achieve certain results. Some SQL exploits will produce valuable user data stored in the database, and some are just precursors to other attacks. The following are the most common purposes of a SQL injection attack:

Identifying SQL Injection Vulnerability   The purpose is to probe a web application to discover which parameters and user input fields are vulnerable to SQL injection.

Performing Database Finger-Printing   The purpose is to discover the type and version of database that a web application is using and "fingerprint" the database. Knowing the type and version of the database used by a web application allows an attacker to craft database-specific attacks.

Determining Database Schema   To correctly extract data from a database, the attacker often needs to know database schema information, such as table names, column names, and column data types. This information can be used in a follow-on attack.

Extracting Data   These types of attacks employ techniques that will extract data values from the database. Depending on the type of web application, this information could be sensitive and highly desirable to the attacker.

Adding or Modifying Data   The purpose is to add or change information in a database.

Performing Denial of Service   These attacks are performed to shut down access to a web application, thus denying service to other users. Attacks involving locking or dropping database tables also fall under this category.

Evading Detection   This category refers to certain attack techniques that are employed to avoid auditing and detection.

Bypassing Authentication   The purpose is to allow the attacker to bypass database and application authentication mechanisms. Bypassing such mechanisms could allow the attacker to assume the rights and privileges associated with another application user.

Executing Remote Commands   These types of attacks attempt to execute arbitrary commands on the database. These commands can be stored procedures or functions available to database users.

Performing Privilege Escalation   These attacks take advantage of implementation errors or logical flaws in the database in order to escalate the privileges of the attacker.

SQL Injection Using Dynamic Strings

Most SQL applications do a specific, predictable job. Many functions of a SQL database receive static user input where the only variable is the user input fields. Such statements do not change from execution to execution. They are commonly called static SQL statements.

However, some programs must build and process a variety of SQL statements at run-time. In many cases the full text of the statement is unknown until application execution. Such statements can, and probably will, change from execution to execution. So, they are called dynamic SQL statements.

Dynamic SQL is an enhanced form of SQL that, unlike standard SQL, facilitates the automatic generation and execution of program statements. Dynamic SQL is a term used to mean SQL code that is generated by the web application before it is executed. Dynamic SQL is a flexible and powerful tool for creating SQL strings. It can be helpful when you find it necessary to write code that can adjust to varying databases, conditions, or servers. Dynamic SQL also makes it easier to automate tasks that are repeated many times in a web application.

A hacker can attack a web-based authentication form using SQL injection through the use of dynamic strings. For example, the underlying code for a web authentication form on a web server may look like the following:

```
SQLCommand = "SELECT Username FROM Users WHERE Username = '"
SQLCommand = SQLComand & strUsername
SQLCommand = SQLComand & "' AND Password = '"
SQLCommand = SQLComand & strPassword
SQLCommand = SQLComand & "'"
strAuthCheck = GetQueryResult(SQLQuery)
```

A hacker can exploit the SQL injection vulnerability by entering a login and password in the web form that uses the following variables:

```
Username: kimberly
Password: graves' OR ''='
```

The SQL application would build a command string from this input as follows:

```
SELECT Username FROM Users
WHERE Username = 'kimberly'
AND Password = 'graves' OR ''=''
```

This is an example of SQL injection: this query will return all rows from the user's database, regardless of whether kimberly is a real username in the database or graves is a legitimate password. This is due to the OR statement appended to the WHERE clause. The comparison ''='' will always return a true result, making the overall WHERE clause evaluate to true for all rows in the table. This will enable the hacker to log in with any username and password.

In Exercise 9.1, you will use HP Scramlr to test for SQL injection vulnerabilities.

EXERCISE 9.1

Using HP's Scrawlr to Test for SQL Injection Vulnerabilities

1. Download Scrawlr from www.HP.com.

2. Install Scrawlr on your Windows lab PC.

3. Open the Scrawlr program.

4. Type a target web address in the URL Of Site To Scan field:

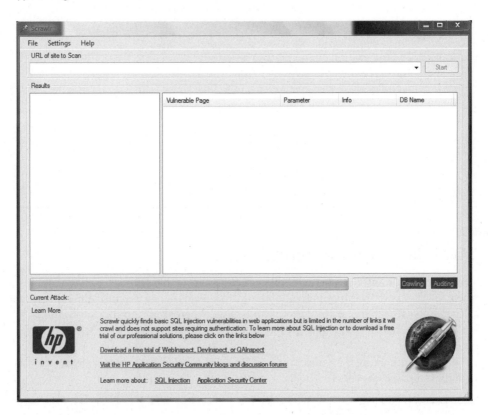

5. Click the Start button to start the audit of the website for SQL injection vulnerabilities.

6. Once the SQL injection vulnerability scan is complete, Scrawlr will display additional hosts linked from the scanned site. It is a best practice to scan the linked sites as well as the main site to ensure no SQL injection vulnerabilities exist.

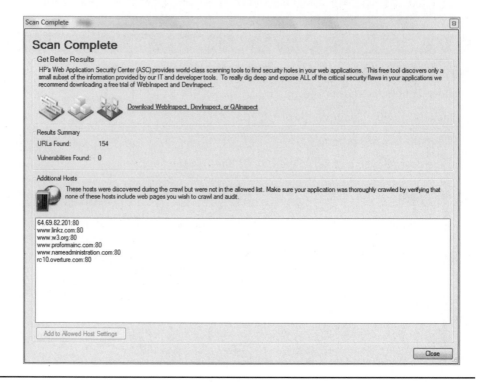

SQL Injection Countermeasures

The cause of SQL injection vulnerabilities is relatively simple and well understood: insufficient validation of user input. To address this problem, defensive coding practices, such as encoding user input and validation, can be used when programming applications. It is a laborious and time-consuming process to check all applications for SQL injection vulnerabilities.

When implementing SQL injection countermeasures, review source code for the following programming weaknesses:

- Single quotes
- Lack of input validation

The first countermeasures for preventing a SQL injection attack are minimizing the privileges of a user's connection to the database and enforcing strong passwords for SA and Administrator accounts. You should also disable verbose or explanatory error messages so no more information than necessary is sent to the hacker; such information could help them determine whether the SQL Server is vulnerable. Remember that one of the purposes of SQL injection is to gain additional information as to which parameters are susceptible to attack.

Another countermeasure for preventing SQL injection is checking user data input and validating the data prior to sending the input to the application for processing.

Some countermeasures to SQL injection are

- Rejecting known bad input
- Sanitizing and validating the input field

Buffer Overflows

As a CEH, you must be able to identify different types of buffer overflows. You should also know how to detect a buffer overflow vulnerability and understand the steps a hacker may use to perform a stack-based overflow attack. We'll look at these topics, as well as provide an overview of buffer-overflow mutation techniques, in the following sections.

Types of Buffer Overflows and Methods of Detection

Buffer overflows are exploits that hackers use against an operating system or application; like SQL injection attacks, they're usually targeted at user input fields. A buffer overflow exploit causes a system to fail by overloading memory or executing a command shell or arbitrary code on the target system. A buffer overflow vulnerability is caused by a lack of bounds checking or a lack of input-validation sanitization in a variable field (such as on a web form). If the application doesn't check or validate the size or format of a variable before sending it to be stored in memory, an overflow vulnerability exits.

The two types of buffer overflows are stack based and heap based.

The *stack* and the *heap* are storage locations for user-supplied variables within a running program. Variables are stored in the stack or heap until the program needs them. Stacks are static locations of memory address space, whereas heaps are dynamic memory address spaces that occur while a program is running. A heap-based buffer overflow occurs in the lower part of the memory and overwrites other dynamic variables. See Figure 9.1.

FIGURE 9.1   Stack versus Heap Memory

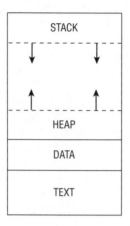

A call stack, or *stack*, is used to keep track of where in the programming code the execution pointer should return after each portion of the code is executed. A stack-based buffer overflow attack (Figure 9.2) occurs when the memory assigned to each execution routine is overflowed. As a consequence of both types of buffer overflows, a program can open a shell or command prompt or stop the execution of a program. The next section describes stack-based buffer overflow attacks.

FIGURE 9.2   A stack-based buffer overflow attack

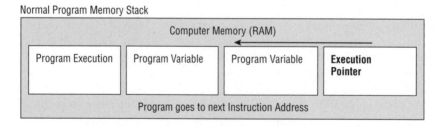

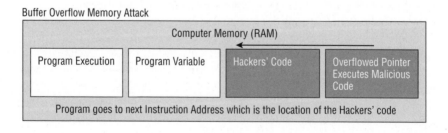

To detect program buffer overflow vulnerabilities that result from poorly written source code, a hacker sends large amounts of data to the application via a form field and sees what the program does as a result.

The following are the steps a hacker uses to execute a stack-based buffer overflow:

1. Enter a variable into the buffer to exhaust the amount of memory in the stack.

2. Enter more data than the buffer has allocated in memory for that variable, which causes the memory to overflow or run into the memory space for the next process. Then, add another variable, and overwrite the return pointer that tells the program where to return to after executing the variable.

3. A program executes this malicious code variable and then uses the return pointer to get back to the next line of executable code. If the hacker successfully overwrites the pointer, the program executes the hacker's code instead of the program code.

Most hackers don't need to be this familiar with the details of buffer overflows. Prewritten exploits can be found on the Internet and are exchanged between hacker groups. Exercise 9.2 walks through using Metasploit to perform a Buffer Overflow attack.

 The memory register that gets overwritten with the return address of the exploit code is known as the EIP.

EXERCISE 9.2

Performing a Buffer Overflow Attack Using Metasploit

1. Open the Metasploit Framework.

2. Start the test machine running Windows Server with IIS.

3. From Metasploit, run the IIS Buffer Overflow attack against the test machine running IIS.

4. Choose a payload to deliver to the IIS target system via the buffer overflow exploit.

Buffer Overflow Countermeasures

As you can see, hackers can graduate from standard buffer overflows to redirecting the return pointer to the code of their choosing. A hacker must know the exact memory address and the size of the stack in order to make the return pointer execute their code. A hacker can use a No Operation (NOP) instruction, which is just padding to move the instruction pointer and does not execute any code. The NOP instruction is added to a string before the malicious code to be executed.

If an intrusion detection system (IDS) is present on the network, it can thwart a hacker who sends a series of NOP instructions to forward to the instruction pointer. To bypass the

IDS, the hacker can randomly replace some of the NOP instructions with equivalent pieces of code, such as x++,x-;?NOPNOP. This example of a mutated buffer overflow attack can bypass detection by an IDS.

Programmers should not use the built-in strcpy(), strcat(), and streadd() C/C++ functions because they are susceptible to buffer overflows. Alternatively, Java can be used as the programming language since Java is not susceptible to buffer overflows.

Summary

SQL injection and buffer overflows are hacking methods used to exploit applications. Web applications are especially vulnerable to attack as they have easy access for hackers in the form of user input fields, such as username, password, forgotten password, and price fields. The strict interpretation and unsanitized input is able to directly interact with the database and can cause the database to reveal confidential information. Buffer overflows exist in two types, stack based and heap based, which attack different areas of the memory allocation space. SQL injection and buffer overflow attacks can be prevented by validating user input and limiting the length of a user input field. These two countermeasures can fix most application vulnerabilities and protect applications from SQL injection and buffer overflow attacks.

Exam Essentials

Know how SQL injection and buffer overflow attacks are similar.   SQL injection and buffer overflows are similar in that both attacks are delivered via a web form field.

Understand the purposes of SQL injection.   The purposes of SQL injection attacks can be to obtain user data from a database or to perform information gathering on the database and application vulnerabilities.

Understand SQL injection countermeasures.   Utilizing correct programming code without single quotes and performing bounds-checking and input validation are SQL injection countermeasures.

Know the difference between a stack-based and a heap-based buffer overflow.   Stacks are static locations of memory address space, whereas heaps are dynamic memory address spaces.

Understand how to bypass an IDS using a buffer overflow attack.   An IDS looks for a series of NOP instructions. By replacing the NOP instruction with other code segments, a hacker can effectively bypass an IDS.

Understand buffer overflow and SQL injection countermeasures.   Bounds-checking and sanitizing the input from a web form can prevent a buffer overflow and SQL injection vulnerability.

Review Questions

1. Entering **Password::blah**' or **1=1-** into a web form in order to get a password is an example of what type of attack?

    A. Buffer overflow

    B. Heap-based overflow

    C. Stack-based overflow

    D. SQL injection

2. Replacing NOP instructions with other code in a buffer overflow mutation serves what purpose?

    A. Bypassing an IDS

    B. Overwriting the return pointer

    C. Advancing the return pointer

    D. Bypassing a firewall

3. Which of the following is used to store dynamically allocated variables?

    A. Heap overflow

    B. Stack overflow

    C. Heap

    D. Stack

4. What is the first step in a SQL injection attack?

    A. Enter arbitrary commands at a user prompt.

    B. Locate a user input field on a web page.

    C. Locate the return pointer.

    D. Enter a series of NOP instructions.

5. What command is used to retrieve information from a SQL database?

    A. INSERT

    B. GET

    C. SET

    D. SELECT

6. Which of the following is a countermeasure for buffer overflows?

    A. Not using single quotes

    B. Securing all login pages with SSL

    C. Bounds checking

    D. User validation

7. What does NOP stand for?

A. No Operation

B. Network Operation Protocol

C. No Once Prompt

D. Network Operation

8. What information does a hacker need to launch a buffer overflow attack?

A. A hacker needs to be familiar with the memory address space and techniques of buffer overflows in order to launch a buffer overflow attack.

B. A hacker needs to understand the differences between heaps and stacks.

C. A hacker must be able to identify a target vulnerable to a buffer overflow attack.

D. A hacker must be able to perform a port scan looking for vulnerable memory stacks.

9. Why are many programs vulnerable to SQL injection and buffer overflow attacks?

A. The programs are written quickly and use poor programming techniques.

B. These are inherent flaws in any program.

C. The users have not applied the correct service packs.

D. The programmers are using the wrong programming language.

10. Which command would a hacker enter in a web form field to obtain a directory listing?

A. `Blah';exec master..xp_cmdshell "dir *.*"--`

B. `Blah';exec_cmdshell "dir c:\*.* /s >c:\directory.txt"--`

C. `Blah';exec master..xp_cmdshell "dir c:\*.* /s >c:\directory.txt"--`

D. `Blah';exec cmdshell "dir c:\*.* "--`

11. What are two types of buffer overflow attacks?

A. Heap and stack

B. Heap and overflow

C. Stack and memory allocation

D. Injection and heap

12. Variables that are gathered from a user input field in a web application for later execution by the web application are known as _____.

A. Delayed execution

B. Dynamic strings

C. Static variables

D. Automatic functions

13. What is one purpose of SQL injection attacks?

   A. To create heap-based buffer overflows

   B. To create stack-based buffer overflows

   C. To perform NOP execution

   D. To identify vulnerable parameters

14. Which application will help identify whether a website is vulnerable to SQL injection attacks?

   A. BlackWidow

   B. Metasploit

   C. Scrawlr

   D. SQL Block

15. A countermeasure to buffer overflows is to use the _____ programming language because it is not susceptible to buffer overflow attacks.

   A. Java

   B. Netscape

   C. Oracle

   D. ASP

16. You are a programmer analyzing the code of an application running on your organization's servers. There are an excessive number of `fgets ()` commands. These are C++ functions that do not perform bounds checking. What kind of attack is this program susceptible to?

   A. Buffer overflow

   B. Denial of service

   C. SQL injection

   D. Password cracking

17. Which of the following are countermeasures to SQL injection attacks? (Choose two.)

   A. Rejecting known bad input

   B. Sanitizing and validating input field

   C. Performing user validation

   D. Ensuring all user input is a variable

18. An ethical hacker is performing a penetration test on a web application. The hacker finds a user input field on a web form and enters a single quotation mark. The website responds with a server error. What does the error indicate?

   A. The web application is susceptible to SQL injection attacks.

   B. The web application is not susceptible to SQL injection attacks.

   C. The server is experiencing a denial of service.

   D. The web application has crashed.

19. SQL statements that vary from execution to execution are known as _____ strings.

   A. Variable

   B. Dynamic

   C. Application-based

   D. Static

20. When is a No Operation (NOP) instruction added to a string?

   A. After the malicious code is executed

   B. Before the malicious code is executed

   C. At exactly the same time the malicious code is executed

   D. During the time the malicious code is executed

Answers to Review Questions

1. D. Use of a single quote indicates a SQL injection attack.

2. A. The purpose of mutating a buffer overflow by replacing NOP instructions is to bypass an IDS.

3. C. A heap is using to store dynamic variables.

4. B. The first step in a SQL injection attack is to locate a user input field on a web page using a web browser.

5. D. The command to retrieve information from a SQL database is SELECT.

6. C. Performing bounds checking is a countermeasure for buffer overflow attacks.

7. A. NOP is an acronym for No Operation.

8. C. All a hacker needs to be able to do to launch a buffer overflow attack is to identify a target system. A hacker can run a prewritten exploit to launch a buffer overflow.

9. A. Programs can be exploited because they're written quickly and poorly.

10. C. The command `Blah';exec master..xp_cmdshell "dir c:\*.* /s >c:\directory .txt"--` obtains a directory listing utilizing SQL injection.

11. A. Heap and stack are the two types of buffer overflows.

12. B. Dynamic strings are user input fields stored for later execution by the application.

13. D. One purpose of attacking a SQL database–based application is to identify user input parameters susceptible to SQL injection attacks.

14. C. HP's Scrawlr will scan a web URL to determine if the site is vulnerable to SQL injection attacks.

15. A. A recommended countermeasure to buffer overflow attacks is to use Java-based applications, which are not susceptible to buffer overflow attacks.

16. A. Applications that do not perform bounds checking on user input fields are susceptible to buffer overflow attacks.

17. A, B. Rejecting known bad input and sanitizing and validating user input prior to sending the command to the SQL database is a countermeasure to SQL injection attacks.

18. A. A server error in response to a single quotation mark in a web application user input field indicates the application is not sanitizing the user data and is therefore susceptible to SQL injection attacks.

19. B. Dynamic strings are built on the fly from user input and will vary each time the command is executed.

20. B. A NOP instruction is added to a string just before the malicious code is to be executed.

Chapter

10

Wireless Network Hacking

CEH EXAM OBJECTIVES COVERED IN THIS CHAPTER:

✓ Overview of WEP, WPA authentication mechanisms, and cracking techniques

✓ Overview of wireless sniffers and locating SSIDs, MAC spoofing

✓ Understand rogue access points

✓ Understand wireless hacking techniques

✓ Describe the methods used to secure wireless networks

Wireless networks add another entry point into a network for hackers. Much has been written about wireless security and hacking because wireless is a relatively new technology and rife with security vulnerabilities. From the increase of Wi-Fi hotspots to the rising number of cell phones, PDAs, and laptops equipped with Wi-Fi radios, wireless security is an ever increasing issue for many organizations.

Because of the broadcast nature of radio frequency (RF) wireless networks and the rapid adoption of wireless technologies for home and business networks, many hacking opportunities exist in wireless networking. Even for organizations with a "no wireless" policy—meaning they do not support any Wi-Fi connectivity—rogue wireless access points placed on the LAN are an increasing threat. The cost of Wi-Fi equipment is dropping and many organizations are pressing the IT staff to install wireless networks to complement or replace existing wired networks.

Wi-Fi and Ethernet

It is important to recognize that Wi-Fi networks are fundamentally different from Ethernet networks. Whereas in an Ethernet network the data is carried in frames on copper or fiber-optic cabling, in a Wi-Fi network the data travels across open air. Additionally, any encryption applied to wireless networks only encrypts the data itself, leaving the header potion of the wireless frame open to many types of attacks. The details of wireless attacks and countermeasures will be covered later in this chapter, but first you need to understand the fundamentals of the 802.11 standards and protocols.

802.11 Wireless LANs operate at layer 1 and 2 of the OSI Model. This means that the protocols in use on a WLAN are the same from Layer 3 (usually IP) on up to Layer 7 (the application layer). See Figure 10.1.

Many people call 802.11 WLANs "wireless Ethernet," which is a big misnomer. 802.11 has a completely different frame format at Layer 2 than does 802.3 (Ethernet). For example, Ethernet Layer 2 frames carry only two MAC addresses, while 802.11 frames have fields for four MAC addresses. Ethernet just defines source and destination addresses, while an 802.11 frame can define source, destination, transmitter and receiver. 802.11 frames also carry a frame control field in the MAC header used to indicate information about the frame, such as if the frame is encrypted. See Figure 10.2.

FIGURE 10.1   Wireless LANs in the OSI Model

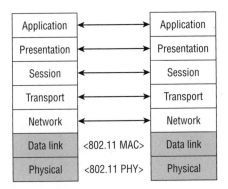

FIGURE 10.2   802.11 MAC Header

			MAC Header					
2	2	6	6	6	6	2	0-2312	4
Frame Control	Duration/ ID	Address 1	Address 2	Address 3	Sequence Control	Address 4	Frame Body	FCS

There are three types of 802.11 frames:

- Management—Used for notification, connection, disconnection, and information.

- Control—Used to control which station has access to the wireless network media.

- Data—Used to carry upper layer data.

Most wireless LANs (WLANs) are based on the IEEE 802.11 standards and amendments, such as 802.11a, 802.11b, 802.11g, and 802.11n. The lettered amendments have been rolled up into a final 802.11 standard and are now referred to by the clause or section number within the 802.11 standard. However, since the lettered amendments are still frequently used when differentiating between the sections of the 802.11 standard, they will be used here in this chapter as well. Table 10.1 shows a comparison of the 802.11 standard amendments.

TABLE 10.1   802.11 comparison

IEEE Standard	Frequency	Speed	Transmission Range	Spread Spectrum
802.11	2.4 GHz	Up to 2 Mbps	Depends on spread spectrum type	DSSS and FHSS
802.11a	5 GHz	Up to 54 Mbps	25 to 75 feet indoors; range can be affected by building materials	OFDM
802.11b	2.4 GHz	Up to 11 Mbps	Up to 150 feet indoors; range can be affected by building materials	DSSS
802.11g	2.4 GHz	Up to 54 Mbps	Up to 150 feet indoors; range can be affected by building materials	DSSS
802.11n	2.4 and 5 GHz	Up to 600 Mbps	At least as far as b, g, and a—and possibly much further	OFDM

The initial 802.11 standard included only rudimentary security features and was fraught with vulnerabilities. The 802.11i amendment is the latest security solution that addresses the 802.11 weaknesses. The Wi-Fi Alliance created additional security certifications known as *Wi-Fi Protected Access* (WPA) and WPA2 to fill the gap between the original 802.11 standard and the latest 802.11i amendment. The security vulnerabilities and security solutions discussed in this chapter are all based on these IEEE and Wi-Fi Alliance standards.

Authentication and Cracking Techniques

Two methods exist in the 802.11 standard for authenticating wireless LAN clients to an access point: open system or shared-key authentication. Open system does not provide any security mechanisms but is simply a request to make a connection to the network. Shared-key authentication has the wireless client hash a string of challenge text with the Wired Equivalent Privacy (WEP) key to authenticate the client to the network. Table 10.2 compares the Wi-Fi security standards type of authentication and encryption.

WEP was the first security option for 802.11 WLANs. WEP is used to encrypt data on the WLAN and can optionally be paired with shared-key authentication to authenticate WLAN clients. WEP uses an RC4 64-bit or 128-bit encryption key to encrypt the Layer 2 data payload. This WEP key comprises a 40-bit or 104-bit user-defined key combined with a 24-bit Initialization Vector (IV), making the WEP key either 64 or 128 bit.

TABLE 10.2 Wi-Fi security comparison

Wi-Fi Security	Authentication	Cipher	Encryption
WPA-Personal	Preshared Key	TKIP	RC4
WPA-Enterprise	802.1X/EAP	TKIP	RC4
WPA2-Personal	Preshared Key	CCMP (default), TKIP (optional)	AES (default), RC4 (optional)
WPA2-Enterprise	802.1X/EAP	CCMP (default), TKIP (optional)	AES (default), RC4 (optional)

The process by which RC4 uses IVs is the real weakness of WEP: it gives a hacker the opportunity to crack the WEP key. The method, knows as the *Fluhrer, Mantin, and Shamir (FMS) attack*, uses encrypted output bytes to determine the most probable key bytes. The ability to exploit the WEP vulnerability was incorporated into products like AirSnort, WEPCrack, and Aircrack. Although a hacker can attempt to crack WEP by brute force, the most common technique is the FMS attack.

WPA employs the Temporal Key Integrity Protocol (TKIP)—which is a safer RC4 implementation—for data encryption and either WPA Personal or WPA Enterprise for authentication. WPA Personal uses an ASCII passphrase for authentication whereas WPA Enterprise uses a RADIUS server to authenticate users. WPA Enterprise is a more secure robust security option but relies on the creation and more complex setup of a RADIUS server. TKIP rotates the data encryption key to prevent the vulnerabilities of WEP and, consequently, cracking attacks.

WPA2 is similar to 802.11i and uses the Advanced Encryption Standard (AES) to encrypt the data payload. AES is considered an uncrackable encryption algorithm. WPA2 also allows for the use of TKIP during a transitional period called *mixed mode security*. This transitional mode means both TKIP and AES can be used to encrypt data. AES requires a faster processor, which means low-end devices like PDAs may only support TKIP.

WPA Personal and WPA2 Personal use a passphrase to authentication WLAN clients. WPA Enterprise and WPA2 Enterprise authenticate WLAN users via a RADIUS server using the 802.1X/Extensible Authentication Protocol (EAP) standards. Figure 10.3 shows the 802.1x/EAP process and the communication process used to authenticate a client using 802.1x/EAP.

FIGURE 10.3   802.1X authentication process

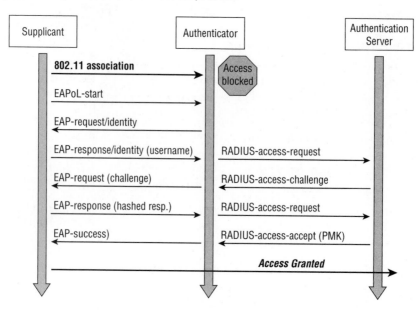

802.11i and WPA use the same encryption and authentication mechanisms as WPA2. However, WPA2 doesn't require vendors to implement preauthorization. Preauthorization enables fast, secure roaming, which is necessary in very mobile environments with time-sensitive applications such as wireless VoIP.

Table 10.3 summarizes the authentication and encryption options for WLANs and associated weaknesses.

TABLE 10.3   802.11 and WPA security solutions and weaknesses

	Encryption	Authentication	Weakness
Original IEEE 802.11 standard	WEP	WEP	IV weakness allows the WEP key to be cracked. The same key is used for encryption and authentication of all clients to the WLAN.
WPA	TKIP	Passphrase or RADIUS (802.1x/EAP)	Passphrase is susceptible to a dictionary attack.
WPA2	AES (can use TKIP while in mixed mode)	Passphrase or RADIUS (802.1x/EAP)	Passphrase is susceptible to a dictionary attack.
IEEE 802.11i	AES (can use TKIP while in mixed mode)	Passphrase or RADIUS (802.1x/EAP)	Passphrase is susceptible to a dictionary attack.

Hacking Tools

Aircrack is a WEP-cracking software tool. It doesn't capture packets; it's used to perform the cracking after another tool has captured the encrypted packets. Aircrack runs on Windows or Linux.

WEPCrack and AirSnort are Linux-based WEP-cracking tools.

NetStumbler and Kismet are WLAN discovery tools. They both discover the Media Access Control (MAC) address, Service Set Identifier (SSID), security mode, and channel of the WLAN. Additionally, Kismet can discover WLANs whose SSIDs are hidden, collect packets, and provide IDS functionality.

 Real World Scenario

Be Careful Where You War Drive

In 2003, hackers used a wireless network at home-improvement retailer Lowe's in an attempt to steal credit card numbers. The three hackers discovered a vulnerable WLAN at a Lowe's store in Southfield, Michigan while scanning for open connections, or "war driving" in the area. The hackers then used the open access point to compromise the entire corporate network of the North Carolina–based home improvement store company, hacking into stores in California, Kansas, South Dakota, and other states over the course of several weeks. They accessed a credit processing program called tcpcredit that skimmed credit account information for every transaction processed at a particular Lowe's store. The hacker's plan was thought to be a way to siphon off millions of credit card numbers through a backdoor installed in the proprietary Lowe's program.

One of the men involved in the hacking attempt pleaded guilty to four counts of wire fraud and unauthorized access to a computer after he and two accomplices hacked into the Lowe's network. In 2004 he was convicted and is currently serving a nine-year prison term even though there is no evidence that he gathered any credit card numbers. During the investigation only six credit card numbers were found in the file that was created from the modified tcpcredit program. This story goes to show that even harmless war driving could draw unwanted attention, so be careful about the WLAN to which you are connecting.

Using Wireless Sniffers to Locate SSIDs

A common attack on a WLAN involves eavesdropping or sniffing. This is an easy attack to perform and usually occurs at hotspots or with any default installation access point (AP), because packets are generally sent unencrypted across the WLAN. Passwords for network access protocols such as FTP, POP3, and SMTP can be captured in cleartext (unencrypted) by a hacker on an unencrypted WLAN.

The *Service Set Identifier (SSID)* is the name of the WLAN and can be located in beacon frames and probe response frames. If two wireless networks are physically close, the SSIDs are used to identify and differentiate the respective networks. The SSID is usually sent in the clear in a beacon frame as well as other frames, such as probe response frames. Most APs allow the WLAN administrator to hide the SSID. However, this isn't a robust security mechanism because some tools can read the SSID from other packets, such as probe requests and other client-side packets.

Exercise 10.1 walks you through installing and using a WLAN sniffer tool called Omnipeek.

EXERCISE 10.1

Installing and Using a WLAN Sniffer Tool

1. Download a trial version of Omnipeek from www.wildpackets.com. You will need to have a wireless LAN adapter that is supported by Omnipeek in promiscuous mode for Omnipeek to properly capture all the traffic on a wireless LAN. Check for the supported wireless LAN adapters and supporting drivers from www.wildpackets.com.

2. Start a new capture by clicking the New Capture button on the Omnipeek start screen.

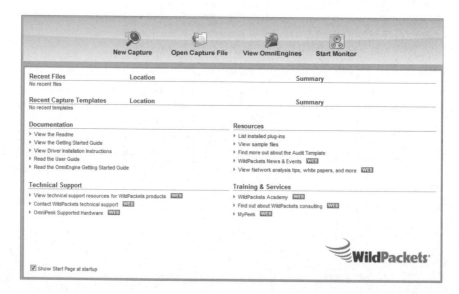

EXERCISE 10.1 *(continued)*

3. Select the wireless adapter from the capture options.

    Note: On the Adapter tab, the WildPackets API must list a description of Yes or the adapter will not work properly in Omnipeek, as shown here:

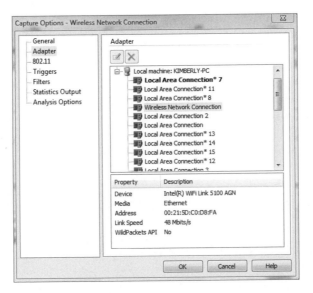

4. Click the 802.11 tab and choose initially to scan all channels. Later, once you have identified a specific WLAN to monitor, you can choose to only capture traffic on that one channel.

EXERCISE 10.1 *(continued)*

5. Click OK to start the capture. The capture window will show frames being captured. Double-click a frame to see more detail.

6. Click the stop capture button to stop capturing. Select the Display filter drop down button (it looks like a funnel) from the toolbar just above the frames. Select POP from the filter drop down list. Only POP email frames will be displayed. You can use a display filter to show only certain types of frames. POP, SMTP, FTP, TELNET, and HTTP frames all carry clear text data. Passwords and other information can be gathered from those frames.

7. To find Access Points (AP) and Stations that are connected, click on the WLAN menu on the left side of the screen. The APs BSSID, STA MAC, Channel, and SSID can all be located on the WLAN screen of Omnipeek. APs not broadcasting the SSID will show 0x00 for the SSID until a station connects and Omnipeek can determine the SSID from the probe frames. Once Omnipeek can determine the SSID, it will be displayed on the WLAN screen.

MAC Filters and MAC Spoofing

An early security solution in WLAN technology used MAC address filters: a network administrator entered a list of valid MAC addresses for the systems allowed to associate with the AP. MAC filters are cumbersome to configure and aren't scalable for an enterprise network because they must be configured on each AP. MAC spoofing is easy to perform (as you'll see in Exercise 10.2) and negates the effort required to implement MAC filters. A hacker can identify a valid MAC address because the MAC headers are never encrypted.

EXERCISE 10.2

MAC Address Spoofing

1. Download and install TMAC from www.technitium.com.

2. Select the wireless adapter from the list of network connections in TMAC. Click the Change MAC button.

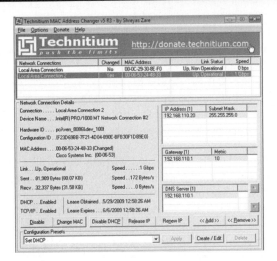

3. Type **00:11:22:33:44:55** as the MAC address; click the Change Now button and confirm the changes to be made to the MAC address.

4. Open a command prompt and type **IPCONFIG /ALL** to confirm the MAC address of the wireless adapter has been changed to 00:11:22:33:44:55.

5. To restore the original MAC address of the network adapter, select the adapter within TMAC, click the Change MAC button, and click the Original MAC button.

6. Configure an access point to allow only the MAC address 00:11:22:33:44:55 to connect to the WLAN. (This step will vary depending on the type of access point—refer to the user guide for your access point to configure the MAC address filtering.)

7. Test the wireless client connecting using the original MAC address. The client should not connect to the AP with the MAC filtering applied. Change the MAC to 00:11:22:33:44:55 using TMAC and attempt to connect again to the AP. It should be able to connect to the AP using the Spoofed MAC address.

Hacking Tool

SMAC is a MAC spoofing tool that a hacker can use to spoof a valid user's address and gain access to the network.

Rogue Access Points

Rogue access points are WLAN access points that aren't authorized to connect to a network. Rogue APs open a wireless hole into the network. A hacker can plant a rogue AP, or an employee may unknowingly create a security hole by plugging an access point into the network. The resulting rogue AP can be used by anyone who can connect to the AP, including a hacker, giving them access to the wired LAN. This is why it's critical for organizations to scan for rogue access points. Even organizations that have a "no wireless" policy need to perform wireless scanning to ensure no rogue APs are connected to the network.

Rogue APs are probably the most dangerous wireless threat that exists because they give a potential hacker direct access to the wired LAN. Clients connecting to rogue access points will usually receive an IP address directly from the network or from the AP and then the traffic is bridged directly on the wired LAN. From there a hacker can perform scanning, enumeration, and system hacking against targets on the wired LAN. Countermeasures to detect and remove rogue access points exist and should be implemented by all organizations.

Many enterprise WLAN controller–based management solutions have the ability to perform rogue access point detection. These controller-based solutions include the ability to monitor the air using either access points or sensors/monitors, or both. Access points by nature must remain on a channel while clients are connected in order to service those clients, whereas sensors and monitors are able to continually scan the air on all channels in the frequency band to capture possible rogue access point wireless transmissions. These wireless MAC addresses are compared to addresses received on the wire to determine if the AP is connected to the same LAN as the wireless intrusion detection system (WIDS) or wireless intrusion prevention system (WIPS). Some WIPSs can also keep clients from connecting to rogue access points by sending spoofed deauthentication frames to any client attempting to connect to the rogue AP—thus keeping clients from sending data through the rogue AP. Overlay WIDS/WIPS systems can also be helpful in detecting rogue access points by triangulating the position of the rogue AP.

Enterprise WLAN WIPS and overlay WIPS are only temporary detection and containment options. The primary goal should be to locate the rogue AP and remove it from the network.

Evil Twin or AP Masquerading

Hackers can use a software-based AP to create an AP that looks like a real Access Point. This is known as the Evil Twin attack or AP Masquerading.

Wireless Hacking Techniques

Most wireless hacking attacks can be categorized as follows:

Cracking Encryption and Authentication Mechanisms   These mechanisms include cracking WEP, WPA preshared key authentication passphrases, and Cisco's Lightweight EAP authentication (LEAP). Hackers can use these mechanisms to connect to the WLAN using stolen credentials or can capture other users' data and decrypt or encrypt it. A protection against this attack is to implement a stronger type of encryption, such as AES.

Eavesdropping or Sniffing   This type of attack involves capturing passwords or other confidential information from an unencrypted WLAN or hotspot. A protection against this attack is to use SSL application-layer encryption or a VPN to secure user data.

Denial of Service   DoS can be performed at the physical layer by creating a louder RF signature than the AP with an RF transmitter, causing an approved AP to fail so users connect to a rogue AP. DoS can be performed at the Logical Link Control (LLC) layer by generating deauthentication frames (deauth attacks), by continuously generating bogus frames, or by having a wireless NIC send a constant stream of raw RF (Queensland attack). A countermeasure is to enforce a security perimeter around your WLAN and detect and remove sources of DoS attacks using an IDS.

AP Masquerading or Spoofing   Rogue APs pretend to be legitimate APs by using the same configuration SSID settings or network name. A countermeasure to AP masquerading is to use a WIDS to detect and locate spoofed APs.

MAC Spoofing   The hacker pretends to be a legitimate WLAN client and bypasses MAC filters by spoofing another user's MAC address. WIDSs can detect MAC spoofing, and not using MAC filtering is a way to avoid MAC spoofing attacks.

Planting Rogue Access Points   The most dangerous attack is a rogue AP that has been planted to allow a hacker access to the target LAN. A countermeasure is to use a WIPS to detect and locate rogue APs.

Wireless networks give a hacker an easy way into the network if the AP isn't secured properly. There are many ways to hack or exploit the vulnerabilities of a WLAN. There are also effective countermeasures to many of these attacks. The next section will detail the best methods to secure wireless network.

Securing Wireless Networks

Because wireless networking is a relatively new technology compared to wired networking technologies, fewer security options are available. Security methods can be categorized by the applicable layer of the OSI model.

Layer 2, or MAC layer, security options are as follows:

- Static WEP (not recommended)

- WPA

- WPA2/802.11i

Layer 3, or Network layer, security options are as follows:

- IPSec

- SSL VPN

Layer 7, or Application layer, security options are as follows:

- Secure applications such as Secure Shell (SSH), HTTP over SSL (HTTPS), and FTP/SSL (FTPS)

 Because of its numerous weaknesses, WEP shouldn't be used as the sole security mechanism for a WLAN.

Securing Home Wireless Networks

Many people setting up wireless home networks rush through the job to get their Internet connectivity working as quickly as possible. The small office, home office (SOHO) networking products on the market make setup quick and easy but not necessarily secure. Configuring additional security features can be time consuming and nonintuitive for some home users, and therefore they may not implement any security mechanism at all.

These days wireless networking products are so ubiquitous and inexpensive that just about anyone can set up a WLAN in a matter of minutes with less than $100 worth of equipment. This widespread use of wireless networks means that there may be dozens of potential network intruders within range of your home or office WLAN. Most WLAN hardware has gotten easy enough to set up that many users simply plug it in and start using the network without giving much thought to security. Nevertheless, taking a few extra minutes to configure the security features of your wireless router or access point is time well spent. The following recommendations will improve the security of your home wireless network:

Change default administrator passwords and usernames. When configuring your home access point, you usually use a web browser to access the configuration interface. Almost all routers and access points have an administrator password that's needed to log into the device and modify any configuration settings. To set up these pieces of equipment, manufacturers provide a default username and password. Many of the default logins are simple (such as username=admin and password=admin) and very well known to hackers on the Internet. Most devices use a weak default password like "password" or the manufacturer's name, and some don't have a default password at all. You should change the default password on your home AP as soon as possible. As soon as you set up a new WLAN router or access point, your first step should be to change the default administrative password to something else.

Use WEP/WPA encryption.   Most Wi-Fi equipment supports some form of *encryption*. Encryption technology scrambles messages sent over wireless networks so that they cannot be easily read by hackers. You should configure the strongest form of encryption that works with your wireless clients. 802.11's WEP (Wired Equivalency Privacy) encryption has well-known weaknesses that make it relatively easy for a determined user with the right equipment to crack the encryption and access the wireless network. A better way to protect your WLAN is with WPA (Wi-Fi Protected Access). WPA provides much better protection and is also easier to use, since your password characters aren't limited to 0–9 and A–F as they are with WEP. (Note: WEP can also use ASCII keys.)

Change the default SSID.   Access points use a network name called an SSID to advertise the network to wireless users. Manufacturers normally ship their products with the same SSID set. For example, the SSID for Linksys devices is normally "Linksys." Just knowing the SSID does not by itself allow your neighbors to break into your network, but it is a start. More importantly, when someone finds a default SSID, it is usually an indication of a poorly configured network. You should change the default SSID immediately when configuring wireless security on your network.

Do not auto-connect to open Wi-Fi networks.   Connecting to an open Wi-Fi network such as a free wireless hotspot or an unknown WLAN exposes your computer to security risks. Most computers have a setting available allowing these connections to happen automatically without notifying you. Most versions of Windows will reconnect to a previously connected SSID. This setting should not be enabled except in temporary situations.

Enable firewall settings on your laptop and home access point.   Most network routers contain built-in firewall capability, but the option also exists to disable them. Ensure that your router's firewall is turned on. You should always install and configure personal firewall software on each computer connected to the router.

Reduce your WLAN transmitter power.   You won't find this feature on all wireless routers and access points, but some allow you to lower the power of your WLAN transmitter and thus reduce the range of the signal. (Normally this feature is only available with enterprise-class access points.) Although it's usually impossible to fine-tune a signal so precisely that it won't leak outside your home or business, with some trial and error you can often limit how far outside your premises the signal reaches, minimizing the opportunity for outsiders to access your WLAN. This will also improve your throughput on your access point by limiting the wireless cell to just your premise.

Disable remote administration.   Most WLAN routers have the ability to be remotely administered via the Internet. Ideally, you should use this feature only if it lets you define a specific IP address or limited range of addresses that will be able to access the router. Otherwise, almost anyone anywhere could potentially find and access your router. As a rule, unless you absolutely need this capability, it's best to keep remote administration turned off.

Summary

The growth of wireless networks has been fueled by convenience and an ever-increasing mobile workforce. More employees are working from home or on the road, and organizations are building larger enterprise WLANs to support greater mobility of the workforce. In the past, many organizations have avoided WLANs because of the inherent lack of security and immature technologies.

The ratification of 802.11n promises greater speeds on wireless LANs, making them comparable to existing Ethernet LANs. This enhanced speed will only increase the number of organizations using wireless for business applications and consequently increase the security risks.

More recently, WLAN security mechanisms have matured to the point that businesses and government offices are beginning to adopt WLAN technology. With proper security mechanisms and implementation, WLANs can be secured to a high standard. By carefully following the security recommendations and countermeasures, you can secure your WLAN against attack.

Exam Essentials

Understand the inherent security vulnerabilities of using a WLAN.   RF is a broadcast medium, like a hub environment, and therefore all traffic is able to be captured by a hacker.

Understand the security solutions implemented in the IEEE 802.11 standard.   WEP, shared key, and MAC filters are security solutions offered in the original IEEE 802.11 standard.

Understand the security solutions offered by the Wi-Fi Alliance.   WPA and WPA2 are Wi-Fi Alliance equipment security certifications.

Know what an SSID is used for on a WLAN.   The SSID identifies the network name and shouldn't be used as a security mechanism.

Know what security mechanisms should not be used for WLAN security.   WEP and MAC filters shouldn't be used as the sole means to secure the WLAN.

Review Questions

1. Which of the following security solutions uses the same key for both encryption and authentication?

   A. WPA

   B. WPA2

   C. WEP

   D. 802.11i

2. What does WEP stands for?

   A. Wireless Encryption Protocol

   B. Wired Equivalent Privacy

   C. Wireless Encryption Privacy

   D. Wired Encryption Protocol

3. What makes WEP crackable?

   A. Same key used for encryption and authentication

   B. Length of the key

   C. Weakness of IV

   D. RC4

4. Which form of encryption does WPA use?

   A. AES

   B. TKIP

   C. LEAP

   D. Shared key

5. Which form of authentication does WPA2 use?

   A. Passphrase only

   B. 802.1x/EAP/RADIUS

   C. Passphrase or 802.1x/EAP/RADIUS

   D. AES

6. 802.11i is most similar to which wireless security standard?

   A. WPA2

   B. WPA

   C. TKIP

   D. AES

7. Which of the following is a Layer 3 security solution for WLANs?

   A. MAC filter

   B. WEP

   C. WPA

   D. VPN

8. A device that sends deauth frames is performing which type of attack against the WLAN?

   A. Denial of service

   B. Cracking

   C. Sniffing

   D. MAC spoofing

9. What is the most dangerous type of attack against a WLAN?

   A. WEP cracking

   B. Rogue access point

   C. Eavesdropping

   D. MAC spoofing

10. 802.11i is implemented at which layer of the OSI model?

    A. Layer 1

    B. Layer 2

    C. Layer 3

    D. Layer 7

11. Which of the following is the best option for securing a home wireless network?

    A. WEP

    B. Shared-key authentication

    C. WPA-Personal

    D. WPA-Enterprise

12. You just installed a new wireless access point for your home office. Which of the following steps should you take immediately to secure your WLAN?

    A. Spoof your clients MAC address.

    B. Change the Admin password on the AP.

    C. Change the channel on the AP to Channel 11.

    D. Set the SSID to SECURE.

13. What can be done on a wireless laptop to increase security when connecting to any WLAN? (Choose two.)

    A. Install and configure personal firewall software.

    B. Disable auto-connect features.

    C. Use WEP.

    D. Use MAC filtering.

14. What is an SSID used for on a WLAN?

    A. To secure the WLAN

    B. To manage the WLAN settings

    C. To identify the WLAN

    D. To configure the WLAN AP

15. What is the best way to enforce a "no wireless" policy?

    A. Install a personal firewall.

    B. Disable WLAN client adapters.

    C. Use a WIDS/WIPS.

    D. Only connect to open APs.

16. Which of the following is a program used to spoof a MAC address?

    A. MAC Again

    B. Big MAC

    C. TMAC

    D. WZC

17. Which of the following are Layer 7 application-secure protocols used to secure data on WLAN hotspots?

    A. HTTPS

    B. HTTP

    C. FTP

    D. VPN

18. Which type of frame is used by a WIPS to prevent WLAN users from connecting to rogue access points?

    A. Disconnect

    B. Deauthentication

    C. Disable

    D. Reject

19. WPA passphrases can consist of which of the following character sets?

   A. Only a–z and A–Z

   B. Only a–z

   C. Only a–z, A–Z, and 0–9

   D. Only 0–9

20. Which of the following is a countermeasure to using WEP?

   A. Use a strong WEP key of at least 20 characters.

   B. Use a WEP key that does not repeat any of the same characters.

   C. Use WPA instead of WEP.

   D. Implement a preshared key with WEP.

Answers to Review Questions

1. C. WEP uses the same key for encryption and authentication.

2. B. WEP is an acronym for Wired Equivalent Privacy.

3. C. WEP is crackable because of the lack of sophistication in using the IV when deploying RC4.

4. B. WPA uses TKIP.

5. C. WPA2 uses either a passphrase in personal mode or 802.1x/EAP/RADIUS in enterprise mode.

6. A. 802.11i is almost the same as WPA2.

7. D. A VPN is a Layer 3 security solution for WLANs.

8. A. A DoS can be performed by a device sending constant deauth frames.

9. B. A rogue AP is the most dangerous attack against a WLAN because it gives a hacker an open door into the network.

10. B. 802.11i is a Layer 2 technology.

11. C. WPA-Personal has the strongest authentication and encryption usable on a home network. WPA-Enterprise requires a RADIUS server, which most home users would not have the ability to set up and configure.

12. B. You should immediately change the Admin password on an AP's web interface when installing a new AP.

13. A, B. Installing and configuring personal firewall software and disabling auto-connect features are two ways to increase the security of WLAN connections.

14. C. A Service Set Identifier (SSID) is used to identify the WLAN to wireless users.

15. C. Using a wireless intrusion detection system or protection system is the best way to enforce a "no wireless" policy.

16. C. TMAC is a program used to spoof a MAC address.

17. A. HTTPS is a secure version of HTTP commonly used to secure data on WLAN hotspots.

18. B. Deauthentication frames are used by a WIPS to prevent users from connecting to rogue APs.

19. C. WPA passphrases can be alphanumeric and include a–z, A–Z, and 0–9.

20. C. Using WPA is a countermeasure to the weakness of WEP.

Chapter

11

Physical Site Security

CEH EXAM OBJECTIVES COVERED IN THIS CHAPTER:

- ✓ Physical security breach incidents

- ✓ Understanding physical security

- ✓ What is the need for physical security?

- ✓ Who is accountable for physical security?

- ✓ Factors affecting physical security

Physical security is arguably the most critical area of IT security for preventing the loss or theft of confidential and sensitive data. If an organization fails to enforce adequate physical security, all other technical security measures such as firewalls and intrusion detection systems (IDSs) can be bypassed. There is a saying: "Once you're inside, you own the network." By physically securing your network and your organization, you prevent somebody from stealing equipment such as laptops or tape drives, placing hardware keyloggers on systems, and planting rogue access points on the network. Physical security relies heavily on individuals to enforce it and therefore is susceptible to social-engineering attacks, such as following an employee into the building without supplying the proper key or credentials (thus bypassing the physical security challenge).

This chapter will explore the need for physical security and define who is responsible for planning and enforcing it.

Components of Physical Security

Physical security is the protection of personnel, hardware, programs, networks, and data from physical circumstances and events that could cause serious losses or damage to an enterprise, agency, or institution. This includes protection from fire, natural disasters, burglary, theft, vandalism, and terrorism.

Physical security is often overlooked (and its importance underestimated) in favor of more technical and dramatic issues such as hacking, viruses, Trojans, and spyware. However, breaches of physical security can be carried out with little or no technical knowledge on the part of an attacker. Moreover, accidents and natural disasters are a part of everyday life, and in the long term, are inevitable.

There are three main components to physical security:

- Obstacles can be placed in the way of potential attackers and sites can be hardened against accidents and environmental disasters. Such measures can include multiple locks, fencing, walls, fireproof safes, and water sprinklers.

- Surveillance and notification systems, such as lighting, heat sensors, smoke detectors, intrusion detectors, alarms, and cameras, can be put in place.

- Methods can be implemented to apprehend attackers (preferably before any damage has been done) and to recover quickly from accidents, fires, or natural disasters.

It seems as though every day, a news article describes another prominent government agency or major corporation that has compromised client information or confidential employee information. For example, a laptop may be stolen in a home-invasion robbery or from a hotel room while an employee is traveling. This confidential or sensitive information can be dangerous in the hands of a hacker.

In physical security, like all security, the best approach is a layered defense. You should never depend 100 percent on a single control to protect your critical assets. Here are two examples of where a layered approach to physical security is better than a single physical security mechanism.

The first example is when a guard is the only defense mechanism in place. If he falls asleep or takes an unscheduled break, then an intruder has the opportunity to walk right into your data center without being detected. A better security measure would be to have an individual be required to possess a unique ID badge to enter the front door. Next, she is challenged by a guard, recorded on a camera, and then needs to have a separate unique key to enter the data center. In this example, there are four layers of defense to protect your assets.

In the second security example, an employee can't afford a laptop, so he decides to take his company computer home to play his favorite video game. He gets distracted on the train or bus on the way home and forgets his bag containing the laptop. The laptop does not have any security controls in place and contains sensitive data. If best practices were followed in this scenario, multiple layers would exist to prevent and discourage this individual from removing the laptop from the controlled environment. An acceptable use policy should be in place to stress the importance and ramifications of removing corporate property and sensitive data from the premises. The laptop should have multi-factor authentication and disk encryption enabled, so that in the event that it is lost or stolen, the data that existed on it is useless to others. If the environment were particularly sensitive, tracking devices could be placed in all mobile devices, and in the event that they travel an unacceptable distance from the office, an alarm is activated to notify security personnel.

It is critical to have multiple lines of defense, as the more layers of defense you have in place, the less vulnerable you are to a threat. Also it is important to remember that you can have many layers of logical security controls protecting an asset and they can generally be circumvented quickly and easily if physical access is gained.

Equipment theft is one of the most common physical security attacks. Most people don't expect their computer to be stolen and are naive about locking down host systems; instead, they rely on standard network security mechanisms.

Many insider attacks are the result of physical security breaches. Once a hacker has gained physical access to a server, a single client system, or a network port, the results can be disastrous. In addition, such breaches are difficult to identify, track, or locate. Some of the common security breaches caused by insufficient physical security are as follows:

- Installation of malware such as keyloggers, viruses, Trojans, backdoors, or rootkits

- Identification and capture of validation or authentication credentials such as passwords or certificates

- Physical connection to the wired network to sniff confidential data such as passwords and credit card numbers

- Access to systems to collect data that can be used to crack passwords stored locally on the system

- Opportunity to plant rogue access points to create an open wireless network with access to the wired network

- Theft of paper or electronic documents

- Theft of sensitive fax information

- Dumpster diving attack (emphasizing the need to shred important documents)

Indications of a physical security breach may include, but are not limited to

- Unauthorized or unexplained door alarms

- Unauthorized personnel recorded on a security camera

- Damage to door lock or outside barrier fence

- Evidence of vehicles or persons outside and inside the perimeter fence

- Loss of communications that cannot be explained

- Missing or unaccounted for equipment

Understanding Physical Security

Generally security measures can be categorized in the following three ways:

Physical   Physical measures to prevent access to systems include security guards, lighting, fences, locks, and alarms. Facility access points should be limited, and they should be monitored/protected by closed-circuit television (CCTV) cameras and alarms. The entrance to the facility should be restricted to authorized people. Access to laptop systems and removable media such as removable drives, backup tapes, and disks should be restricted and protected. Computer screens should be positioned such that they can't be seen by passers-by, and a policy should be implemented and enforced that requires users to lock their systems when they leave the computer for any reason. Computer systems with highly sensitive data should be protected in an enclosed and locked area such as a credential-access room with a rack-mount case and lock.

Technical   Technical security measures such as firewalls, IDS, spyware content filtering, and virus and Trojan scanning should be implemented on all remote client systems, networks, and servers. Technical security measures such as access control are implemented through the use of authentication, passwords, and file and folder permissions. Other technical controls can be implemented through computer software such as virus scanning and host firewalls. Essentially a technical control is any security mechanism implemented through computer hardware or software.

Operational   Operational security is addressed through administrative controls such as acceptable use policies, hiring policies, and security policies. Operational security measures to analyze threats and perform risk assessments should be a documented process in the organization's security policy.

Technical and operational security measures are dealt with in other chapters of this book. Technical countermeasures are listed in every chapter of this book (except the first and last chapters).

You need physical security measures for the same reason you need other types of security (such as technical or operational): to prevent hackers from gaining access to your network and your information. A hacker can easily get such access through weaknesses in physical security measures. In addition, data can be lost or damaged by natural causes, so risk managers must add natural disasters to the equation when planning appropriate security. Physical security measures are designed to prevent the following:

- Unauthorized access to a computer system

- Stealing of data from systems

- Corruption of data stored on a system

- Loss of data or damage to systems caused by natural causes

 Real World Scenario

Data Stolen from VA Laptop

In 2006, a laptop computer was stolen from the home of a Department of Veterans Affairs data analyst who (against department policy) took the computer home. The laptop contained data on about 26.5 million U.S. military veterans.

It is believed that this was a random burglary and the person who stole the laptop did not know the data was on the computer. The thieves took both his laptop and the external hard drive containing names, birth dates, and Social Security numbers of every veteran who had been discharged after 1975.

The VA commented that the employee "took home a considerable amount of electronic data from the VA which he was not authorized to do. It was in violation of our rules and regulations and policies." This security breach is an example of how your most personal data can easily get into the hands of identity thieves.

Several veterans groups took legal action against the VA after the breach was discovered. Now, three years later, the parties have come to an agreement. Veterans who can show proof of actual harm, such as emotional distress leading to physical symptoms, or expenses for credit monitoring, will be eligible to receive payments up to $1,500. This settlement totals $20 million in costs to the VA. This is just one example of how important physical site security and enforcing policies is to maintain security for personal data. Organizations found liable for not protecting the data to which they have been entrusted may face heavy fines.

The following people in an organization should be accountable for physical security:

- The organization's physical security officer
- Information system professionals
- Chief information officer
- Employees

Essentially, everyone in an organization is responsible for enforcing physical security policies. It's the physical security officer's responsibility to set the physical security standard and implement physical security measures.

Organizations have a responsibility to train all employees in security awareness training. The best countermeasure to prevent physical security attacks is to train employees to be aware of breaches to physical security.

Physical security is affected by factors outside the physical security controls. Factors that can affect an organization's physical security include the following:

- Vandalism
- Theft
- Natural causes, such as earthquake, fire, or flood

Security professionals need to be aware of these risk factors and plan accordingly. Many organizations create a business continuity plan (BCP) or disaster recovery plan (DRP) to prepare for these possibilities.

Physical Site Security Countermeasures

There are some simple ways to improve physical security in your organization. Many times improving security involves enforcing the guidelines that are already in place. People tend to get loose in their enforcement of policies and procedures after a period of time. To maintain a high level of security, everyone in the organization must be vigilant in protecting the data assents of the organization.

The following countermeasures should be implemented to ensure strong physical site security:

Lock the server room.   Before you lock down the servers using technical mechanisms and before you even turn them on for the first time, you should ensure that there are good locks on the server room door. Of course, the best lock in the world does no good if it isn't used, so you also need policies requiring that those doors be locked any time the room is unoccupied. The policies should set out who has the key or keycode to get in. The server room is the heart of your physical network, and someone with physical access to the servers, switches, routers, cables, and other devices in that room can do enormous damage.

Set up and monitor video surveillance.   Locking the door to the server room is a good first step, but someone could break in, or someone who has authorized access could misuse that authority. You need a way to know who goes in and out and when. A log book for signing in and out is the most elemental way to accomplish this, but that approach has a lot of draw-backs. A person with malicious intent is likely to just bypass it. A better solution than the log book is an authentication system incorporated into the locking devices, so that a smart card, token, or biometric scan is required to unlock the doors and a record is made of the identity of each person who enters. A video surveillance camera, placed in a location that makes it difficult to tamper with or disable but gives a good view of persons entering and leaving, should supplement the log book or electronic access system. Surveillance cameras can monitor continuously, or they can use motion detection technology to record only when someone is moving about. They can even be set up to send email or cell phone notification if motion is detected when it shouldn't be, such as after hours.

Make sure the most vulnerable devices are in a locked room.   It's not just the servers that you have to physically secure. Other networking equipment also needs to be secured. A hacker can plug a laptop into a hub and use sniffer software to capture data traveling across the network. Make sure that as many of your network devices as possible are in that locked room. Wiring closets and phone rooms are easy targets if not secured.

Secure the workstations.   Hackers can use any unsecured computer that's connected to the network to access or delete information that's important to your business. Workstations at unoccupied desks or in empty offices—such as those used by employees who are on vacation or who have left the company and not yet been replaced—or at locations easily accessible to outsiders—such as the front receptionist's desk—are particularly vulnerable. Disconnect and/or remove computers that aren't being used and/or lock the doors of empty offices, including those that are temporarily empty while an employee is at lunch or out sick. For computers that must remain in open areas, sometimes out of view of employees, enable smart card or biometric readers so that it's more difficult for unauthorized persons to log on.

Keep intruders from opening the computer.   Both servers and workstations should be pro-tected from thieves who can open the case and grab the hard drive. It's much easier to make off with a hard disk in your pocket than to carry a full tower off the premises. Many com-puters come with case locks to prevent opening the case without a key.

Protect the portable devices.   Laptops and handheld computers pose special physical secu-rity risks. A thief can easily steal the entire computer, including any data stored on its disk as well as network logon passwords that may be saved. If employees use laptops at their desks, they should take them along when they leave or secure them to a permanent fixture with a cable lock. Handhelds can be locked in a drawer or safe when the employee leaves the area. Motion-sensing alarms are also available to alert you if your portable is moved. For portables that contain sensitive information, full disk encryption, biometric readers, and software that "phones home" if the stolen laptop connects to the Internet can supple-ment physical precautions.

Many smart phones have the ability to do a remote wipe if a device is lost or stolen.

Pack up the backups.   Backing up important data is an essential element in disaster recovery, but don't forget that the information on those backup tapes, disks, or discs can be stolen and used by someone outside the company. Many IT administrators keep the backups next to the server in the server room. They should be locked in a drawer or safe at the very least. Ideally, a set of backups should be kept off site, and you must take care to ensure that they are secured in that offsite location. Don't overlook the fact that some workers may back up their work on floppy disks, USB keys, or external hard disks. If this practice is allowed or encouraged, be sure to have policies requiring that the backups be locked up at all times.

Disable removable media drives.   To prevent employees from copying company information to removable media, you can disable or remove floppy drives, USB ports, and other means of connecting external drives. Simply disconnecting the cables may not deter technically savvy workers. Some organizations go so far as to fill ports with glue or other substances to permanently prevent their use, although there are software mechanisms that disallow that and allow for an administrator to reenable the drive.

Protect your printers.   You might not think about printers posing a security risk, but many of today's printers store document contents in their own onboard memories. If a hacker steals the printer and accesses that memory, he or she may be able to make copies of recently printed documents. Printers, like servers and workstations that store important information, should be located in secure locations and bolted down so nobody can walk off with them. Also think about the physical security of documents that workers print out. It's best to implement a policy of immediately shredding any unwanted printed documents, even those that don't contain confidential information. This establishes a habit and frees the end user of the responsibility for determining whether a document should be shredded.

Enforce badges for all employees and contractors.   Initiate a badge program that includes an employee picture, and color-code specific areas of access. Contractors and visitors should also have badges and be escorted, observed, and supervised for their entire visit. It should be standard policy for all employees to question anyone who doesn't have a visible ID badge.

Watch out for "tailgaters."   These people wait for someone with access to enter a controlled area such as one with a locked door and then follow the authorized person through the door. Tailgaters enter without using their own key, card key, or lock combination. Smokers who stand outside the building seem to be especially susceptible to "tailgating"; after sharing some time and a smoke together, it is normal to hold the door open for other smokers when the smoke break is over.

Exercise 11.1 is viewing a video on lockpicking. It is useful to understand how to pick a lock in order to understand how an intruder can gain physical access.

EXERCISE 11.1

View a Video on Lockpicking

1. Open a web browser to www.youtube.com.

2. Search for "lock picking video" or "lock picking door".

3. Watch a video on lock picking.

4. Search for "How Lock Picking Works" on www.howstuffworks.com.

5. Follow the interactive tutorial on using the correct and incorrect keys in a lock.

6. Answer the following questions about lock picking based on the YouTube video and HowStuffWorks tutorial:

   - What is the purpose of a tension wrench?

   - How do you keep the tumblers from falling down when picking a lock?

   - What is raking?

   - What is the shear line?

   - What types of locks are the most difficult to pick?

Not all attacks on your organization's data come across the network, and not all attacks are technical in nature. It's imperative that companies remember that maintaining a strong network security program doesn't immunize them against the physical assault or theft of data and the resources that contain that data. Physical attacks can be from outside an organization, but they can also be insiders—disgruntled employees or contractors are commonly found to be the source of physical site attacks. See Exercise 11.2.

EXERCISE 11.2

Audit Your Organization's Physical Site Security

Review the following physical site security checklist to evaluate your organization's physical security.

Public Parking Areas

- If appropriate, are employee, tenant, and public parking areas clearly designated?

- Are nighttime lighting levels adequate? *Test: Can you comfortably read a newspaper under existing lighting conditions?*

- Are parking areas and entrances observable by as many people as possible?

- Are parking areas fully lit during all hours that people are on the property?

EXERCISE 11.2 *(continued)*

- If appropriate, have parking areas been properly posted to permit law enforcement personnel to take enforcement action when necessary? *Examples: restricted parking zones, handicapped parking.*

Restricted Access Areas

- Are barriers such as fences and locked gates installed to prevent unauthorized vehicle and pedestrian access to restricted areas?

- Are employees instructed to report unauthorized individuals in restricted areas and other suspicious persons and activities?

- Are restricted areas properly posted to keep out unauthorized individuals?

- Is outdoor signage prominently displayed near areas of restricted access?

- Is signage indicating the phone number for reporting suspicious activity in an easy-to-see location?

Storage Areas

- Are outside storage areas and yards fully enclosed?

- Are fences and walls in good repair?

- Are fences high enough?

- Are gates in good repair?

- Are storage areas and yards provided with adequate lighting during the hours of darkness?

- Are gates secured with high security padlocks or equivalent locking devices?

- Are padlocks locked in place when gates open?

- Are high value storage areas protected by an electronic security system?

Building Exterior

- Are public entrances clearly defined by walkways and signage?

- Are landscape features maintained to provide good visibility around buildings?

- Is vegetation trimmed to eliminate potential hiding places near doors, windows, walkways, and other vulnerable areas of the property?

- Do trees or other landscape features provide access to the roof or other upper levels of buildings?

- Are trees and vegetation kept trimmed to prevent them from interfering with lighting and visibility?

- Do dumpsters and trash enclosures create blind spots or hiding areas?

- Are perimeter fences designed to maintain visibility from the street?

- Are exterior private areas easily distinguishable from public areas?

Lighting

- Are building exteriors and other critical areas illuminated to recommended levels during hours of darkness?

- Are proper lighting levels maintained at all door and window openings and other vulnerable points during hours of darkness?

- Has a maintenance inspection schedule been established to ensure that lights are in good working order at all times?

Doors

- Are all exterior doors of a metal, metal and glass, or solid core wood design?

- Are all unused doors permanently sealed?

- Is exterior hardware removed from all doors that are not used to provide access from the outside?

- Are all doors designed so that the lock release cannot be reached by breaking out glazing or lightweight panels?

- Are sliding glass doors equipped with supplemental pin locks and anti-lift devices?

- Do exposed hinges have nonremovable pins?

- Is a good-quality deadbolt lock used whenever possible?

- Is the lock designed, or the doorframe constructed, so that the door cannot be forced open by spreading the frame?

- Are keys issued only to persons who actually need them?

- Is there a policy in place mandating that all doors that are not required to be unlocked during business hours be closed and secured when not in use?

Windows

- Are unused windows permanently sealed?

- Are window locks designed or located so they cannot be defeated by breaking the glass?

- Where appropriate, are landscaping features such as thorny shrubs or similar vegetation used to prevent access to vulnerable windows?

EXERCISE 11.2   *(continued)*

- Where necessary, are accessible windows adequately lit during hours of darkness?

- Are roof ladders and other roof access points either removed or secured against unauthorized use?

- Are roll-up and sliding doors properly mounted and secured with high-quality locking devices?

- Are utility rooms both inside and outside the building properly secured?

Public Access Areas

- Are security and/or reception areas positioned to view all public entrances?

- Are all public areas of the building clearly marked?

- Are the boundaries between public and nonpublic areas clearly defined?

- Have secure barriers been installed to prevent easy movement between public and nonpublic areas?

- Are all doors leading to private offices and other nonpublic areas secured by high-quality locking devices such as electronic or keypad style locks?

- Are security guards employed in areas where there is a strong likelihood of criminal activity or trespassing?

- Are interior public restrooms observable from nearby offices or reception areas?

Office Security

- Do you restrict office keys to those who actually need them?

- Do you keep complete, up-to-date records of the disposition of all office keys?

- Do you have adequate procedures for collecting keys from terminated employees?

- Do you secure all typewriters, calculators, computers, and similar items with some type of locking device?

- Do you prohibit duplication of office keys except for those that are specifically ordered by you in writing?

- Do you require that all office keys be marked "Do not duplicate" to prevent legitimate locksmiths from making copies without your knowledge?

- Have you established a policy that keys will not be left unguarded on desks or cabinets—and do you enforce the policy?

- Have you established a policy that facility keys and key rings will not be marked with information that identifies the facility to which they belong?

- Do you require that filing cabinet keys be removed from locks and placed in a secure location when not in use?

- Do you have a responsible person in charge of your key-control program?

- Do you shred sensitive documents before discarding them?

- Do you lock briefcases and bags containing important material in a safe place when not in use?

- Do you insist on proper identification from all vendors and repair persons who come into your facility?

- Do you clear desks of important papers every night?

- Do you frequently change the combination to your safe?

- Is computer access restricted to authorized personnel?

- Have you instituted an employee identification badge system?

- If you employ guards after hours, do you periodically make unannounced visits to ensure that they are doing their job properly?

Alarms

- Do your buildings have an alarm system?

- Is the alarm system certified by Underwriters Laboratory?

- Is the system tested daily?

- Does the system report to an alarm company central station or police facility?

- Does the system have an automatic backup power supply that activates during power failures?

- Is the system free from false alarms?

- Does the system employ anti-tamper technology?

What to Do After a Security Breach Occurs

Even if an organization applies physical site countermeasures, a security breach may still occur. If such a breach occurs, there are some recommended steps your organization should take to prevent it from occurring again:

- Establish a physical security incident response process, including identification of the threat, response, recovery, and post-incident review to manage a physical attack or security incident.

- Set policies, standards, and procedures to support the physical security incident response process.

- Identify the stakeholders—including the security incident response team, personnel within the organization, and external parties who are likely to be involved in managing and reviewing the information security incident.

Summary

Remember that network security starts at the physical level. All the firewalls in the world won't stop an intruder who is able to gain physical access to your network and computers, so lock up as well as lock down. Physical access to corporate data by an unauthorized person is an assault on your organization's security. Once someone gains physical access to your data—whether it's a stolen laptop or lost documents or media—you become vulnerable to further attacks, not to mention a lot of bad publicity. It is critical to implement physical site security measures to prevent attacks before they occur.

Exam Essentials

Understand the attacks that can be performed via physical access.   Physical access gives a hacker the ability to perform password cracking, install rogue wireless access points, and steal equipment.

Know some factors that affect the enforcement of physical security.   Vandalism, theft, and natural causes affect the enforcement of physical security.

Know who is accountable for physical security.   The organization's security officer, information system professionals, chief information officer, and employees are all responsible for physical security.

Understand the need for physical security.   Physical security is necessary to prevent unauthorized access to a building or computer system, theft of data, corruption of data stored on a system, and loss of data or damage to systems caused by natural causes.

Review Questions

1. Who is responsible for implementing physical security? (Choose all that apply.)
   A. The owner of the building
   B. Chief information officer
   C. IT managers
   D. Employees

2. Which of these factors impacts physical security?
   A. Encryption in use on the network
   B. Flood or fire
   C. IDS implementation
   D. Configuration of firewall

3. Which of the following is physical security designed to prevent? (Choose all that apply.)
   A. Stealing confidential data
   B. Hacking systems from the inside
   C. Hacking systems from the Internet
   D. Gaining physical access to unauthorized areas

4. Which of the following is often one of the most overlooked areas of security?
   A. Operational
   B. Technical
   C. Internet
   D. Physical

5. A hacker who plants a rogue wireless access point on a network in order to sniff the traffic on the wired network from outside the building is causing what type of security breach?
   A. Physical
   B. Technical
   C. Operational
   D. Remote access

6. Which area of security usually receives the least amount of attention during a penetration test?
   A. Technical
   B. Physical
   C. Operational
   D. Wireless

7. Which of the following attacks can be perpetrated by a hacker against an organization with weak physical security controls?

A. Denial of service

B. Radio frequency jamming

C. Hardware keylogger

D. Banner grabbing

8. Which type of access allows passwords stored on a local system to be cracked?

A. Physical

B. Technical

C. Remote

D. Dial-in

9. Which of the following is an example of a physical security breach?

A. Capturing a credit card number from a web server application

B. Hacking a SQL Server in order to locate a credit card number

C. Stealing a laptop to acquire credit card numbers

D. Sniffing a credit card number from packets sent on a wireless hotspot

10. What type of attack can be performed once a hacker has physical access?

A. Finding passwords by dumpster diving

B. Stealing equipment

C. Performing a DoS attack

D. Performing session hijacking

11. What is the most important task after a physical security breach has been detected?

A. Lock down all the doors out of the building.

B. Shut down the servers to prevent further hacking attempts.

C. Call the police to begin an investigation.

D. Gather information for analysis to prevent future breaches.

12. Which of the following is a recommended countermeasure to prevent an attack against physical security?

A. Lock the server room.

B. Disconnect the servers from the network at night.

C. Do not allow anyone in the server room.

D. Implement multiple ID checks to gain access to the server room.

13. What are some physical measures to prevent a server hard drive from being stolen? (Choose all that apply.)

    A. Lock the server room door.

    B. Lock the server case.

    C. Add a software firewall to the server.

    D. Enforce badges for all visitors.

14. What is the name for a person who follows an employee through a locked door without their own badge or key?

    A. Tailgater

    B. Follower

    C. Visitor

    D. Guest

15. Which of the following should be done after a physical site security breach is detected?

    A. Implement security awareness training.

    B. Establish a security response team.

    C. Identify the stakeholders.

    D. Perform penetration testing.

16. Which of the following should be physically secured? (Choose all that apply.)

    A. Network hubs/switches

    B. Removable media

    C. Confidential documents

    D. Backup tapes

    E. All of the above

17. Which of the following are physical ways to protect portable devices? (Choose all that apply.)

    A. Strong user passwords

    B. Cable locks to prevent theft

    C. Motion-sensing alarms

    D. Personal firewall software

18. Which of the following are physical security measures designed to prevent?

    A. Loss of data or damage to systems caused by natural causes

    B. Access to data by employees and contractors

    C. Physical access to a customer database

    D. Access to an employee database via the Internet

19. Which of the following could be caused by a lack of physical security?

   A. Web server attack

   B. SQL injection

   C. Attack on a firewall

   D. Implementation of a rogue wireless access point

20. Which of the following are indications of a physical site breach?

   A. Unauthorized personnel recorded on a security camera

   B. IDS log event recording an intruder accessing a secure database

   C. An antivirus scanning program indicating a Trojan on a computer

   D. An employee inappropriately accessing the payroll database

Answers to Review Questions

1. B, C, D. The chief information officer, along with all the employees, including IT managers, is responsible for implementing physical security.

2. B. A fire or flood can affect physical security; all the other options are technical security issues.

3. A, B, D. Physical security is designed to prevent someone from stealing confidential data, hacking systems from the inside, and gaining physical access to unauthorized areas. Technical security defends against hacking systems from the Internet.

4. D. Physical security is one of the most overlooked areas of security.

5. A. In order to place a wireless access point, a hacker needs to have physical access.

6. B. Physical security usually receives the least amount of testing during a penetration test.

7. C. A hardware keylogger can be installed to capture passwords or other confidential data once a hacker gains physical access to a client system.

8. A. Physical access allows a hacker to crack passwords on a local system.

9. C. Theft of equipment is an example of a physical security breach.

10. B. Stealing equipment requires physical access.

11. D. The most important task after a physical security breach has been detected is to gather information and analyze to prevent a future attack.

12. A. Locking the server room is a simple countermeasure to prevent a physical security breach.

13. A, B, D. Locking the server room and server cases and enforcing badges for all visitors are physical controls. A software firewall is a technical control.

14. A. A tailgater is the name for an intruder who follows an employee with legitimate access through a door.

15. C. After a physical site security breach, the stakeholders in the incident response process need to be identified. Implement security awareness training, establish a security response team, and perform penetration testing before another physical site security breach is detected.

16. E. Network hubs and switches, removable media, confidential documents, and all backup media tapes should be physically secured and then destroyed when they are no longer needed.

17. B, C. Cable locks and motion-sensing alarms are physical countermeasures to prevent theft of portable devices.

18. A. Physical security measures are designed to prevent loss of data or damage to systems caused by natural causes.

19. D. A lack of physical security could allow a hacker to plant a rogue wireless access point on the network.

20. A. Unauthorized personnel recorded on a security camera is an indication of a physical site security breach.

Chapter

12

Hacking Linux Systems

CEH EXAM OBJECTIVES COVERED IN THIS CHAPTER:

- ✓ Understand how to compile a Linux kernel
- ✓ Understand GCC compilation commands
- ✓ Understand how to install LKM modules
- ✓ Understand Linux hardening methods

Linux is a popular operating system with system administrators because of its open source code and its flexibility, which allows anyone to modify it. Because of the open source nature of Linux, there are many different versions, known as *distributions* (or *distros*). Several of the Linux distributions have become robust commercial operating systems for use on workstations as well as servers. Popular commercial distributions include Red Hat, Debian, Mandrake, and SUSE; some of the most common free versions are Gentoo and Knoppix.

Linux's flexibility and the fact that it's open source, together with the increase in Linux applications, have made Linux the operating system of choice for many systems. Although Linux has inherently tighter security than Windows operating systems, it also has vulnerabilities that can be exploited. This chapter covers the basics of getting started using Linux as an operating system and knowing how to harden the system to attacks.

Linux Basics

Linux is loosely based on Unix, and anyone familiar with working in a Unix environment should be able to use a Linux system. All standard commands and utilities are included on most distros.

Many text editors are available inside a Linux system, including vi, ex, pico, jove, and GNU emacs. Many Unix users prefer "simple" editors like vi. But vi has many limitations due to its age, and most modern editors like emacs have gained popularity in recent years.

Most of the basic Linux utilities are GNU software, meaning they are freely distributed to the community. GNU utilities also support advanced features that are not found in the standard versions of BSD and UNIX System. However, GNU utilities are intended to remain compatible with BSD.

A shell is a command-line program interface that allows a user to enter commands, and the system executes commands from the user. In addition, many shells provide features like job control, the ability to manage several processes at once, input and output redirection, and a command language for writing shell scripts. A shell script is a program written in the shell's command language and is similar to an MS-DOS batch file.

Many types of shells are available for Linux. The most important difference among shells is the command language. For example, the C SHell (csh) uses a command language similar to the C programming language. The classic Bourne SHell (sh) uses another command language. The choice of a shell is often based on the command language it provides, and determines which features will be available to the user.

The GNU Bourne Again Shell (bash) is a variation of the Bourne Shell, which includes many advanced features like job control, command history, command and filename completion, and an interface for editing files. Another popular shell is tcsh, a version of the C Shell with advanced functionality similar to that found in bash. Other shells include zsh, a small Bourne-like shell; the Korn Shell (ksh); BSD's ash; and rc, the Plan 9 shell.

Moving around the Linux files system may take a little getting used to if you are primarily a Windows user. The commands in Table 12.1 will help you start to navigate the Linux file system.

TABLE 12.1 Linux file system navigation

Command	Purpose
cd ..	Used to go back one directory in most Unix shells. It is important that the space be between the cd and the two dots (..).
cd –	When in a Korn shell, used to go back one directory.
ls -a	Lists all contents of a directory, including hidden files.
ls -l	Lists all the information about files such as permissions, owners, size, and last modified date.
cp	Copies a file.
mv	Moves a file.
mkdir	Makes a new directory.
rm	Removes a file or directory.

Most Linux file systems are organized with common directories. The directories in Table 12.2 are located on most Linux distros.

TABLE 12.2 Linux directories

Directory	Contents
bin	Binary (executable) files
sbin	System binaries
etc	Configuration files

TABLE 12.2 *Linux directories (continued)*

Directory	Contents
include	Include files
lib	Library files
src	Source files
doc	Documentation files
man	Manual (help) files
share	Shared files

Linux networking commands are similar to the Windows networking commands. For the CEH exam, you should be familiar with the commands in Table 12.3.

TABLE 12.3 Linux networking commands

Command	Description
arp	Used to view the ARP table of MAC addresses mapped to IP addresses
ifconfig	Used to view network interface configuration
netstat	Presents a summary of network connections and sockets
nslookup	Resolves domain names to IP addresses
ping	Tests IP connectivity
ps	Lists all running processes
route	Lists the routing table
shred	Securely deletes a file
traceroute	Traces the path to a destination

Compiling a Linux Kernel

Because of the open source nature of Linux, the source code is freely distributed. The source code is available as binary files, which must be compiled in order to properly operate as an operating system. The binary files are available to anyone and may be downloaded and modified to add or change functionality. There are three reasons a user might want to recompile the Linux kernel:

- You may have some hardware that is so new that there's no kernel module for it in on your distribution CD.

- You may have come across some kind of bug that is fixed in a revision of the operating system.

- You may have some new software application that requires a newer version of the operating system.

Compiling your own linux kernel is great for flexibility, but users should be careful where they download the source code. A site may have bad or infected code, Trojans, or other backdoors added to the source code. For security reasons, only download Linux from known and trusted Internet websites or purchase a commercial distro. A good website to use for downloading Linux distros is www.frozentech.com.

In Exercise 12.1 you will compile a Linux Kernel, and Exercise 12.2 shows how to create a USB bootable Linux Distro.

The site I recommend for downloading the Linux kernel is ftp.kernel.org.

EXERCISE 12.1

Configuring and Compiling the Kernel

To download, configure, and compile the Linux kernel, follow these steps:

1. Locate the file for the latest version of the operating system and download it to the /usr/src directory on your Linux system. Then use the tar zxf command to unpack it.

2. The next step is to configure the Linux kernel. Change directory to /usr/src/Linux and type **make menuconfig**. This command will build a few programs and then quickly pop up a window. The window menu lets you alter many aspects of kernel configuration.

EXERCISE 12.1   *(continued)*

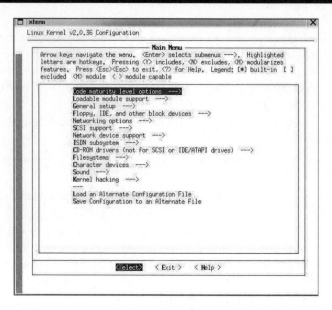

3. After you have made any necessary changes, save the configuration and type **make dep; make clean** at the command prompt. The first of these commands builds the tree of interdependencies in the kernel sources. These dependencies may have been affected by the options you have chosen in the configuration step. The make clean command purges any unwanted files left from previous builds of the kernel.

4. Issue the commands **make zImage** and **make modules**. These may take a long time because they are compiling the kernel.

5. The last step is installing the new kernel. On an Intel-based system the kernel is installed in /boot with the command:

    cp /usr/Linux/src/arch/i386/boot/zImage /boot/newkernel

6. Issue the command **make modules_install**. This will install the modules in /lib/modules.

7. Edit /etc/lilo.conf to add a section like this:

    image = /boot/newkernellabel = newread-only

8. At the next reboot, select the new kernel in lilo and it will load the new kernel. If it works, move it to the first position in the lilo.conf file so it will boot every time by default. Lilo is a boot loader that most Linux users use for booting a Linux system.

Example of a "lilo.conf" file (usually located in "/etc/"):

```
# This line is a comment line
#LILO global section
    boot = /dev/hda2
    timeout = 500
    prompt
    default = linuxbox #"linuxbox" is default kernel
    vga = normal
    read-only
#End of globol section ends
# bootable kernel "vmlinuz-2.0.36-1" in directory "/boot/"
# kernel number one
    image = /boot/vmlinuz-2.0.36-1
    label = linuxbox
    vga = normal
    root = /dev/hda2
#end of kernel one section
```

Linux live CDs are a good choice if you're new to Linux. Using the live CD, you can test and use the operating system without installing Linux on the system. To use a live CD, first visit www.distrowatch.com to choose a distribution. Then, download the ISO file and write it to a CD. That CD can be put in any system and booted to a fully functioning version of Linux.

Using a Live CD

In this exercise you will create a Linux live USB drive. Essentially the OS will boot off the USB drive, and then you will have a fully functioning Linux OS to learn how to use some of the Linux commands.

1. Download UNetbootin from sourceforge.net.

2. Run the UNetbootin program.

3. Select the Distribution radio button and click the drop-down menu.

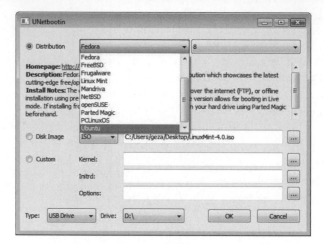

4. Choose the Linux version from the drop-down menu. The suggested Linux distro for CEH tools is BackTrack, but check the distrowatch.com site to learn which tools are included with each distro. Another option is to download your own Linux ISO file and select the Disk Image radio button.

5. Insert a blank USB drive into your computer. All data on the USB drive will be erased, so ensure it does not contain any files you wish to keep. Make sure your USB drive is large enough to contain the entire ISO image.

6. Choose USB Drive for the type and choose the drive letter for your USB drive.

7. Click OK and wait for UNetbootin to finish formatting and copying the distro files onto the drive.

GCC Compilation Commands

GNU Compiler Collection (GCC) is a command-line compiler that takes source code and makes it an executable. You can download it from http://gcc.gnu.org (many Linux distributions also include a version of GCC). GCC can be used to compile and execute C, C++, and FORTRAN applications so they are able to run on a Linux system.

The following command compiles C++ code with the GCC for use as an application:

```
g++ filename.cpp -o outputfilename.out
```

The command to compile C code with the GCC for use as an application is as follows:

```
gcc filename.c -o outputfilename.out
```

Installing Linux Kernel Modules

Linux Kernel Modules (LKMs) let you add functionality to your operating system without having to recompile the OS.

A danger of using LKMs is that a rootkit can easily be created as an LKM, and if loaded, it infects the kernel. For this reason, you should download LKMs only from a verified good source.

Examples of LKM rootkits are Knark, Adore, and Rtkit. Because they infect the kernel, these rootkits are more difficult to detect than those that do not manifest themselves as LKMs. Once a system has been compromised, the hacker can put the LKM in the /tmp or the /var/tmp directory, which can't be monitored by the system administrator, thereby hiding processes, files, and network connections. System calls can also be replaced with those of the hacker's choosing on a system infected by an LKM rootkit.

The command to load a LKM is modprobe *LKM*.

Linux Hardening Methods

Hardening is the process of improving security on a system by making modifications to the system. Linux can be made more secure by employing some of these hardening methods.

The first step in securing any server, Linux or Windows, is to ensure that it's in a secure location such as a network operations center, which prevents a hacker from gaining physical access to the system.

The next and most obvious security measure is to use strong passwords and not give out usernames or passwords. Administrators should make sure the system doesn't have null passwords by verifying that all user accounts have passwords in the Linux /etc/shadow file.

The default security stance of deny all is a good one for hardening a system from a network attack. After applying deny all, the administrator can open certain access for specific users. By using the deny all command first, the administrator ensures that users aren't being given access to files that they shouldn't have access to. The command to deny all users access from the network looks like this:

```
Cat "All:All">> /etc/hosts.deny
```

Another good way to harden a Linux server is to remove unused services and ensure that the system is patched with the latest bug fixes. Administrators should also check system logs frequently for anything unusual that could indicate an attack.

The following are other overall recommended steps to improve the security of a Linux server:

Operating System Selection and Installation

- Use a widely recognized and known good Linux distribution.
- Set up disk partitioning (or logical volumes), taking into account any security considerations.

- After the initial operating system installation, apply any operating system patches that have been released since the installation media was created.

- Set up and enable IP tables.

- Install a host-based intrusion detection system (HIDS).

- Don't install unnecessary applications or services.

- Enable the high security/trusted operating system version if appropriate.

- Secure the boot loader program (such as lilo or GRUB) with a password.

- Enable the single-user mode password if necessary.

Securing Local File Systems

- Look for inappropriate file and directory permissions, and correct any problems you find. The most important of these are:

  - Group and/or world writable system executables and directories

  - Group and/or world writable user home directories

- Select mount options (such as `nosuid`) for local file systems that take advantage of security features provided by the operating system.

- Encrypt sensitive data present on the system.

Configuring and Disabling Services

- Remove or disable all unneeded services. Services are started in several different ways: within `/etc/inittab`, from system boot scripts, or by inetd. When possible, the software for an unneeded service should be removed from the system completely.

- Use secure versions of daemons when they are available.

- If at all possible, run server processes as a special user created for that purpose and not as root.

- When appropriate, run servers in an isolated directory tree via the chroot facility.

- Set a maximum number of instances for services if possible.

- Specify access control and logging for all services. Install TCP Wrappers if necessary. Allow only the minimum access necessary. Include an entry in `/etc/hosts.deny` that denies access to everyone (so only access allowed in `/etc/hosts.allow` will be permitted).

- Use any per-service user-level access control that is provided. For example the cron and at subsystems allow you to restrict which users can use them at all. Some people recommend limiting at and cron to administrators.

- Secure all services, whether they seem security related or not (such as the printing service).

Securing the Root Account

- Select a secure root password, and plan a schedule for changing it regularly.
- If possible, restrict the use of the su command to a single group.
- Use sudo or system roles to grant other ordinary users limited root privilege when needed.
- Prevent direct root logins except on the system console.

Defining User Account Password Selection and Aging Settings

- Set up default user account restrictions as appropriate.
- Set up default user initialization files in /etc/skel, as well as the system-wide initialization files.
- Ensure that administrative and other system accounts to which no one should ever log in have a disabled password and /bin/false or another non-login shell.
- Remove unneeded predefined default accounts.

Securing Remote Authentication

- Disable /etc/hosts.equiv and .rhosts password-less authentication.
- Use ssh and its related commands for all remote user access. Disable rlogin, rsh, telnet, ftp, rcp, and so on.

Performing Ongoing System Monitoring

- Configure the syslog facility. Send or copy syslog messages to a central syslog server for redundancy.
- Enable process accounting.
- Install Tripwire, configure it, and record system baseline data. Write the data to removable media and then remove it from the system. Finally, configure Tripwire to run on a daily basis.
- Design and implement a plan for monitoring log information for security-related events.

Performing Miscellaneous Activities

- Remove any remaining source code for the kernel or additional software packages from the system.
- Add the new host to the security configuration on other systems, in router access control lists, and so forth.
- Check for vendor security updates for any installed software.

Exercise 12.3 shows how to detect listening ports on a Linux system.

EXERCISE 12.3

Detecting Listening Network Ports

One of the most important tasks in securing Linux is to detect and close network ports that are not needed. This exercise will show you how to get a list of listening network ports (TCP and UDP sockets).

1. Boot the BackTrack Linux USB drive you created in an earlier exercise. Note that BackTrack is not necessary for this exercise. These commands will work with any Linux installation.

2. Open a command window and type **netstat -tulp**. This command will display a list of open ports on your system.

Network Destination	Netmask	Gateway	Interface	Metric
0.0.0.0	0.0.0.0	10.122.56.1	10.122.56.61	25
10.122.56.0	255.255.255.128	On-link	10.122.56.61	281
10.122.56.61	255.255.255.255	On-link	10.122.56.61	281
10.122.56.127	255.255.255.255	On-link	10.122.56.61	281
127.0.0.0	255.0.0.0	On-link	127.0.0.1	306
127.0.0.1	255.255.255.255	On-link	127.0.0.1	306
127.255.255.255	255.255.255.255	On-link	127.0.0.1	306
192.168.192.0	255.255.255.0	On-link	192.168.192.1	276
192.168.192.1	255.255.255.255	On-link	192.168.192.1	276
192.168.192.255	255.255.255.255	On-link	192.168.192.1	276
192.168.227.0	255.255.255.0	On-link	192.168.227.1	276
192.168.227.1	255.255.255.255	On-link	192.168.227.1	276
192.168.227.255	255.255.255.255	On-link	192.168.227.1	276

Another method for listing all the TCP and UDP sockets to which programs are listening is lsof. The syntax to run this command is:

```
# lsof -i -n | egrep 'COMMAND|LISTEN|UDP'
```

3. The next step to harden the Linux installation is to disable unused services. The start/stop scripts of all runlevel services can be found in the /etc/init.d directory. For example, if you don't know what the atd service does, go to /etc/init.d and open the file atd. In the script look for lines that start programs. In the atd script, the daemon /usr/sbin/atd line starts the binary atd. Then, having the name of the program that is started by this service, you can check the online pages of atd by running man atd. This will help you to find out more about a system service.

To permanently disable a service—in this example, the runlevel service nfs—type the following command:

```
chkconfig nfs off
```

Real World Scenario

Hacking a Default Linux Installation

I worked at a small consulting company where most of the consultants were experts on Windows systems but lacked experience in other operating systems. One of our customers wanted to use Linux for the e-commerce site, and so, because our company wanted to keep them as a customer, we agreed to install the Linux system for them. Because none of the consultants had much experience with Linux, the system was installed with many default options and standard services.

Soon after the new system was installed, the e-commerce portal was hacked and the customer database was compromised. Customer personal information and credit card numbers were exposed by the hackers. Additionally, the company experienced a denial-of-service attack and the site was not available to customers, causing a loss of business.

After the attack, another consulting company specializing in security performed some forensics analysis and determined that access rights for the users and groups on the Linux system were set to the defaults, which hackers exploited to attack the systems. The consulting company recommended to our organization that in the future Linux should be hardened after installation by setting up and enabling IP tables, configuring the Linux security-related kernel parameters, disabling the unnecessary daemons and network services, changing default passwords, and disabling the remote root logins over ssh.

Summary

It is important to understand the basics of the Linux operating system as many application and web servers run an underlying version of Linux. For the CEH exam, you should be familiar with how to use the Linux OS and know the steps you should take to harden a default Linux installation. Live CDs or USB drives are a great way to learn how to use the basic tools if you are new to Linux.

Exam Essentials

Understand the use of Linux in the marketplace.   Linux has become popular with the introduction of commercial versions and available applications. Linux can be used as a hacking platform, as a server, or as a workstation.

Know how to use a Linux live CD.   Locate and download an ISO file. Write it to a CD, and boot a system from the CD to use the Linux operating system.

Know the steps to create a Linux operating system.   Locate and download the binary files, and compile the Linux source files; then, install the compiled OS.

Know how to harden a Linux system.   Use a known good distribution, change the default passwords, disable the root login, use IP tables, use an HIDS, apply the latest fixes, and monitor log files to harden a Linux system.

Understand how LKMs are used.   LKMs add functionality to a Linux system, but they should be used only from a known good source.

Know about GCC compilation.   GCC compilers are used to create executable applications from C or C++ source code.

Review Questions

1.   What does LKM stand for?

   A.   Linux Kernel Module

   B.   Linux Kernel Mode

   C.   Linked Kernel Module

   D.   Last Kernel Mode

2.   What GCC command is used to compile a C++ file called source into an executable file called game?

   A.   g++ source.c –o game

   B.   gcc source.c –o game

   C.   gcc make source.cpp –o game

   D.   g++ source.cpp –o game

3.   What is the command to deny all users access from the network?

   A.   Cat "All:All">> /etc/hosts.deny

   B.   Set "All:All">> /etc/hosts.deny

   C.   IP deny "All:All"

   D.   Cat All:All deny

4.   Of the following, which are common commercial Linux distributions?

   A.   SUSE, Knark, and Red Hat

   B.   SUSE, Adore, Debian, and Mandrake

   C.   SUSE, Debian, and Red Hat

   D.   SUSE, Adore, and Red Hat

5.   What is a Linux live CD?

   A.   A Linux operating system that runs from a CD

   B.   A Linux operating system installed from a CD onto a hard drive

   C.   A Linux tool that runs applications from a CD

   D.   A Linux application that makes CDs

6.   What type of attack can be disguised as an LKM?

   A.   DoS

   B.   Trojan

   C.   Spam virus

   D.   Rootkit

7. Which of the following is a reason to use Linux?

   A. Linux has no security holes.

   B. Linux is always up-to-date on security patches.

   C. No rootkits can infect a Linux system.

   D. Linux is flexible and can be modified.

8. Which of the following is *not* a way to harden Linux?

   A. Physically secure the system.

   B. Maintain a current patch level.

   C. Change the default passwords.

   D. Install all available services.

9. What type of file is used to create a Linux live CD?

   A. ISO

   B. CD

   C. LIN

   D. CDFS

10. Why is it important to use a known good distribution of Linux?

   A. Source files can become corrupted if not downloaded properly.

   B. Only certain distributions can be patched.

   C. Source files can be modified, and a Trojan or backdoor may be included in the source binaries of some less-known or free distributions of Linux.

   D. Only some versions of Linux are available to the public.

11. What command will give you the most information Linux files?

   A. ls -a

   B. ls -m

   C. ls -t

   D. ls -l

12. What is the purpose of the man command?

   A. Lists help and documentation

   B. Manually configures a program

   C. Performs system maintenance

   D. Installs a program

13. In which directory are Linux system source files located?

   A. source

   B. src

   C. sys

   D. system

14. What is the Linux command that lists all current running processes?

A. ps

B. list ps

C. show ps

D. process

15. What is the Linux command for viewing the IP address of a network interface?

A. ifconfig

B. ipconfig

C. ipconfig /all

D. interface /ip

16. Which Linux command would produce the following output?

```
Proto Recv-Q Send-Q Local Address          Foreign Address        State
tcp        0      0 *:ssh                  *:*                    LISTE
tcp        0      0 *:10000                *:*                    LISTE
tcp        0      0 localhost:smtp         *:*                    LISTE
udp        0      0 *:56315                *:*
udp        0      0 *:icpv2                *:*
```

A. routing

B. route print

C. route

D. show routes

17. What is a recommended way to secure the Linux root account? (Choose all that apply.)

A. Prevent direct root logins except from the system console.

B. Restrict the use of su to a single group.

C. Install su protect to prevent misuse of the su command.

D. Grant the admin privilege to any user needing to install programs.

18. When you are securing local Linux file systems, which two types of directories should you be check for appropriate permissions? (Choose two.)

A. Root directory

B. Services directory

C. Writable system executable directories

D. Writable user home directories

19. What is the Cat command you would use to harden the file system of a Linux system?

   A. Cat "source=All:destination=All">> /etc/hosts.deny

   B. Cat "All:All">> /etc/hosts.deny

   C. Cat "Any:Any">> /etc/hosts.deny

   D. Cat "All:All" /etc/hosts.deny

20. In which file should you check to ensure users do not have a null password in a Linux system?

   A. Password file

   B. Passwd file

   C. Shadow file

   D. Shdw file

Answers to Review Questions

1. A. LKM stands for Linux Kernel Module.

2. D. `g++ source.cpp -o game` is the GCC command to create an executable called game from the source file `source`.

3. A. Use the `Cat "All:All">> /etc/hosts.deny` command to deny all users access from the network on a Linux system.

4. C. SUSE, Debian, and Red Hat are all commercial versions of Linux.

5. A. A Linux live CD is a fully functioning operating system that runs from a CD.

6. D. A rootkit can be disguised as an LKM.

7. D. Linux is flexible and can be modified because the source code is openly available.

8. D. Linux should not have unused services running, because each additional service may have potential vulnerabilities.

9. A. An ISO file is used to create a Linux live CD.

10. C. Known good distributions have been reviewed by the Linux community to verify that a Trojan or backdoor does not exist in the source code.

11. D. The command `ls -l` lists all the information about files such as permissions, owners, size, and last modified date.

12. A. The `man` command will list help and documentation in Linux.

13. B. The `src` directory contains the Linux source files.

14. A. The `ps` command lists all running processes.

15. A. Use the `ifconfig` command to view the IP address of a network interface. `ipconfig` and `ipconfig/all` are Windows commands to view IP address information.

16. C. `route` displays the routing table. `route print` is a Windows command to display the routing table. `show routes` is a command commonly used to view a routing table.

17. A, B. The recommended way to secure the Linux root account is to prevent direct root logins and to restrict the use of su to one group.

18. C, D. Writable system executable directories and writable user home directories should both be checked as they could be used to execute malicious code.

19. B. Use the command `Cat "All:All">> /etc/hosts.deny` to harden a Linux system and ensure all users are denied access to certain files from the network.

20. C. User passwords in a Linux system are stored in the shadow file. To harden a system, check the shadow file for null passwords.

Chapter

13

Bypassing Network Security: Evading IDSs, Honeypots, and Firewalls

CEH EXAM OBJECTIVES COVERED IN THIS CHAPTER:

✓ List the types of intrusion detection systems and evasion techniques

✓ List firewall types and honeypot evasion techniques

Intrusion detection systems (IDS), firewalls, and honeypots are all security measures used to ensure a hacker is not able to gain access to a network or target system. An IDS and a firewall are both essentially packet filtering devices and are used to monitor traffic based on a predefined set of rules. A honeypot is a fake target system used to lure hackers away from the more valuable targets. As with other security mechanisms, IDSs, firewalls, and honeypots are only as good as their design and implementation. It is important to be familiar with how these devices operate and provide security as they are commonly subjects of attack.

Types of IDSs and Evasion Techniques

Intrusion detection systems (IDSs) inspect traffic and look for known signatures of attacks or unusual behavior patterns. A *packet sniffer* views and monitors traffic and is a built-in component of an IDS. An IDS alerts a command center or system administrator by pager, email, or cell phone when an event appearing on the company's security event list is triggered. *Intrusion prevention systems* (IPSs) initiate countermeasures such as blocking traffic when suspected traffic flow is detected. IPSs automate the response to an intrusion attempt and allow you to automate the deny-access capability.

There are two main types of IDS:

Host Based   Host-based IDSs (HIDSs) are applications that reside on a single system or host and filter traffic or events based on a known signature list for that specific operating system. HIDSs include Norton Internet Security and Cisco Security Agent (CSA). Many worms and Trojans can turn off an HIDS. HIDSs can also be installed directly on servers to detect attacks against corporate resources and applications.

Network Based   Network-based IDSs (NIDSs) are software-based appliances that reside on the network. They're used solely for intrusion detection purposes to detect all types of malicious network traffic and computer usage that can't be detected by a conventional firewall. This includes network attacks against vulnerable services; data attacks on applications; host-based attacks such as privilege escalation, unauthorized logins, and access to sensitive files; and malware. NIDSs are *passive* systems: the IDS sensor detects a potential security breach, logs the information, and signals an alert on the console.

The location of a network-based IDS in a network architecture is depicted in Figure 13.1. A network IDS sensor can be located as a first point of detection between the firewall and the Internet or on the semi-private DMZ, detecting attacks on the organization's servers. Finally, a network IDS can be located on the internal private network, with the corporate servers detecting possible attacks on those servers.

FIGURE 13.1   Network-based IDS

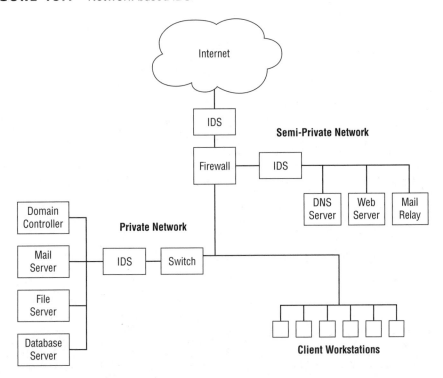

An IDS can perform either signature analysis or anomaly detection to determine if the traffic is a possible attack. Signature detection IDSs match traffic with known signatures and patterns of misuse. A *signature* is a pattern used to identify either a single packet or a series of packets that, when combined, execute an attack. An IDS that employs anomaly detection looks for intrusion attempts based on a person's normal business patterns and alerts when there is an anomaly in the behavior of access to systems, files, logins, and so on.

A hacker can evade an IDS by changing the traffic so that it does not match a known signature. This may involve using a different protocol such as UDP instead of TCP or HTTP instead of ICMP to deliver an attack. Additionally, a hacker can break an attack up into several smaller packets to pass through an IDS but, when reassembled at the receiving station, will result in a compromise of the system. This is known as session splicing. Other methods of evading detection involve inserting extra data, obfuscating addresses or data by using encryption, or desynchronizing and taking over a current client's session.

Hacking Tool

ADMmutate takes an attack script and creates a different—but functionally equivalent—script to perform the attack. The new script isn't in the database of known attack signatures and therefore can bypass the IDS.

Understanding Snort Rules and Output

For the CEH exam, you should be familiar with Snort rules and output. You may need to read a Snort rule or output and answer a question pertaining to what the rule is doing or what type of attack is indicated by the output.

Snort is a real-time packet sniffer, HIDS, and traffic-logging tool deployed on Linux and Windows systems. Snort can analyze protocols, perform content searching/matching, and detect a variety of attacks and probes, such as buffer overflows, stealth port scans, CGI attacks, SMB probes, OS fingerprinting attempts, and much more. You can configure Snort and the IDS rules in the `snort.conf` file. The command to install and run Snort is:

```
snort -l c:\snort\log -c C:\snort\etc\snort.conf -A console
```

Snort consists of two major components:

Snort Engine   An IDS detection engine that utilizes a modular plug-in architecture

Snort Rules   A flexible rule language to describe traffic to be collected

The Snort Engine is distributed both as source code and binaries for popular Linux distributions and Windows. It's important to note that the Snort Engine and Snort rules are distributed separately. The Snort IDS Engine and rules can be downloaded from `snort.org`. The installation methods and software dependencies vary by OS, so this chapter does not include a lab on installing Snort. Detailed installation instructions can be found at `snort.org`.

Configuring Snort

Snort has one configuration file: `snort.conf`. It usually resides in `/etc/snort`. The file contains variables that need to be modified for your specific installation and customized to the events you want to alert on. The file variables are organized in the following sections:

- Network variables
- Preprocessors
- Postprocessors
- Rules

The `snort.conf` file network variables that need to be customized to your network are listed in Table 13.1.

TABLE 13.1   Snort variables

Variable	Meaning
HOME_NET	Local IP address space
EXTERNAL_NET	External IP address space
SMTP	Your SMTP servers
HTTP_SERVERS	Your web servers
SQL_SERVERS	Your SQL Servers
DNS_SERVERS	Your DNS servers
RULE_PATH	The directory that contains your rule files

Here is a sample Snort configuration file using the 192.168.1.0 network as the home network:

```
var HOME_NET 192.168.1.0/24
var EXTERNAL_NET any
var SMTP $HOME_NET
var HTTP_SERVERS $HOME_NET
var SQL_SERVERS $HOME_NET
var DNS_SERVERS $HOME_NET
var RULE_PATH /etc/snort/rules
```

The following are the rule locations identified in the config file:

```
include $RULE_PATH/exploit.rules
include $RULE_PATH/scan.rules
include $RULE_PATH/ftp.rules
include $RULE_PATH/telnet.rules
include $RULE_PATH/smtp.rules
include $RULE_PATH/rpc.rules
include $RULE_PATH/dos.rules
include $RULE_PATH/ddos.rules
include $RULE_PATH/dns.rules
include $RULE_PATH/web-cgi.rules
include $RULE_PATH/web-coldfusion.rules
include $RULE_PATH/web-iis.rules
```

```
include $RULE_PATH/web-frontpage.rules
include $RULE_PATH/web-misc.rules
include $RULE_PATH/web-attacks.rules
include $RULE_PATH/sql.rules
include $RULE_PATH/netbios.rules
include $RULE_PATH/misc.rules
```

Snort Rules

Snort rules are used to generate alerts based on the traffic that is viewed by the IDS processing engine.

All rules have a rule header composed of the following fields:

- `<rule action>`

- `<protocol>`

- `<src address & port>`

- `<dest address & port>`

Here's an example of a Snort rule:

```
alert tcp $EXTERNAL_NET any -> $HOME_NET 23
```

This rule says to generate an alert (and a log message) for any TCP packet coming from an external address space (and any port) destined to the local address space (and port 23).

The Snort rule header is followed by rule options, which are a delimited list of features to use in Snort. Here are some rule options and explanations. The line

```
msg:"TELNET SGI telnetd format bug"
```

specifies to the logging and alerting engines what message to print. The line

```
flags: A+
```

matches the TCP ACK flag (plus any other set flag). The line

```
content: "bin/sh"
```

matches the given string in the packet's payload. The line

```
classtype:attempted-admin
```

associates a high priority to this alert by giving it an *attack class* of `attempted-admin` (attempted administrator privilege gain).

Snort Output

For the CEH exam, it is important to understand a Snort output report. Here is an example of a Snort alert. First, here is the timestamp:

`04/21-19:26:37.353790`

These are the source and destination MAC addresses:

`0:8:2:FB:36:C6 -> 0:6:5B:57:A6:3F`

The type of Ethernet frame (0x800 means Ethernet) and the length are next:

`type:0x800 len:0x3C`

This line specifies the source IP 202.185.44.43 to the destination IP 202.185.44.28 and source port 445 and destination port 2202:

`202.185.44.43:445 -> 202.185.44.28:2202`

This line states that the protocol is TCP and the Time To Live (TTL) is 128:

`TCP TTL:128`

Next is the type of service, the ID, the IP length, and the datagram length:

`TOS:0x0 ID:17467 IpLen:20 DgmLen:41 DF`

The ***A**** means the ACK flag is on, so the packet is an acknowledgment of a previous packet:

`***A****`

In this line, Seq is the sequence number, and Ack is the numbered response to the previous packet:

`Seq: 0x9D08DD67 Ack: 0x83EB1E02`

Finally, in the following line Win is the window size and the TCP length is 2000:
`Win: 0x3FE1 TcpLen: 2000`

In many cases, reading and interpreting Snort output reports on the CEH exam is just a matter of knowing the TCP flags and TCP well-known port numbers.

Firewall Types and Honeypot Evasion Techniques

A *firewall* is a software program or hardware appliance that allows or denies access to a network and follows rules set by an administrator to direct where packets are allowed to go on the network. A *perimeter hardware firewall* appliance (Figure 13.2) is set up either at the network edge where a trusted network connects to an untrusted network, such as the Internet, or between networks. A *software firewall* protects a personal computer, a system, or a host from unwanted or malicious packets entering the network interface card (NIC) from the network.

FIGURE 13.2 Perimeter hardware firewall

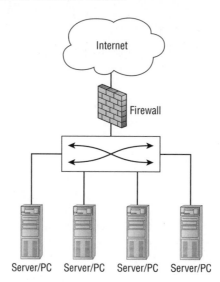

A *honeypot* (Figure 13.3) is a decoy box residing inside your network demilitarized zone (DMZ), set up by a security professional to trap or aid in locating hackers, or to draw them away from the real target system.

FIGURE 13.3   Honeypot Location

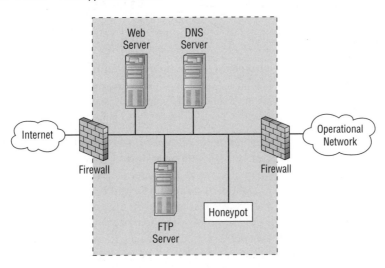

The honeypot is a decoy system that a malicious attacker might try to attack; software on the system can log information about the attacker such as the IP address. This information can be used to try to locate the attacker either during or after the attack. The best location for a honeypot is in front of the firewall on the DMZ, making it attractive to hackers. A honeypot with a static address is designed to look like a real production server (see Figure 13.4). Exercise 13.1 walks you through installing and using a honeypot.

FIGURE 13.4   Honeypot

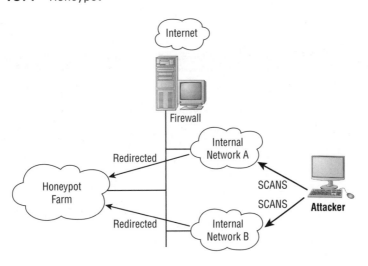

Real World Scenario

Finding a Honeypot

I was performing a wireless network security audit for a large corporation a few years ago. I drove around the corporate campus scanning for open access points (APs), and I was a bit surprised at how many open unsecured APs could be seen by my wireless scanning sniffer. I found over 30 APs to which I could connect and gain network access.

Of course, the next step after connecting to the APs was to scan the network. So, as part of the security audit, I connected from outside the building and ran a port scan against the entire network range; I found several systems with open ports. There was a mail server and a couple of web servers, as well as a Domain Controller that was not totally patched. As per the scope of the audit, I was just to report the vulnerabilities I found and not attempt to exploit the services I found running on the systems. I was surprised that such a large organization would have vulnerabilities so easily found on the open wireless network. I documented all the target systems and the vulnerable ports and services in my security auditing report.

When I presented my report to the customer the following day, the IT manager simply said, "Good, you found our honeynet, now go find the real systems." They had taken all the rogue APs discovered on the network and shunted them to a separate VLAN. Then on the shunted VLAN they had created fake systems, or honeypots, to attract potential hackers. These honeypots can keep a hacker busy trying to attack the honeypot system with no real data while the real services are untouched.

EXERCISE 13.1

Installing and Using KFSensor as a Honeypot

1. Download and install a trial version of KFSensor from www.keyfocus.net.

2. Open and run KFSensor. A pop-up window will appear to start the configuration wizard. Click Next to continue.

EXERCISE 13.1 *(continued)*

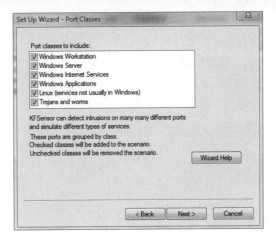

3. Click Next to select all ports.

4. Type *your name*.com (or another domain name of your choosing) in the Domain Name field and click Next.

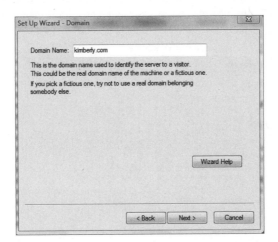

5. Type your email address in the Send To and Send From fields to receive email alerts from KFSensor.

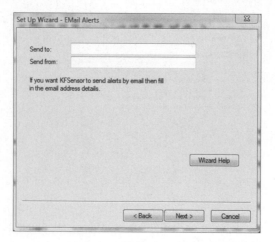

6. From the Port Activity drop-down, select 8 hours. Choose Enable Packet Dump Files from the Network Protocol Analyzer drop-down. Other options can remain at their defaults.

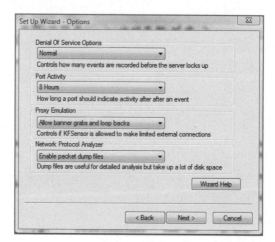

7. Click Next to accept the default to install as a system service.

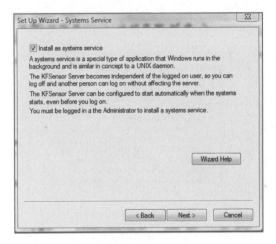

8. Click Finish to complete the wizard configuration.

9. The Main scenario for KFSensor should appear on the left. You may receive a message indicating that some of the ports have been disabled because they are in use by the system services; the strikeout text indicates the ports are not available in KFSensor.

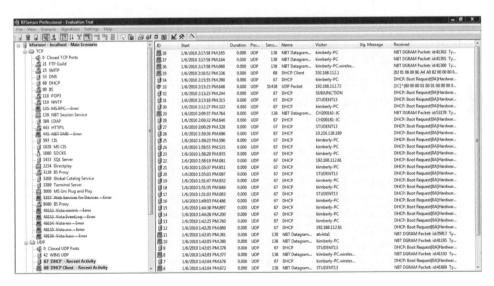

Perform a port scan against the system running KFSensor to identify the services.

EXERCISE 13.1   *(continued)*

10. Attempt to connect to a service running on the KFSensor system.

11. View the visitor to the KFSensor Honeypot by clicking the View menu and choosing Visitors.

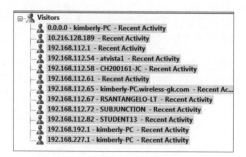

12. Click the IP address of a visitor to view the connections.

13. KFSensor will continue to run even when the program is closed. To stop the servers completely, right-click the KFSensor icon in the system tray and choose Stop Server.

The easiest way to bypass a firewall is to compromise a system on the trusted or internal side of the firewall. The compromised system can then connect through the firewall, from the trusted to the untrusted side, to the hacker's system. A common method of doing this is to make the compromised system connect to the hacker with destination port 80, which looks just like a web client connecting to a web server through the firewall. This is referred to as a *reverse WWW shell*.

This attack works because most firewalls permit outgoing connections to be made to port 80 by default.

Using a tunnel to send HTTP traffic, the hacker bypasses the firewall and makes the attack look innocuous to the firewall; such attacks are virtually untraceable by system administrators. Hacking programs can create covert channels, which let the attack traffic travel down an allowed path such as an Internet Control Message Protocol (ICMP) ping request or reply. Another method of utilizing a covert channel tunnels the attack traffic as a TCP acknowledgment.

To evade the trap set by a honeypot, a hacker can run anti-honeypot software, which tries to determine whether a honeypot is running on the target system and warn the hacker about it. In this way, a hacker can attempt to evade detection by not attacking a honeypot. Most anti-honeypot software checks the software running on the system against a known list of honeypots such as honeyd.

Hacking Tools

007 Shell is a shell-tunneling program that lets a hacker use a covert channel for the attack and thus bypass firewall rules.

ICMP Shell is a program similar to telnet that a hacker uses to make a connection to a target system using just ICMP commands, which are usually allowed through a firewall.

AckCmd is a client/server program that communicates using only TCP ACK packets, which can usually pass through a firewall.

Covert_TCP is a program that a hacker uses to send a file through a firewall one byte at a time by hiding the data in the IP header.

Send-Safe Honeypot Hunter is a honeypot-detection tool that checks against a proxy server for honeypots.

Countermeasures

Specter is a honeypot system that can automatically capture information about a hacker's machine while they're attacking the system.

Honeyd is an open source honeypot that creates virtual hosts on a network that is then targeted by hackers.

KFSensor is a host-based IDS that acts as a honeypot and can simulate virtual services and Trojan installations.

Sobek is a data-capturing honeypot tool that captures an attacker's keystrokes.

The Nessus vulnerability scanner (www.nessus.org) can also be used to detect honeypots.

Summary

Intrusion detection systems can be either network or host based. It is important to implement both types to protect valuable data on servers from attack. In both cases it is critical to keep the rules and definitions up-to-date to ensure the IDS has the latest attack vectors to compare traffic. Firewalls can also be network or host based, and in many cases network appliances' and systems software will perform both IDS detection and firewalling actions. Just because a firewall and IDS are implemented on a network or server, you should not be lulled into a false sense of security; tunneling and encryption can defeat both IDSs and firewalls because the real traffic headers and data cannot be read by the appliance. A CEH uses such techniques in an attempt to bypass the protection of firewalls and IDSs.

Exam Essentials

Know the two main types of IDSs. IDSs can be either host based or network based. A host-based IDS is operating system specific and protects a single system. A network-based IDS can protect the entire network.

Be able to define a honeypot. A honeypot resides in a DMZ as a vulnerable host and advertises services and software to entice a hacker to hack the system.

Be able to define a firewall. A firewall is a packet-filtering device that compares traffic to a list of rules and filters traffic from an untrusted network to a trusted network.

Understand how to detect a honeypot. A honeypot can be detected by comparing the system information to a known list of honeypots in a proxy server.

Understand how an IDS works. An IDS can either perform anomaly analysis or signature-based detection.

Know how to perform firewall evasion techniques. Firewall evasion can be performed by using a protocol such as ICMP or HTTP to carry attack traffic. Another technique is to split the packets into several smaller packets so the entire attack string cannot be detected.

Review Questions

1. What is a system that performs attack recognition and alerting for a network?

    A. HIDS

    B. NIDS

    C. Anomaly detection HIDS

    D. Signature-based NIDS

2. Which of the following tools bypasses a firewall by sending one byte at a time in the IP header?

    A. Honeyd

    B. Nessus

    C. Covert_TCP

    D. 007 Shell

    E. TCP to IP Hide

3. Which of the following is a honeypot-detection tool?

    A. Honeyd

    B. Specter

    C. KFSensor

    D. Sobek

4. Which of the following is a system designed to attract and identify hackers?

    A. Honeypot

    B. Firewall

    C. Honeytrap

    D. IDS

5. Which of the following is a tool used to modify an attack script to bypass an IDS's signature detection?

    A. ADMmutate

    B. Script Mutate

    C. Snort

    D. Specter

6. What is a reverse WWW shell?

   A. A web server making a reverse connection to a firewall

   B. A web client making a connection to a hacker through the firewall

   C. A web server connecting to a web client through the firewall

   D. A hacker connecting to a web server through a firewall

7. A reverse WWW shell connects to which port on a hacker's system?

   A. 80

   B. 443

   C. 23

   D. 21

8. What is the command used to install and run Snort?

   A. `snort -l c:\snort\log -c C:\snort\etc\snort.conf -A console`

   B. `snort -c C:\snort\etc\snort.conf -A console`

   C. `snort -c C:\snort\etc\snort.conf console`

   D. `snort -l c:\snort\log -c -A`

9. What type of program is Snort?

   A. NIDS

   B. Sniffer, HIDS, and traffic-logging tool

   C. Sniffer and HIDS

   D. NIDS and sniffer

10. What are the ways in which an IDS is able to detect intrusion attempts? (Choose all that apply.)

   A. Signature detection

   B. Anomaly detection

   C. Traffic identification

   D. Protocol analysis

11. You are viewing a snort output report and see an entry with the following address information: `168.175.44.80:34913 -> 142.155.44.28:443`. What type of server is the destination address?

   A. HTTP

   B. FTP

   C. SSL

   D. HTTPS

12. What is the `snort.conf` file variable for the local IP subnet?

A. INTERNAL_NET

B. DESTINATION_NETWORK

C. SOURCE_NET

D. HOME_NET

13. How is the rule location identified in the `snort.conf` file?

A. RULE_PATH

B. RULE_DIR

C. RULES

D. RULE_NET

14. Which field is *not* located in the rule header in a Snort rule?

A. Rule Action

B. Protocol

C. Source Address

D. HOME_NET

15. Which Snort rule option would associate a high priority to an alert?

A. `class:attempted-admin`

B. `classtype:High`

C. `classtype:attempted-admin`

D. `class:admin`

16. What are the two components needed when installing Snort?

A. Snort rules

B. Snort signatures

C. Snort Engine

D. Snort processor

17. What is an attack signature in an IDS?

A. A pattern of packets that indicates an attack

B. The first packet that indicates the start of an attack

C. The TCP header that indicates an attack

D. The confirmation that an attack has occurred

18. What is a method used to defeat an IDS signature match?

A. Anomaly detection

B. Tunneling

C. Packet smashing

D. Buffer overflows

19. You are reviewing a Snort output report with the following content:

```
10/17-20:28:15.014784 0:10:5A:1:D:5B -> 0:2:B3:87:84:25 type:0x800 len:0x3C
192.168.1.4:1244 -> 192.168.1.67:443 TCP TTL:128 TOS:0x0 ID:39235
IpLen:20 DgmLen:40 DF
***A**** Seq: 0xA18BBE Ack: 0x69749F36 Win: 0x2238 TcpLen: 20
0x0000: 00 02 B3 87 84 25 00 10 5A 01 0D 5B 08 00 45 00  .....%..Z..[..E.
0x0010: 00 28 99 43 40 00 80 06 DD F4 C0 A8 01 04 C0 A8  .(.C@...........
0x0020: 01 43 04 DC 01 BB 00 A1 8B BE 69 74 9F 36 50 10  .C........it.6P.
0x0030: 22 38 6E 63 00 00 00 00 00 00 00 00             "8nc........
```

What TCP flags are set in the packet?

A. ACK

B. SYN

C. FIN

D. RST

20. A Snort file has been retrieved with the following output:

```
10/17-20:28:15.080091 0:2:B3:87:84:25 -> 0:10:5A:1:D:5B type:0x800 len:0x13B
192.168.1.67:443 -> 192.168.1.4:1244 TCP TTL:64 TOS:0x0 ID:6664
IpLen:20 DgmLen:301 DF
***AP*** Seq: 0x6974A4F2 Ack: 0xA18F51 Win: 0x1E51 TcpLen: 20
0x0000: 00 10 5A 01 0D 5B 00 02 B3 87 84 25 08 00 45 00  ..Z..[.....%..E.
0x0010: 01 2D 1A 08 40 00 40 06 9C 2B C0 A8 01 43 C0 A8  .-..@.@..+...C..
0x0020: 01 04 01 BB 04 DC 69 74 A4 F2 00 A1 8F 51 50 18  ......it.....QP.
0x0030: 1E 51 5B AF 00 00 17 03 01 01 00 9D 6D 31 27 DB  .Q[.........m1'.
0x0040: 5C 57 B7 39 48 C5 FE 3C 92 77 65 E4 95 49 F4 C5  \W.9H..<.we..I..
0x0050: 5B 98 CB A2 A5 F9 DF C1 F1 6D A2 1A 22 04 E4 DB  [........m..."...
0x0060: 4A 1F 18 A9 F8 11 54 57 E6 AF 9A 6C 55 43 8D 37  J.....TW...lUC.7
0x0070: 76 E9 DB 61 2C 62 63 3C 7D E0 F4 08 E0 44 96 03  v..a,bc<}....D..
0x0080: 72 72 16 0C 87 B9 BC FF 08 52 C1 41 22 59 D7 B9  rr.......R.A"Y..
0x0090: 8E 4B 77 DE B8 11 AE AF B2 CB 8D 01 92 E8 26 4A  .Kw...........&J
0x00A0: 8C 24 00 8E C3 07 36 7F 84 9F 08 AF 2B 83 F8 13  .$....6.....+...
0x00B0: 1F 61 93 A8 2E 9D 5E 11 A1 DE CF 5E CF 1A 69 1B  .a....^....^..i.
0x00C0: 24 F9 A8 B1 CF C7 6C 08 69 ED BF 75 0A 46 C6 63  $.....l.i..u.F.c
0x00D0: CF D2 29 5B 2D 25 C1 44 0E 3F 4C 40 8D 30 75 74  ..)[-%.D.?L@.0ut
0x00E0: A4 C3 06 90 45 65 AC 73 0C C8 CD 4E 0E 22 DD C3  ....Ee.s...N."..
0x00F0: 37 48 FD 8B E6 77 02 9C 76 84 3F E9 7C 0E 9F 28  7H...w..v.?.|..(
0x0100: 06 C1 07 B8 88 4D 22 F2 D0 EF EA B4 37 40 F4 6D  .....M".....7@.m
0x0110: F8 79 47 25 85 AC 12 BB 92 94 0E 66 D9 2C 88 53  .yG%.......f.,.S
0x0120: F7 25 D7 DE 44 BF FF F2 54 4F 5B EF AB 6E E1 A0  .%..D...TO[..n..
0x0130: 38 BB DD 36 BF 5B 26 65 58 F8 8A              8..6.[&eX..
```

What is the web client's port number?

A. 443

B. 1244

C. 64

D. 080091

Answers to Review Questions

1. B. An NIDS performs attack recognition for an entire network.

2. C. Covert_TCP passes through a firewall by sending one byte at a time of a file in the IP header.

3. D. Sobek is a honeypot-detection tool.

4. A. A honeypot is a system designed to attract and identify hackers.

5. A. ADMmutate is a tool used to modify an attack script to bypass an IDS's signature detection.

6. B. A reverse WWW shell occurs when a compromised web client makes a connection back to a hacker's computer and is able to pass through a firewall.

7. A. The hacker's system, which is acting as a web server, uses port 80.

8. A. Use the command `snort -l c:\snort\log -c C:\snort\etc\snort.conf -A console` to install and run the Snort program.

9. B. Snort is a sniffer, HIDS, and traffic-logging tool.

10. A, B. Signature analysis and anomaly detection are the ways an IDS detects instruction attempts.

11. D. The destination port 443 indicates the traffic destination is an HTTPS server.

12. D. The `HOME_NET` variable is used in a `snort.conf` file to identify the local network.

13. A. The rule location is identified by the `RULE_PATH` variable in a `snort.conf` file.

14. D. Rule Action, Protocol, Source Address, and Destination Address are all included in a Snort rule header. `HOME_NET` is the variable to define the Internal Network in the `snort.conf` file.

15. C. This Snort option associates a high priority to this alert by giving it an *attack class* of `attempted-admin`.

16. A, C. Snort rules and the Snort Engine need to be installed separately during installation of Snort.

17. A. An attack *signature* is a pattern used to identify either a single packet or a series of packets that, when combined, execute an attack.

18. B. Tunneling is a method used to defeat an IDS signature match.

19. A. ***A**** indicates the ACK flag is set.

20. B. The destination address is 192.168.1.4:1244 and 1244 indicates the client port number. The source port of 443 indicates an HTTPS server.

Chapter

14

Cryptography

CEH EXAM OBJECTIVES COVERED IN THIS CHAPTER:

- ✓ Overview of cryptography and encryption techniques
- ✓ Describe how public and private keys are generated
- ✓ Overview of MD5, SHA, RC4, RC5, Blowfish algorithms

Cryptography is the study of encryption and encryption algorithms. In a practical sense, encryption is the conversion of messages from a comprehensible form (cleartext) into an incomprehensible one (cipher text), and back again. The purpose of encryption is to render data unreadable by interceptors or eavesdroppers who do not know the secret of how to decrypt the message. Encryption attempts to ensure secrecy in communications. Cryptography defines the techniques used in encryption. This chapter will discuss encryption algorithms and cryptography.

Cryptography and Encryption Techniques

Encryption can be used to encrypt data while it is in transit or while it's stored on a hard drive. Cryptography is the study of protecting information by mathematically scrambling the data so it cannot be deciphered without knowledge of the mathematical formula used to encrypt it. This mathematical formula is known as the encryption algorithm. Cryptography is composed of two words: *crypt* (meaning secret or hidden) and *graphy* (meaning writing). Cryptography literally means secret or hidden writing.

Cleartext is the readable and understandable data, and cipher text is the scrambled text as a result of the encryption process. Cipher text should be unreadable and show no repeatable pattern to ensure the confidentiality of the data. Figure 14.1 shows cleartext versus cipher text.

FIGURE 14.1 Cleartext and cipher text

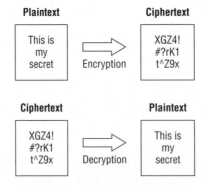

There are three critical elements to data security. Confidentiality, integrity, and authentication are known as the CIA triad (Figure 14.2). Data encryption provides confidentiality, meaning the data can only be read by authorized users. Message hashing provides integrity, which ensures the data sent is the same data received and the information was not modified in transit. Message digital signatures provide authentication (ensuring users are who they say they are) as well as integrity. Message encrypting and digital signatures together provide confidentiality, authentication, and integrity.

FIGURE 14.2 The CIA triad

Confidentiality
Integrity
Authentication

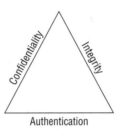

Encryption algorithms can use simple methods of scrambling characters, such as *substitution* (replacing characters with other characters) and *transposition* (changing the order of characters). *Encryption algorithms* are mathematical calculations based on substitution and transposition.

Here are some early cryptographic systems:

Caesar's Cipher A simple substitution cipher (Figure 14.3).

FIGURE 14.3 Substitution cipher

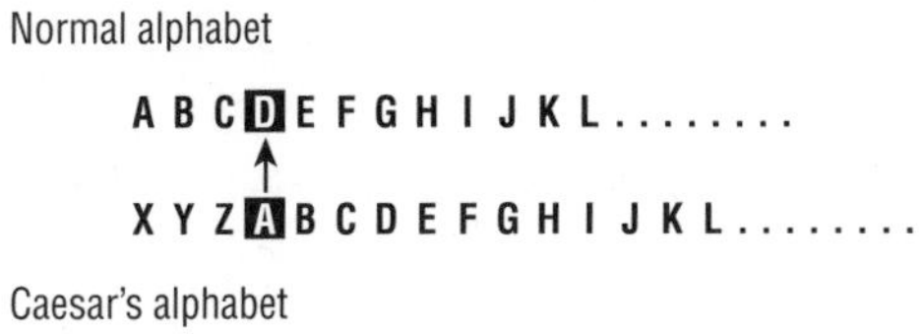
Normal alphabet
A B C D E F G H I J K L........
X Y Z A B C D E F G H I J K L........
Caesar's alphabet

Atbash Cipher Used by the ancient Hebrews, Atbash (Figure 14.4) is a substitution cipher and works by replacing each letter used with another letter the same distance away from the end of the alphabet; for example, A would be sent as a Z and B would be sent as a Y.

FIGURE 14.4 Atbash cipher

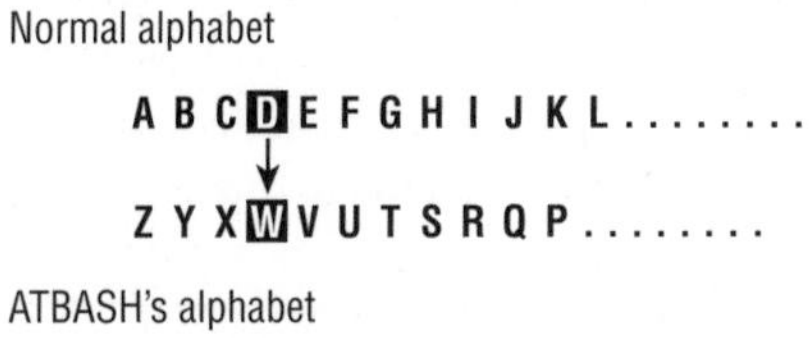
Normal alphabet
A B C D E F G H I J K L........
Z Y X W V U T S R Q P........
ATBASH's alphabet

Vigenere Cipher   Sixteenth-century French cryptographer Blaise de Vigenere created a polyalphabetic cipher to overcome the shortcomings of simple substitution ciphers. The Vigenere cipher (Figure 14.5) uses a table to increase the available substitution values and make the substitution more complex. The substitution table consists of columns and rows labeled "A" to "Z." To get cipher text, first you select the column of plain text and then you select the row of the key. The intersection of row and column is called cipher text. To decode cipher text, you select the row of the key and find the intersection that is equal to cipher text; the label of the column is called plain text.

FIGURE 14.5   Vigenere cipher

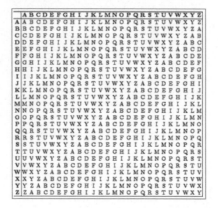

Vernam Cipher   In 1917, AT&T Bell Labs engineer Gilbert Vernam sought to improve the Vigenere cipher and ended up creating the Vernam cipher, or "one-time pad." The Vernam cipher is an encryption algorithm where the plain text is combined with a random key, or "pad," that is the same length as the message. One-time pads are the only algorithm that is provably unbreakable by brute force.

Concealment Cipher   A concealment cipher creates a message that is concealed in some way. For example, the following paragraph includes a secret message:

I have been trying to buy Sally some nice jewelry, like gold or silver earrings, but prices now have increased.

The key is to look at every sixth word in a sentence. So the secret message is "buy gold now."

Types of Encryption

The two primary types of encryption are symmetric and asymmetric key encryption.

Symmetric key encryption means both sender and receiver use the same secret key to encrypt and decrypt the data. A secret key, which can be a number, a word, or just a string of random letters, is applied to the text of a message to change the content in a particular way. This might be as simple as shifting each letter by a number of places in the alphabet.

As long as both sender and recipient know the secret key, they can encrypt and decrypt all messages that use this key.

The drawback to symmetric key encryption is there is no secure way to share the key between multiple systems. Systems that use symmetric key encryption need to use an offline method to transfer the keys from one system to another. This is not practical in a large environment such as the Internet, where the clients and servers are not located in the same physical place.

The strength of symmetric key encryption is fast, bulk encryption. Weaknesses of symmetric key encryption include

- Key distribution
- Scalability
- Limited security (confidentiality only)
- The fact that it does not provide nonrepudiation, meaning the sender's identity can be proven

Examples of symmetric algorithms are as follows:

- DES (data encryption standard)
- 3DES
- AES (Advanced Encryption Standard)
- IDEA (International Data Encryption Algorithm)
- Twofish
- RC4 (Rivest Cipher 4)

Asymmetric (or public) key cryptography was created to address the weaknesses of symmetric key management and distribution. But there's a problem with secret keys: how can they be exchanged securely over an inherently insecure network such as the Internet? Anyone who knows the secret key can decrypt the message, so it is important to keep the secret key secure. Asymmetric encryption uses two related keys known as a key pair. A public key is made available to anyone who might want to send you an encrypted message. A second, private key is kept secret, so that only you know it.

Any messages (text, binary files, or documents) that are encrypted by using the public key can only be decrypted by using the matching private key. Any message that is encrypted by using the private key can only be decrypted by using the matching public key. This means that you do not have to worry about passing public keys over the Internet as they are by nature available to anyone. A problem with asymmetric encryption, however, is that it is slower than symmetric encryption. It requires far more processing power to both encrypt and decrypt the content of the message.

The relationship between the two keys in asymmetric key encryption is based on complex mathematical formulas. One method of creating the key pair is to use factorization of prime numbers. Another is to use discrete logarithms. Asymmetric encryption systems are based on one-way functions that act as a trapdoor. Essentially the encryption is one-way in that the same key cannot decrypt messages it encrypted. The associated private key provides information to make decryption feasible. The information about the function is included in the public key, whereas information about the trapdoor is in the private key. Anyone who has the private key knows the trapdoor function and can compute the public key.

To use asymmetric encryption, there needs to be a method for transferring public keys. The typical technique is to use X.509 digital certificates (also known simply as certificates). A certificate is a file of information that identifies a user or a server, and contains the organization name, the organization that issued the certificate, and the user's email address, country, and public key.

When a server and a client require a secure encrypted communication, they send a query over the network to the other party, which sends back a copy of the certificate. The other party's public key can be extracted from the certificate. A certificate can also be used to uniquely identify the holder.

Asymmetric encryption can be used for

- Data encryption
- Digital signatures

Asymmetric encryption can provide

- Confidentiality
- Authentication
- Nonrepudiation

Strengths of asymmetric key encryption include

- Key distribution
- Scalability
- Confidentiality, authentication, and nonrepudiation

The weakness of asymmetric key encryption is that the process is slow and typically requires a significantly longer key. It's only suitable for small amounts of data due to its slow operation.

Stream Ciphers vs. Block Ciphers

Block ciphers and stream ciphers are the two types of encryption ciphers. Block ciphers are encryption ciphers that operate by encrypting a fixed amount, or "block," of data. The most common block size is 64 bits of data. This chunk or block of data is encrypted as one unit of cleartext. When a block cipher is used for encryption and decryption, the message is divided into blocks of bits. Blocks are then put through one or more of the following scrambling methods:

- Substitution
- Transposition
- Confusion
- Diffusion
- S-boxes

A stream cipher encrypts single bits of data as a continuous stream of data bits. Stream ciphers typically execute at a higher speed than block ciphers and are suited for hardware usage. The stream cipher then combines a plain text bit with a pseudorandom cipher bit stream by means of an XOR (exclusive OR) operation. The XOR process (see Figure 14.6) is to compare the plain text and key one bit at a time and, based on the XOR logic, create cipher text. If the plain text and secret key are the same bit, the result is a 0; if they are different, such as 1 and 0, then the resulting encrypted bit is a 1.

FIGURE 14.6   XOR table

XOR LOGIC		
	$0 \text{ xor } 0 = 0$	Same Bits
	$1 \text{ xor } 1 = 0$	Same Bits
XOR Symbol	$1 \text{ xor } 0 = 1$	Different Bits
$\oplus$	$0 \text{ xor } 1 = 1$	Different Bits

ENCRYPT

$\oplus$ 0 0 1 1 0 1 0 1   Plaintext
   1 1 1 0 0 0 1 1   Secret Key
= 1 1 0 1 0 1 1 0   Ciphertext

DECRYPT

$\oplus$ 1 1 0 1 0 1 1 0   Ciphertext
   1 1 1 0 0 0 1 1   Secret Key
= 0 0 1 1 0 1 0 1   Plaintext

Generating Public and Private Keys

When a client and a server use asymmetric cryptography, both create their own pairs of keys for a total of four keys: the server's public key, the server's private key, the client's public key, and the client's private key. A system's key pair has a mathematical relationship that allows data encrypted with one of the keys to be decrypted with the other key. These keys have a mathematical relationship based on factoring prime numbers such that each key can be used to decrypt data encrypted with the other key. When a client and a server want to mutually authenticate and share information, they each send their own public key to the remote system, but they never share their private keys. Each message is encrypted with the receiver's public key. Only the receiver's private key can decrypt the message. The server would encrypt a message to the client using the client's public key. The only key that can decrypt the message is held by the client, which ensures confidentiality.

A *public key infrastructure (PKI)* is necessary in order to create digital certificates. PKI is a framework that consists of hardware; software; policies that exist to manage, create, store, and distribute keys; and digital certificates. Additionally, a complete PKI solution (like the one in Figure 14.7) involves symmetric algorithms, asymmetric algorithms, hashing, and digital authentication (usually certificates, but could also be Kerberos).

FIGURE 14.7   Certificate authority

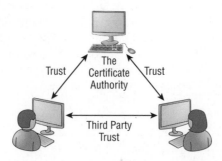

One of the major strengths of public key encryption is its ability to facilitate communication between parties previously unknown to each other, a process that is made possible by the PKI hierarchy of trust relationships. The important parts of the PKI infrastructure are as follows:

- Digital certificates
- Certificate authorities
- Certificate generation and destruction
- Key management

 Real World Scenario

Understanding Certificate Authorities

Using a certificate authority (CA) to validate a client is similar to providing a driver's license for identification. When I am traveling on an airplane, I have to present a valid form of identification to prove my identity. The airport security will generally require a third party such as the state to issue the identification in the case of a driver's license. The security staff might question an ID card that I made at home using my digital camera and color printer. It is also unlikely that they'd accept a library card as a form of identification because it most likely does not contain all the necessary information about me. The state that issues a driver's license is much like the certificate authority: a trusted third party who is trusted to validate my identity. The certificate itself is similar to the driver's license as it contains all the necessary information to validate my identity.

CAs are the glue that binds the public key infrastructure together. They are essentially neutral third-party organizations that provide notarization services for digital certificates. To obtain a digital certificate from a reputable CA, you must identify and prove identity.

Digital certificates are formatted to the X.509 standard and contain set fields. These fields include

- Version
- Serial Number
- Algorithm ID
- Issuer
- Validity
- Not Before (a specified date)
- Not After (a specified date)
- Subject
- Subject Public Key Information
- Public Key Algorithm
- Subject Public Key
- Issuer-Unique Identifier (optional)
- Subject-Unique Identifier (optional)
- Extensions (optional)

In Exercise 14.1, you will view a digital certificate from a secure website.

EXERCISE 14.1

Viewing a Digital Certificate

Connect to any website that requires a login, such as a bank, webmail, or e-commerce site. If you do not have a login to a secure website, then create a Google email account (Gmail) at www.gmail.com for free. If you are creating a Gmail account, you will need to change the settings to always use HTTPS to secure your email. Once you have logged in using SSL, you will be able to view the x.509 certificate from the web server.

1. Open Internet Explorer and log into the secure website.

2. Click the Page menu and choose Properties, or click the yellow lock icon in the lower-right side on the Internet Explorer screen.

EXERCISE 14.1 *(continued)*

3. Click the Certificates button on the page's properties sheet.

4. Click the Details tab to see all the certificate fields. Click each field to see the values.

EXERCISE 14.1 *(continued)*

5. Determine the issuer of the certificate.

6. Determine the validity date of the certificate.

7. View the public key of the certificate.

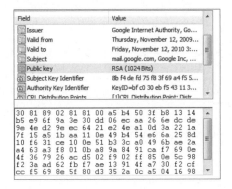

Other Uses for Encryption

Integrity is one of the components of the CIA triad and ensures that information remains unchanged and is in its true original form. A hash is a common method of providing integrity of a message. A hash is the conversion of a string of characters into a shorter fixed-length value that represents the original. It is similar to a shorthand version of the full data.

Common hashing algorithms for digital signatures include

- SHA-1
- MD5
- RIPEMD-160

EXERCISE 14.2

Using WinMD5 to Compute File Hashes

1. Download and install WinMD5 from www.blisstonia.com/software/WinMD5.

2. Run the WinMD5.exe program.

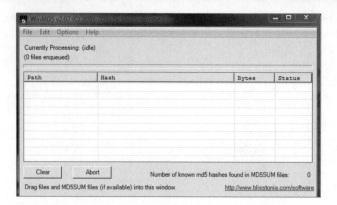

3. Click the File menu in WinMD5 and choose Open. Select any file from your system.

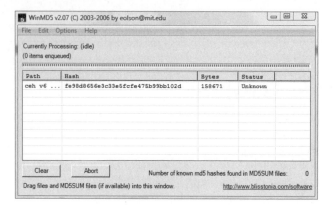

Here is an example of a bad MD5 hash on a file:

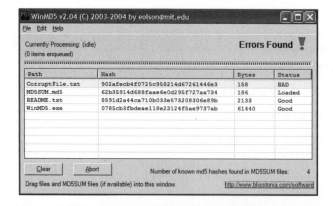

If you've downloaded a file from the Internet, you may be concerned that the file is not complete or was corrupted. One of the ways to ensure the file sent is the same file received is through the MD5 hashing algorithm. MD5 hashes are fingerprints of files. You can compare the fingerprints of two files to see if the files themselves are the same.

You have to have the correct fingerprint for a file to compare the file you receive with the original; otherwise, you cannot tell your file has integrity. When you download a large file, it may contain another file called MD5SUM or something similar. This file contains the correct fingerprints. Dragging an MD5SUM file onto WinMD5 causes the fingerprints to be compared automatically.

The MD5SUM program allows you to compute the MD5 hashes of files. It also makes it easy to compare the fingerprints against the correct fingerprints stored in an MD5SUM file. Red Hat, for example, provides MD5SUM files for all of its large downloadable files.

When you perform hashing, two messages with the same digest are extremely unlikely. However, if this does occur and two messages produce the same hash, it is called a collision. Collisions allow for cryptographic attacks against the algorithm.

Cryptography Algorithms

Algorithms vary in key length from 40 bits to 448 bits. The longer the key length, the stronger the encryption algorithm. Using brute force to crack a key of 40 bits takes from 1.4 minutes to 0.2 seconds, depending on the strength of the processing computer. In comparison, a 64-bit key requires between 50 years and 37 days to break, again depending on the speed of the processor. Currently, any key with a length over 256 bits is considered uncrackable.

Message Digest 5 (MD5), Secure Hash Algorithm (SHA), RC4, RC5, and Blowfish are all names for different mathematical algorithms used for encryption. As a CEH, you need to be familiar with these algorithms:

MD5   MD5 is a hashing algorithm that uses a random-length input to generate a 128-bit digest. It is popular to create a digital signature to accompany documents and emails to prove the integrity of the source. The digital signature process involves the creation of an MD5 message digest of the document, which is then encrypted by the sender's private key. MD5 message digests are encrypted by a private key in the digital signature process.

SHA   SHA is also a message digest, which generates a 160-bit digest of encrypted data. SHA takes slightly longer than MD5 and is considered a stronger encryption. It is the preferred algorithm for use by the government.

- SHA-0: Message of arbitrary length
  - Output: 160-bit fingerprint or message digest
- SHA-1: Message of arbitrary length
  - Output: 160-bit fingerprint or message digest. Corrected a flaw in the original SHA-0 algorithm.
- SHA-2: Message of arbitrary length
  - Output: 256-bit fingerprint or 512-bit fingerprint

RC4 and RC5   RC4 is a symmetric key algorithm and is a *stream cipher*, meaning one bit is encrypted at a time. It uses random mathematical permutations and a variable key size. RC5 is the next-generation algorithm: it uses a variable block size and variable key size. RC5 has been broken with key sizes smaller than 256.

Blowfish   Blowfish is a 64-bit block cipher, which means that it encrypts data in chunks or blocks. It is stronger than a stream cipher and has a variable key length between 32 and 448 bits.

MAC (Message Authentication Code)   MACs require the sender and receiver to share a secret key.

HMAC (Hashed Message Authentication Code)   HMAC was designed to be immune to the multicollision attack. HMAC functions by using a hashing algorithm, such as MD5 or SHA-1, and altering the initial state by use of a symmetric key.

Even if someone can intercept and modify the data, it's of little use if that person does not possess the secret key. There is no easy way for the person to re-create the hashed value without the key.

Digital signatures (see Figure 14.8) are based on public key cryptography and used to verify the authenticity and integrity of a message. A digital signature is created by passing a message's contents through a hashing algorithm. The hashed value is then encrypted with the sender's private key. Upon receiving the message, the recipient decrypts the encrypted sum and then recalculates the expected message hash.

Values should match in order to

- Ensure validity of the message

- Prove that it was sent by the party believed to have sent it

- Prove that only that party has access to the private key

FIGURE 14.8   Digital signature process

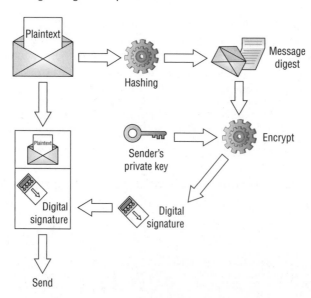

Cryptography Attacks

Cryptographic attacks are methods of evading the security of a cryptographic system by finding weaknesses in the cipher, protocol, or key management. The following are cryptographic attacks that can be performed by an attacker:

Cipher Text–Only Attack   This attack requires the attacker to obtain several messages encrypted using the same encryption algorithm. The key indicators of a cipher text–only attack are the following:

- The attacker does not have the associated plain text.
- The attacker attempts to crack the code by looking for patterns and using statistical analysis.

Known–Plain Text Attack   This attack requires the attacker to have the plain text and cipher text of one or more messages. The goal is to discover the key. This attack can be used if you know a portion of the plain text of a message.

Chosen–Plain Text Attack   This type of attack is carried out when an attacker has the plain text messages of their choosing encrypted. An attacker can analyze the cipher text output of the encryption.

Chosen–Cipher Text Attack   This type of attack is carried out when the attacker can decrypt portions of the cipher text message of their choosing. The attacker can use the decrypted portion of the message to discover the key.

A replay attack occurs when the attacker can intercept cryptographic keys and reuse them at a later date to either encrypt or decrypt messages to which they may not have access.

A brute-force attack involves trying all possible combinations (such as keys or passwords) until the correct solution is identified. Brute-force attacks are usually successful but require time and are usually costly.

Summary

Cryptography has been created to keep secrets from those not authorized to view the information. Cryptography's goal is to keep that information private while also ensuring it can travel across unsecure networks such as the Internet unmolested and unaltered. In many cases, cryptography is just a means of delaying viewing of information for a period of time until the information is no longer useful. Symmetric encryption secret keys are used primarily for performing bulk data encryption whereas asymmetric keys are used for transferring a secret key securely to a system.

Exam Essentials

Define the two types of encryption.   Symmetric key and asymmetric key encryption are the two main types of encryption.

Understand the methods used to scramble data during encryption.   Substitution and transposition methods are the basis of encryption and are used to scramble data during the encryption process.

Identify the common encryption algorithms.   MD5, SHA, RC4, RC5, and Blowfish are the most common encryption algorithms.

Know how public and private keys are created.   A public key and a private key are created simultaneously as a key pair and are used to encrypt and decrypt data.

Data encrypted with one member of the key pair can only be decrypted by the other.

Know the definition of cryptography.   Cryptography is the process of encrypting data through a mathematical process of scrambling data known as an encryption algorithm.

Review Questions

1. How many keys exist in a public/private key pair?

   A. 1

   B. 2

   C. 3

   D. 4

2. How many keys are needed for symmetric key encryption?

   A. 1

   B. 2

   C. 3

   D. 4

3. Which of the following key lengths would be considered uncrackable? (Choose all that apply.)

   A. 512

   B. 256

   C. 128

   D. 64

4. What algorithm outputs a 128-bit message digest regardless of the length of the input?

   A. SHA

   B. MD5

   C. RC4

   D. RC6

5. What algorithm outputs a 160-bit key with variable-length input?

   A. SHA

   B. MD5

   C. RC4

   D. RC6

6. Which algorithm is used in the digital signature process?

   A. RC4

   B. RC5

   C. Blowfish

   D. MD5

7. What is cryptography?
   A. The study of computer science
   B. The study of mathematics
   C. The study of encryption
   D. The creation of encryption algorithms

8. What is the process of changing the order of some characters in an encryption key?
   A. Transposition
   B. Subtraction
   C. Substitution
   D. Transrelation

9. Data encrypted with the server's public key can be decrypted with which key?
   A. The server's public key
   B. The server's private key
   C. The client's public key
   D. The client's private key

10. Which type of encryption is the fastest to use for large amounts of data?
    A. Symmetric
    B. Public
    C. Private
    D. Asymmetric

11. What is the goal of a known–plain text attack?
    A. To read the encrypted data
    B. To gain access to the public key
    C. To discover the encryption key
    D. To validate the sender of the data

12. Which cryptographic attack attempts to crack the code by looking for patterns and using statistical analysis?
    A. Cipher text–only attack
    B. Chosen–plain text attack
    C. Chosen–cipher text attack
    D. Brute-force attack

13. Which two factors are of concern when using brute-force attacks against encryption?
    A. Time
    B. Money
    C. Knowledge of the sender
    D. The ability to capture data

14. Which program is useful in ensuring the integrity of a file that has been downloaded from the Internet?

    A. Tripwire

    B. Norton Internet Security

    C. Snort

    D. WinMD5

15. What are some of the common fields in an x.509 certificate? (Choose all that apply.)

    A. Secret Key

    B. Expiration Date

    C. Issuer

    D. Public Key

16. What is the standard format for digital certificates?

    A. x.500

    B. x.509

    C. x.25

    D. XOR

17. What would the cipher text result be of a value of 1 in plain text and 0 in the secret key after an XOR process?

    A. 1

    B. 0

18. What are two components of a PKI?

    A. User passwords

    B. Digital certificates

    C. Encrypted data

    D. CA

19. What element of the CIA triad ensures that the data sent is the same data received?

    A. Confidentiality

    B. Integrity

    C. Authentication

20. What is the purpose of a hash?

    A. To ensure confidentiality when using a public network such as the Internet

    B. To ensure integrity of a transferred file

    C. To ensure only authorized users are accessing a file

    D. To ensure the data is available to authorized users

Answers to Review Questions

1. B. Two keys, a public key and a private key, exist in a key pair.

2. A. The same key is used to encrypt and decrypt the data with symmetric key encryption.

3. A, B. A key length of 256 bits or more is considered uncrackable.

4. B. MD5 outputs a 128-bit digest with variable-length input.

5. A. SHA outputs a 160-bit key with variable-length input.

6. D. MD5 is used in the digital signature process.

7. C. Cryptography is the study of encryption.

8. A. Transposition is the process of changing the order of some characters in an encryption process.

9. B. Data can be decrypted with the other key in the pair—in this case, the server's private key.

10. A. Symmetric key encryption is fast and best to use when you have large amounts of data.

11. C. The goal of a known–plain text attack is to discover the encryption key.

12. A. A cipher text–only attack attempts to crack the encryption using cryptoanalysis.

13. A, B. Time and money are the two biggest concerns when attempting to break encryption using a brute-force method.

14. D. WinMD5 can be used to verify the integrity of a file downloaded from the Internet.

15. C, D. An x.509 certificate includes a field for Issuer and Public Key.

16. B. x.509 is the standard for digital certificates.

17. A. Different values such as 1 and 0 in an XOR process result in a value of 1.

18. B, D. CA (certificate authorities) and digital certificates are two components of a PKI.

19. B. Integrity ensures the data is not modified in transit.

20. B. A hash is a one-way encryption used to validate the integrity of a file.

Chapter

15

Performing a Penetration Test

CEH EXAM OBJECTIVES COVERED IN THIS CHAPTER:

- ✓ Overview of penetration testing methodologies
- ✓ List the penetration testing steps
- ✓ Overview of the Pen-Test legal framework
- ✓ Overview of the Pen-Test deliverables
- ✓ List the automated penetration testing tools

A penetration test simulates methods that intruders use to gain unauthorized access to an organization's network and systems and to compromise them.

The purpose of a penetration test is to test the security implementations and security policy of an organization. The goal is to see if the organization has implemented security measures as specified in the security policy.

A hacker whose intent is to gain unauthorized access to an organization's network is different from a professional penetration tester. The professional tester lacks malice and intent and uses their skills to improve an organization's network security without causing a loss of service or a disruption to the business.

In this chapter, we'll look at the aspects of penetration testing (pen testing) that you must know as a CEH.

Defining Security Assessments

A *penetration tester* assesses the security posture of the organization as a whole to reveal the potential consequences of a real attacker compromising a network or application. Security assessments can be categorized as security audits, vulnerability assessments, or penetration testing. Each security assessment requires that the people conducting the assessment have different skills based on the scope of the assessment.

A *security audit* and a *vulnerability assessment* scan IP networks and hosts for known security weaknesses with tools designed to locate live systems, enumerate users, and identify operating systems and applications, looking for common security configuration mistakes and vulnerabilities.

A vulnerability or security assessment only identifies the potential vulnerabilities whereas a *pen test* tries to gain access to the network. An example of a security assessment is looking at a door and thinking if that door is unlocked it could allow someone to gain unauthorized access, whereas a pen test tries to open the door to see where it leads. A pen test is usually a better indication of the weaknesses of the network or systems but is more invasive and therefore has more potential to cause disruption to network service.

Penetration Testing

There are two types of security assessments: external and internal assessments. An *external assessment* tests and analyzes publicly available information, conducts network scanning and enumeration, and runs exploits from outside the network perimeter, usually via the Internet. An *internal assessment* is performed on the network from within the organization, with the tester acting either as an employee with some access to the network or as a black hat with no knowledge of the environment.

A black-hat penetration test usually involves a higher risk of encountering unexpected problems. The team is advised to make contingency plans in order to effectively utilize time and resources.

You can outsource your penetration test if you don't have qualified or experienced testers or if you're required to perform a specific assessment to meet audit requirements, such as the Health Insurance Portability and Accountability Act (HIPAA).

An organization employing an assessment term must specify the scope of the assessment, including what is to be tested and what is not to be tested. For example, a pen test may be a targeted test limited to the first 10 systems in a demilitarized zone (DMZ) or a comprehensive assessment uncovering as many vulnerabilities as possible. In the scope of work, a service-level agreement (SLA) should be defined to determine any actions that will be taken in the event of a serious service disruption.

Other terms for engaging an assessment team can specify a desired code of conduct, the procedures to be followed, and the interaction or lack of interaction between the organization and the testing team.

A security assessment or pen test can be performed manually with several tools, usually freeware or shareware, though the test may also include sophisticated fee-based software. A different approach is to use more expensive automated tools. Assessing the security posture of your organization using a manual test is sometimes a better option than just using an automated tool based on a standard template. The company can benefit from the expertise of an experienced professional who analyzes the information. While the automated approach may be faster and easier, something may be missed during the audit. However, a manual approach requires planning, scheduling, and diligent documentation.

The only difference between true "hacking" and pen testing is permission. It is critical that a person performing a penetration test get written consent to perform the pen testing.

Real World Scenario

Ensure You Have Permission Before Pen Testing

About eight years ago I worked as a network administrator for an organization of some 500 users. My boss asked if I would do a security assessment of the organization's perimeter network. I told him to send me an email describing what he wanted to come out of the assessment, and within hours I was scanning my heart out.

After initial reviews, I found that the previous administrator had several "Allow All" exceptions set in the firewall. Our organization shared a connection, data, servers, and facilities with another organization that did much the same job as ours. Once I did the review and fixed a number of issues, my boss told other managers of the progress, and they decided that they wanted me to test the other organization's perimeter. I requested first thing that they make sure we had authorization to do that testing. After a day or two, my manager told me that we were good to go on the testing. Management was concerned about someone attacking the other organization and tunneling through our dedicated line to our network.

I did not get a copy of the written authorization to conduct the testing (that is, the very important "Get Out of Jail Free" card).

During the scan, I found a network—which had no firewall and mostly unpatched servers—running IIS web services, with only antivirus software for protection. The network was also running an Oracle database.

I stopped doing anything on that machine and network once I was able to login as admin on the server because doing anything further was pointless. I wrote a report and submitted it to my manager.

About a month later someone on our staff read in the newspaper that the other organization "got hacked." The office of the state attorney general became involved, and my managers and I were threatened with prosecution. Ultimately, nothing happened to me or my manager. The moral of the story: always carry your Get Out of Jail Free card, and make sure you have a signed copy. Don't ever take anyone's word for it.

Penetration Testing Steps

Penetration testing includes three phases:

- Preattack phase
- Attack phase
- Postattack phase

The *preattack phase* involves reconnaissance or data gathering. This is the first step for a pen tester. Gathering data from Whois, DNS, and network scanning can help you map a target network and provide valuable information regarding the operating system and applications running on the systems. The pen test involves locating the IP block and using Whois domain name lookup to find personnel contact information, as well as enumerating information about hosts. This information can then be used to create a detailed network diagram and identify targets. You should also test network filtering devices to look for legitimate traffic, stress-test proxy servers, and check for default installation of firewalls to ensure that default users IDs, passwords, and guest passwords have been disabled or changed and no remote login is allowed.

Next is the *attack phase*, and during this phase tools can range from exploitive to responsive. They're used by professional hackers to monitor and test the security of systems and the network. These activities include but aren't limited to the following:

Penetrating the Perimeter   This activity includes looking at error reports, checking access control lists by forging responses with crafted packets, and evaluating protocol filtering rules by using various protocols such as SSH, FTP, and telnet. The tester should also test for buffer overflows, SQL injections, bad input validation, output sanitization, and DoS attacks. In addition to performing software testing, you should allocate time to test internal web applications and wireless configurations, because the insider threat is the greatest security threat today.

Acquiring the Target   This set of activities is more intrusive and challenging than a vulnerability scan or audit. You can use an automated exploit tool like CORE IMPACT or attempt to access the system through legitimate information obtained from social engineering. This activity also includes testing the enforcement of the security policy, or using password cracking and privilege escalation tools to gain greater access to protected resources.

Escalating Privileges   Once a user account has been acquired, the tester can attempt to give the user account more privileges or rights to systems on the network. Many hacking tools are able to exploit a vulnerability in a system and create a new user account with administrator privileges.

Executing, Implanting, and Retracting   This is the final phase of testing. Your hacking skills are challenged by escalating privileges on a system or network while not disrupting business processes. *Leaving a mark* can show where you were able to gain greater access to protected resources. Many companies don't want you to leave marks or execute arbitrary code, and such limitations are identified and agreed upon prior to starting your test.

The *postattack* phase involves restoring the system to normal pretest configurations, which includes removing files, cleaning Registry entries if vulnerabilities were created, and removing shares and connections.

Finally, you analyze all the results and create two copies of the security assessment reports, one for your records and one for management. These reports include your objectives, your observations, all activities undertaken, and the results of test activities, and may recommend fixes for vulnerabilities.

Exercise 15.1 shows a framework for a comprehensive penetration test.

EXERCISE 15.1

Viewing a Pen Testing Framework of Tools

1. Open a web browser to www.vulnerabilityassessment.co.uk.

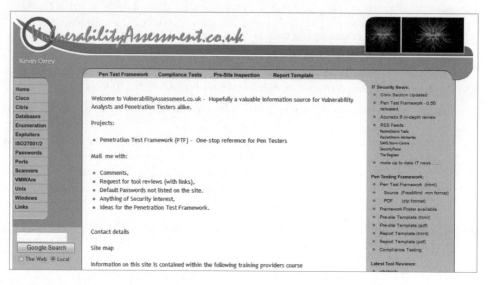

2. Click the Pen Test Framework link near the top.

3. Expand the Network Footprinting section and view the subheadings.

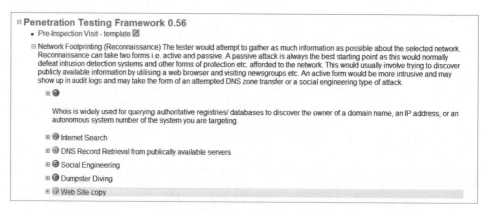

4. Continue down the major heading, expanding each of the subheadings for the pen test framework. You can use this list to locate all the tools necessary in each step of the pen testing process.

The Pen Test Legal Framework

A penetration tester must be aware of the legal ramifications of hacking a network, even in an ethical manner. We explored the laws applicable to hacking in Chapter 1. The documents that an ethical hacker performing a penetration test must have signed with the client are as follows:

- Scope of work, to identify what is to be tested
- Nondisclosure agreement, in case the tester sees confidential information
- Liability release, releasing the ethical hacker from any actions or disruption of service caused by the pen test

Automated Penetration Testing Tools

A 2006 survey of the hackers mailing list created a top-10 list of vulnerability scanning tools; more than 3,000 people responded. Fyodor (http://insecure.org/fyodor/), who created the list, says, "Anyone in the security field would be well advised to go over the list and investigate tools they are unfamiliar with." The following should be considered the top pen testing tools in a hacker's toolkit:

Nessus   This freeware network vulnerability scanner has more than 11,000 plug-ins available. Nessus includes remote and local security checks, a client/server architecture with a GTK graphical interface, and an embedded scripting language for writing your own plug-ins or understanding the existing ones.

GFI LANguard   This is a commercial network security scanner for Windows. GFI LANguard scans IP networks to detect what machines are running. It can determine the host operating system, what applications are running, what Windows service packs are installed, whether any security patches are missing, and more.

Retina   This is a commercial vulnerability assessment scanner from eEye. Like Nessus, Retina scans all the hosts on a network and reports on any vulnerabilities found.

CORE IMPACT   CORE IMPACT is an automated pen testing product that is widely considered to be the most powerful exploitation tool available (it's also very costly). It has a large, regularly updated database of professional exploits. Among its features, it can exploit one machine and then establish an encrypted tunnel through that machine to reach and exploit other machines.

ISS Internet Scanner   This is an application-level vulnerability assessment. Internet Scanner can identify more than 1,300 types of networked devices on your network, including desktops, servers, routers/switches, firewalls, security devices, and application routers.

X-Scan   X-Scan is a general multithreaded plug-in-supported network vulnerability scanner. It can detect service types, remote operating system types and versions, and weak usernames and passwords.

SARA   Security Auditor's Research Assistant (SARA) is a vulnerability assessment tool derived from the System Administrator Tool for Analyzing Networks (SATAN) scanner. Updates are typically released twice a month.

QualysGuard   This is a web-based vulnerability scanner. Users can securely access QualysGuard through an easy-to-use web interface. It features more than 5,000 vulnerability checks, as well as an inference-based scanning engine.

SAINT   Security Administrator's Integrated Network Tool (SAINT) is a commercial vulnerability assessment tool.

MBSA   Microsoft Baseline Security Analyzer (MBSA) is built on the Windows Update Agent and Microsoft Update infrastructure. It ensures consistency with other Microsoft products and, on average, scans more than 3 million computers each week.

In addition to this list, you should be familiar with the following vulnerability exploitation tools:

Metasploit Framework   This is an open source software product used to develop, test, and use exploit code.

Canvas   Canvas is a commercial vulnerability exploitation tool. It includes more than 150 exploits.

Pen Test Deliverables

The main deliverable at the end of a penetration test is the pen testing report. The report should include the following:

- A list of your findings, in order of highest risk
- An analysis of your findings
- A conclusion or explanation of your findings
- Remediation measures for your findings
- Log files from tools that provide supporting evidence of your findings
- An executive summary of the organization's security posture
- The name of the tester and the date testing occurred
- Any positive findings or good security implementations

EXERCISE 15.2

Viewing a Sample Pen Testing Report Framework

1. Open a web browser to www.desktopauditing.com.

2. Click the link on the left side for IT Security Audit Report and Findings Template.

EXERCISE 15.2 *(continued)*

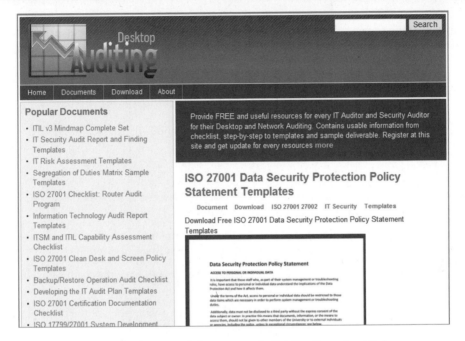

3. Scroll all the way to the bottom of the page and click the Download link.

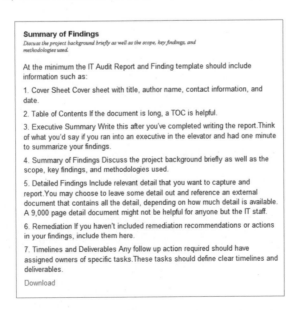

4. Use the sample report as a template for creating your own security auditing reports.

Summary

Security auditing or pen testing is a necessary part of running a secure networking environment. It is critical that a trusted and knowledgeable individual such as a CEH test the systems, applications, and components to ensure all security findings can be addressed by the organization. The organization can use the pen testing report as a measure of how successfully they have implemented the security plan and to make improvements on the data security.

Exam Essentials

Be able to define a security assessment.   A security assessment is a test that uses hacking tools to determine an organization's security posture.

Know pen testing deliverables.   A pen testing report of the findings of the penetration test should include suggestions to improve security, positive findings, and log files.

Know the legal requirements of a pen test.   A pen tester should have the client sign a liability release, a scope of work, and a nondisclosure agreement.

List the penetration testing steps.   Preattack, attack, and postattack are the three phases of pen testing.

Know the two types of security assessments.   Security assessments can be performed either internally or externally.

Review Questions

1. What is the purpose of a pen test?
   A. To simulate methods that intruders take to gain escalated privileges
   B. To see if you can get confidential network data
   C. To test the security posture and policies and procedures of an organization
   D. To get passwords

2. Security assessment categories include which of the following? (Choose all that apply.)
   A. White-hat assessments
   B. Vulnerability assessments
   C. Penetration testing
   D. Security audits
   E. Black-hat assessments

3. What type of testing is the best option for an organization that can benefit from the experience of a security professional?
   A. Automated testing tools
   B. White-hat and black-hat testing
   C. Manual testing
   D. Automated testing

4. Which type of audit tests the security implementation and access controls in an organization?
   A. A firewall test
   B. A penetration test
   C. An asset audit
   D. A systems audit

5. What is the objective of ethical hacking from the hacker's prospective?
   A. Determine the security posture of the organization
   B. Find and penetrate invalid parameters
   C. Find and steal available system resources
   D. Leave marks on the network to prove they gained access

6. What is the first step of a pen test?
   A. Create a map of the network by scanning.
   B. Locate the remote access connections to the network.
   C. Sign a scope of work, NDA, and liability release document with the client.
   D. Perform a physical security audit to ensure the physical site is secure.

7. Which tools are *not* essential in a pen tester's toolbox?

   A. Password crackers

   B. Port scanning tools

   C. Vulnerability scanning tools

   D. Web testing tools

   E. Database assessment tools

   F. None of the above

8. What are not the results to be expected from a preattack passive reconnaissance phase? (Choose all that apply.)

   A. Directory mapping

   B. Competitive intelligence gathering

   C. Asset classification

   D. Acquiring the target

   E. Product/service offerings

   F. Executing, implanting, and retracting

   G. Social engineering

9. Once the target has been acquired, what is the next step for a company that wants to confirm the vulnerability was exploited? (Choose all that apply.)

   A. Use tools that will exploit a vulnerability and leave a mark.

   B. Create a report that tells management where the vulnerability exists.

   C. Escalate privileges on a vulnerable system.

   D. Execute a command on a vulnerable system to communicate to another system on the network and leave a mark.

10. An assessment report for management may include which of the following? (Choose all that apply.)

   A. Suggested fixes or corrective measures.

   B. Names of persons responsible for security.

   C. Extensive step by step countermeasures.

   D. Findings of the penetration test.

11. What makes penetration testing different from hacking?

   A. The tools in use

   B. The location of the attack

   C. Permission from the owner

   D. Malicious intent

12. What documents should be signed prior to beginning a pen test? (Choose two.)

 A. Liability release

 B. Nondisclosure agreement

 C. Hold harmless agreement

 D. Contract agreement

13. What is another name for a pen test?

 A. Compliance audit

 B. Network audit

 C. Security audit

 D. Validation audit

14. What is the first part of the pen testing report?

 A. Findings

 B. Remediation

 C. Compliance

 D. Executive summary

15. What is a type of security assessment in which the test is performed as if the tester were an employee working from within the organization?

 A. Internal assessment

 B. Black hat testing

 C. Full-knowledge test

 D. Organization audit

16. Which type of test involves a higher risk of encountering unexpected problems?

 A. White-hat test

 B. Black-hat test

 C. Grey-hat test

 D. Internal assessment

17. What is one reason to outsource a pen test?

 A. Specific audit requirements

 B. Less risky

 C. More findings

 D. Effective countermeasures

18. In which phase of a pen test is scanning performed?

 A. Preattack phase

 B. Information gathering phase

 C. Attack phase

 D. Fingerprinting phase

19. Which component of a pen testing scope of work defines actions to be taken in the event of a serious service disruption?

    A. Service requirements

    B. Service-level agreement (SLA)

    C. Minimum performance levels

    D. Failback plan

20. Which automated pen testing tool can identify networked devices on the network, including desktops, servers, routers/switches, firewalls, security devices, and application routers?

    A. ISS Internet Scanner

    B. Core Impact

    C. Retina

    D. Nessus

Answers to Review Questions

1. C. A penetration test is designed to test the overall security posture of an organization and to see if it responds according to the security policies.

2. B, C, D. Security assessments can consist of security audits, vulnerability assessments, or penetration testing.

3. C. Manual testing is best, because knowledgeable security professionals can plan, test designs, and do diligent documentation to capture test results.

4. B. A penetration test produces a report of findings on the security posture of an organization.

5. A. An ethical hacker is trying to determine the security posture of the organization.

6. C. The first step of a pen test should always be to have the client sign a scope of work, NDA, and liability release document.

7. F. All these tools must be used to discover vulnerabilities in an effective security assessment.

8. D, F. Acquiring the target and executing, implanting, and retracting are part of the active reconnaissance preattack phase.

9. A, D. The next step after target acquisition is to use tools that will exploit a vulnerability and leave a mark or execute a command on a vulnerable system to communicate to another system on the network and leave a mark.

10. A, D. An assessment will include findings of the penetration test and may also include corrective suggestions to fix the vulnerability.

11. C. Permission from the owner is the difference in hacking and pen testing.

12. A, B. A pen tester should have the client sign a liability release, a scope of work, and a nondisclosure agreement prior to beginning the test.

13. C. Security audits are another name for pen tests.

14. D. An executive summary should be the first part of a pen testing report.

15. A. An *internal assessment* is performed on the network from within the organization, with the tester acting as an employee with some access to the network.

16. B. A black-hat penetration test usually involves a higher risk of encountering unexpected problems. The team is advised to make contingency plans in order to effectively utilize time and resources.

17. A. You can outsource your penetration test if you don't have qualified or experienced testers or if you're required to perform a specific assessment to meet audit requirements such as HIPAA.

18. A. Gathering data from Whois, DNS, and network scanning can help you map a target network and provide valuable information regarding the operating system and applications running on the systems during the preattack phase.

19. B. In the scope of work, a service-level agreement (SLA) should be defined to determine any actions that will be taken in the event of a serious service disruption.

20. A. ISS Internet Scanner is an application-level vulnerability assessment. Internet Scanner can identify more than 1,300 types of networked devices on the network, including desktops, servers, routers/switches, firewalls, security devices, and application routers.

Appendix

About the Companion CD

IN THIS APPENDIX:

- ✓ What you'll find on the CD
- ✓ System requirements
- ✓ Using the CD
- ✓ Troubleshooting

What You'll Find on the CD

The following sections are arranged by category and summarize the software and other goodies you'll find on the CD. If you need help with installing the items provided on the CD, refer to the installation instructions in the "Using the CD" section of this appendix.

Sybex Test Engine

For Windows

The CD contains the Sybex test engine, which includes two bonus exams located only on the CD.

PDF of Glossary of Terms

For Windows

We have included an electronic version of the Glossary in `.pdf` format. You can view the electronic version of the Glossary with Adobe Reader.

Adobe Reader

For Windows

We've also included a copy of Adobe Reader so you can view PDF files that accompany the book's content. For more information on Adobe Reader or to check for a newer version, visit Adobe's website at `www.adobe.com/products/reader/`.

Electronic Flashcards

For PC

These handy electronic flashcards are just what they sound like. One side contains a question or fill-in-the-blank question, and the other side shows the answer.

System Requirements

Make sure your computer meets the minimum system requirements shown in the following list. If your computer doesn't match up to most of these requirements, you may have problems using the software and files on the companion CD. For the latest and greatest information, please refer to the ReadMe file located at the root of the CD-ROM.

- A PC running Microsoft Windows 98, Windows 2000, Windows NT4 (with SP4 or later), Windows Me, Windows XP, Windows Vista, or Windows 7

- An Internet connection

- A CD-ROM drive

Using the CD

To install the items from the CD to your hard drive, follow these steps:

1. Insert the CD into your computer's CD-ROM drive. The license agreement appears.

Windows users: The interface won't launch if you have Autorun disabled. In that case, click Start ➢ Run (for Windows Vista or Windows 7, Start ➢ All Programs ➢ Accessories ➢ Run). In the dialog box that appears, type **D:\Start.exe**. (Replace *D* with the proper letter if your CD drive uses a different letter. If you don't know the letter, see how your CD drive is listed under My Computer.) Click OK.

2. Read the license agreement, and then click the Accept button if you want to use the CD.

The CD interface appears. The interface allows you to access the content with just one or two clicks.

Troubleshooting

Wiley has attempted to provide programs that work on most computers with the minimum system requirements. Alas, your computer may differ, and some programs may not work properly for some reason.

The two likeliest problems are that you don't have enough memory (RAM) for the programs you want to use or you have other programs running that are affecting installation or running of a program. If you get an error message such as "Not enough memory" or "Setup cannot continue," try one or more of the following suggestions and then try using the software again:

Turn off any antivirus software running on your computer. Installation programs sometimes mimic virus activity and may make your computer incorrectly believe that it's being infected by a virus.

Close all running programs. The more programs you have running, the less memory is available to other programs. Installation programs typically update files and programs; so if you keep other programs running, installation may not work properly.

Have your local computer store add more RAM to your computer. This is, admittedly, a drastic and somewhat expensive step. However, adding more memory can really help the speed of your computer and allow more programs to run at the same time.

Customer Care

If you have trouble with the book's companion CD-ROM, please call the Wiley Product Technical Support phone number at (800) 762-2974. Outside the United States, call +1 (317) 572-3994. You can also contact Wiley Product Technical Support at `http://sybex.custhelp.com`. John Wiley & Sons will provide technical support only for installation and other general quality-control items. For technical support on the applications themselves, consult the program's vendor or author.

To place additional orders or to request information about other Wiley products, please call (877) 762-2974.

Glossary

A

access control list (ACL)   A table that maintains a detailed list of permissions or access rights granted to users or groups with respect to file directory, individual file, or network resource access.

access point (AP)   A piece of wireless communications hardware that creates a central point of wireless connectivity.

active attack   An attack that can be detected and is therefore said to leave a footprint.

Active Directory (AD)   A Windows directory that stores information about resources on the network and provides a means of centrally organizing, managing, and controlling access to those resources.

Address Resolution Protocol (ARP)   A TCP/IP protocol used to resolve a node's physical address from a provided IP address.

agent   A software routine that performs designated functions, such as waiting in the background and performing an action when a specified event occurs.

anonymizer   A website that allows a user to access other websites undetected by a proxy server.

anonymous   Having no known name, identity, or source.

anti-Trojan   Software specifically designed to help detect and remove Trojans.

antivirus   A program that attempts to recognize, prevent, and remove computer viruses and other malicious software from the computer.

archive   A place or collection containing records, documents, or other materials of historical interest.

auditing   Checking a computer system to verify intended programs and reliable data and to see whether the data is corrupted or displaying inaccurate results.

B

backdoor   A gap in the security of a computer system that's purposely left open to permit access. Hackers may create backdoors to a system once it has been compromised.

banner grabbing   A technique that enables a hacker to identify the type of operating system or application running on a target server. A specific request for the banner is often allowed through firewalls because it uses legitimate connection requests such as Telnet.

black hat   A malicious hacker.

black-box testing   Testing a system or network without any knowledge of the internal structure.

buffer   A portion of memory available to store data.

buffer overflow   A situation where a program writes data beyond the buffer space allocated in memory. This can result in other valid memory being overwritten. Buffer overflows can occur as a consequence of bugs, improper configuration, and lack of bounds checking when receiving program input.

bug   A software or hardware error that triggers the malfunction of a particular program.

C

cache   A fast storage buffer, such as that found directly on the central processing unit of a computer.

calling procedure   A software routine that passes control to a different software routine. When these routines exist on separate computers, the systems often use Remote Procedure Call (RPC) libraries. Also refers to function calls and subroutines.

certificate authority (CA)   The organization or program that issues digital certificates.

client   A system or software process that accesses a remote service on another computer.

Common Internet File System/Server Message Block   The standard for file sharing used with Microsoft Windows and IBM OS/2 operating systems.

countermeasure   An action taken to offset another action. Usually a fix for a vulnerability in a system.

covert channel   A channel that transfers communication in a nonstandard way, often such that it can't be easily detected. Too frequently, this form of communication violates the security policy by using a channel in an unintended manner.

cross-site scripting   A computer security exploit that is used to execute a malicious script.

D

daemon   A background program that resides on a computer and services requests.

database   A collection of data or information that's organized for easy access and analysis.

decryption   The process of converting encrypted data to plain text.

demilitarized zone (DMZ)   A network area that sits between an organization's internal network and an external network, usually the Internet. Most publicly available servers, such as web and FTP servers, reside in the DMZ.

digital certificate   Credentials that contain personal information such as a name, a public key, an expiration date, and the digital signature of the certificate authority that issued the certificate.

digital signature   A hash of a message that has been encrypted with an individual's private key. It serves as validation of a message's authenticity.

DNS enumeration   Locating DNS records from a DNS server.

domain name   A unique name that identifies a company or organization on the Internet.

Domain Name System (DNS)   The name resolution system that translates alphabetic domain names into numeric IP addresses.

E

encryption   The process of encoding information in an attempt to make it secure from unauthorized access.

enumeration   The creation of a list or inventory of items.

Ethernet   A frame-based computer networking technology for LANs. It defines wiring and signaling for the physical layer, frame formats, and protocols for the media access control (MAC) and data link layer of the OSI model.

exploit   A defined procedure or program that takes advantage of a security hole in a computer program.

Extended Stack Pointer (ESP)   A location identifier used to access parameters passed into a subroutine as arguments.

F

Fiber Distributed Data Interface (FDDI)   A standard for data transmission in a LAN.

File Allocation Table (FAT)   A file system used in DOS, Windows, and OS/2. It keeps track of where data is stored on disk.

firewalking   A method to collect information about a remote network protected by a firewall. Firewalking uses trace route–like IP packet analysis to determine whether a data packet can pass through the packet-filtering device/firewall from the attacker's host to the victim's host.

firewall   Rules created to enforce an access control list (ACL) and designed to prevent unauthorized access to or from a private network.

footprinting   Gathering information about a target to identify weaknesses.

fragmentation   The means of breaking a larger message into smaller chunks for the purpose of sending or storing the data more efficiently.

FreeBSD   A free, open source operating system based on Unix.

File Transfer Protocol SSL   A secure form of FTP software in which Secure Sockets Layer/Transport Layer Security (SSL/TLS) protocols are used to secure the control and data connections.

G

gateway   Software or hardware capable of decision making, which permits or denies access based on general rules. Firewalls are Layer 3 and Layer 4 gateways.

GET   An HTTP command used to request a file from a web server.

gray hat   A hacker who uses skills for defensive or offensive purposes as necessary.

H

hacktivism   Hacking for a cause—for example, hacking to take down a child pornography site.

hash   A function that transforms a string of characters into a number known as the *message digest*.

Hierarchical File System (HFS)   A file system used in Mac OS X. It stores data in a top-to-bottom organization structure.

honeynet   An entire virtual network that is presented as a large honeypot.

honeypot   A system that is designed to attract probes, attacks, and potential exploits. Because honeypots attract attacks, they can be a liability. However, by having honeypots on the network, you can gain enormous amounts of information about how a malicious hacker, or even a script kiddie, gains access to systems. This information can lead to security improvements and/or help a security professional track down a hacker.

hybrid attack   A password attack that combines features of a brute-force attack with a dictionary attack. Characteristics of a hybrid attack include using dictionary terms that substitute numbers or special characters for letters or append numbers to words.

Hypertext Transfer Protocol (HTTP)   A communication protocol that facilitates browsing the World Wide Web.

Hypertext Transport Protocol Secure (HTTPS)   A secure version of the HTTP protocol used to access secure web servers.

I

Institute of Electrical and Electronics Engineers (IEEE)   An organization (sometimes referred to as the I Triple E) that creates standards that assist with the advancement of society's use of technology. It includes engineers, scientists, and students.

Internet Control Message Protocol (ICMP)   An encapsulated IP packet that is used to send error and control messages. The `ping` command uses ICMP Echo requests and ICMP Echo responses to verify connectivity.

Internet Protocol Security Architecture (IPSec)   A Layer 3 protocol that provides secure tunneled communication with authentication and encryption over the Internet. It's often used to create a virtual private network (VPN).

intrusion detection system (IDS)   A mechanism to monitor packets passing through computer networks. The IDS can be monitored as a security check on all transactions that take place in and out of a system.

iris scanner   A biometric device containing a small camera that examines the iris of the eye for purposes of authentication.

K

Kerberos   A computer network authentication protocol.

keylogger   A software or hardware device that records information typed by users. Data is saved in a log file, which could be retrieved by a hacker.

L

Lightweight Directory Access Protocol (LDAP)   A protocol used to access simple directory structures.

local area network (LAN)   A network made up of system nodes and peripherals within a small geographical area.

logic bomb   A program with a delayed payload that is released only when certain conditions are met in the system or program environment.

M

malicious   Deliberately harmful.

mantrap   A secured entrance, normally reserved for high-security facilities. The trap usually involves a series of doors that someone must pass through and in which a trespasser could be detained by locking the doors.

Multipurpose Internet Mail Extensions (MIME)   A communication protocol that allows for the transmission of data in many forms, such as audio, binary, or video, in email messages.

N

NetBSD   The first freely redistributable, open source version of the BSD Unix operating system.

Network Address Translation (NAT)   A technique of mapping multiple IP addresses to a single external IP address belonging to the NAT device. This method is frequently used to connect multiple computers to the Internet.

Network Basic Input/Output System (NetBIOS)   An interface that provides communication between a PC and the network. It was created by IBM and adopted by Microsoft. NetBIOS includes a name service, a session service, and a datagram service.

network interface card (NIC)   A Layer 1 and Layer 2 device that provides upper-layer communication to a physical medium or medium type. Also known as a *network adapter*.

network scanning   Enumerating the available live hosts or IP addresses on a network.

NOP   A command that tells the processor to do nothing. Almost all processors have a NOP instruction that performs a null operation. In the Intel architecture, the NOP instruction is one byte long and translates to 0x90 in machine code. A long run of NOP instructions is called a *NOP slide* or *sled*. The CPU does nothing until it gets back to the main event (which precedes the return pointer).

NT LAN Manager (NTLM)   A challenge/response authentication protocol used in a variety of Microsoft network protocols for authentication purposes.

null session   An unauthenticated connection to a network share by an anonymous user on an unidentified system.

O

Open Systems Interconnection (OSI)   A standard created by the International Organization for Standards (ISO) that describes seven layers with distinct responsibilities in moving data as it's exchanged between two networked devices.

OpenBSD   An open source Unix-based operating system that has many available security measures.

overt channel   An obvious and defined communication path within a computer system or network, used for the transfer of data.

P

passive attack   An attack that violates the security of a system without directly interacting with the system.

password cracker   A program designed to decode passwords.

patch   A short set of instructions to correct a vulnerability in a computer program.

personal identification number (PIN)   An alphanumeric value often used as a secondary form of identification when using two-form authentication.

phraselist   A list of passphrases that a password-cracking tool uses to attempt to crack a password.

physical security   Nondigital methods and mechanisms in place to prevent attackers from getting access to a facility, resource, or information stored on physical media. It can be as simple as a locked door or as elaborate as multiple security layers, including armed guards.

ping   A common connection verification tool that uses ICMP messages to test a target's response. It's been nicknamed the Packet InterNet Groper.

ping sweep   A scan of a range of IP addresses that shows which IP addresses are in use and which aren't. Ping sweeps may include retrieving the DNS name for each live IP address.

Point-to-Point Protocol (PPP)   A protocol used for transporting IP packets over a serial link between the user and ISP.

policy   A set of rules and regulations specified by an organization as a basis for behavior, operation, or performance.

port scanning   Trying to identify the services running on a system by probing ports and viewing the responses from the system. This technique can be used to find services that indicate a weakness in the computer or network device.

POST   An HTTP command used to send text to a web server for processing.

Post Office Protocol 3 (POP3)   A standard interface for retrieving mail by an email client program and from an email server.

Pretty Good Privacy (PGP)   A software package that provides cryptographic routines for email and file-storage applications.

private key   Half of the formula to perform public key cryptography. It's used to create a digital signature and to decrypt data that has been encrypted with the corresponding public key.

probing   Investigating or examining thoroughly.

process   An entity that is uniquely identifiable as it executes in memory.

protocol   A convention or standard that controls and enables communications, connections, and data transfers.

proxy server   A system that acts on behalf of other systems. Proxy servers are often focal points of a network and may contain firewalls.

public key   Half of the formula to perform public key cryptography. Messages that have been encrypted with someone's public key can only be decrypted by the person's private key.

R

remote access   A communication method that allows access to a system or network from a remote location via a telephone line or the Internet.

Request for Comments (RFC)   A solicitation for professional discussion on a topic of interest. RFCs are often released when developing standards for protocols, systems, or procedures used by the Internet community.

rootkit   A collection of tools utilized by an intruder after gaining access to a computer system. These tools assist the attackers in any number of malicious purposes. Rootkits have been developed for all common operating systems, including Linux, Solaris, and Windows, as well as network-connected gaming systems.

S

script   A text file containing ordered commands that a user can perform interactively at the keyboard.

Secure Hash Algorithm (SHA)   A cryptographic message digest algorithm, similar to the message digest family of hash functions developed by Ron Rivest.

Secure Shell (SSH)   Software that produces a secure logon for Windows and Unix using Layer 7 of the OSI model.

Security Accounts Manager (SAM)   A database of usernames, passwords, and permissions in the Windows architecture.

security token   A small physical device used in multifactor authentication that can store cryptographic keys and /or biometric data for identity verification.

Sendmail   An SMTP implementation used in Unix.

Serial Line IP (SLIP)   A communications protocol for dial-up access to TCP/IP networks. It's commonly used to gain access to the Internet as well as to provide dial-up access between LANs.

server   A computer system in a network that provides services to client applications and/or computers.

Server Message Block (SMB)   A protocol for sharing files, printers, serial ports, and communications abstractions such as named pipes and mail slots between computers.

session   An active communication between a user and the system or between two computers. It also refers to Layer 5 (the session layer) of the OSI model.

sheep dip   A stand-alone computer that houses antivirus software and is used under strictly controlled norms to check all media devices before they're connected to a network.

shell   A command language interpreter that is an interface between an operating system kernel and a user.

shellcode   Assembler code that can interact with the operating system and then exit. Hackers often use shellcode to launch exploits, such as stack-based overflows.

shredding   The physical destruction of the platters of a hard disk to ensure that the contents can never be recovered.

Simple Mail Transfer Protocol (SMTP)   A network protocol used when sending email.

Simple Network Management Protocol (SNMP)   An application layer protocol that facilitates the set and/or read management information in the Management Information Base (MIB) of a network device.

Simple Object Access Protocol (SOAP)   A protocol for exchanging XML-based messages using HTTP or SMTP as the transport.

smart card   A device with an embedded microprocessor and storage space, often used with an access code to permit certificate-based authentication.

social engineering   The art of exploiting weaknesses common in human nature to trick a person into revealing useful information such as a user ID, password, or other confidential information.

spyware   Malicious software intended to intervene in or monitor the use of a computer without the user's permission. Spyware doesn't self-replicate like worms and Trojans.

steganography   The practice of hiding a message within an image, audio, or video file. It's a form of a covert channel.

System Integrity Verifier (SIV)   A program that monitors system file hashes to determine whether a file has been changed, such as if an intruder altered or overwrote a system file. Tripwire is one of the most popular SIVs.

T

TCP/IP   The protocol suite of definitions for communications at Layers 3 and 4 of the OSI model. TCP/IP is the standard communication method that computers use to communicate over the Internet.

Telnet   An application used to create a remote session with a computer.

Temporal Key Integrity Protocol (TKIP)   An encryption standard defined in IEEE 802.11i and WPA for Wi-Fi networks designed to replace WEP. TKIP was structured to replace WEP with a more secure solution without replacing legacy hardware.

third party   A person, group, or business indirectly involved in a transaction or other relationship between principals.

threat   An intentional or unintentional action that has the capability of causing harm to an information system.

time bomb   A type of logic bomb, with a delayed payload that is triggered by reaching some preset time, either once or periodically.

time to live (TTL)   A field in the IP header that indicates the amount of time a transmitted packet will be valid. The TTL defines how many router hops a packet can make before it must be discarded. If a packet is discarded by a router, an ICMP error message is generated to the sender.

timestamp   A number that represents the date and time. Recording timestamps is important for tracking events as they occur on a computer.

traceroute   A tool to trace a path to a destination system.

traffic   The data being transferred across the network media.

Trojan   A program that seems to be useful or harmless but in fact contains hidden code embedded to take advantage of or damage the computer on which it's run.

tunneling   Encapsulating one protocol or session inside the data structure of another protocol.

tunneling virus   A virus that attempts to tunnel underneath antivirus software so that it's not detected.

U

Uniform Resource Locator (URL)   The address that defines the route to a file on a web server (HTTP server).

User Datagram Protocol (UDP)   The connectionless, unreliable Internet protocol that functions at Layer 4 of the OSI model.

V

virus   Malicious code written with an intention to damage the user's computer. Viruses are parasitic and attach to other files or boot sectors. They need the movement of a file to infect other computers.

virus hoax   A bluff in the name of a virus. Creators attempt to arouse fear, and sometimes encourage the removal of system files.

virus signature   A unique string of bits that forms a recognizable binary pattern. This pattern is a fingerprint that can be used to detect and eradicate viruses.

vulnerability   A bug or glitch in computer software, an operating system, or architecture that can be exploited, leading to a system compromise.

vulnerability scanning   Searching for devices, processes, or configurations on your network that have known vulnerabilities.

W

war dialer   A malicious application that randomly calls phone numbers while trying to detect the response of a computer modem.

warchalking   A technique to identify key features of Wi-Fi networks for others by drawing symbols in public places (where anyone can intrude easily) and encourage open access.

web server   The computer that delivers web pages to browsers and other files to applications via the HTTP protocol.

web spider   Scanning web sites for certain information such as email accounts.

white-box testing   Testing software, a system, or a network with knowledge of the internal structure. Also called *glass box testing*.

Wi-Fi   A certification from the Wi-Fi alliance to promote interoperability of wireless equipment for 802.11 networks (including 802.11a, 802.11b, 802.11g, and 802.11n). This term was popularized by the Wi-Fi Alliance.

Wired Equivalent Privacy (WEP)   A technically obsolete protocol for wireless local area networks (WLAN). WEP was proposed to present a level of security similar to that of a wired LAN.

wiretapping   A process by which a third party intervenes in a telephone conversation, usually through a secret medium.

worm   A malicious software application that is structured to spread through computer networks. These applications are self-propagating.

Index

Note to the Reader: Throughout this index **boldfaced** page numbers indicate primary discussions of a topic. *Italicized* page numbers indicate illustrations.

E

The Best Certified Ethical Hacker Book/CD Package on the Market!

Get ready for your Certified Ethical Hacker (CEH) certification with the most comprehensive and challenging sample tests anywhere!

The Sybex Test Engine features the following:

- All the review questions, as covered in each chapter of the book
- Challenging questions representative of those you'll find on the real exam
- Two bonus exams available only on the CD

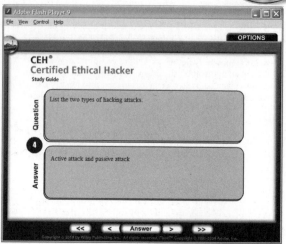

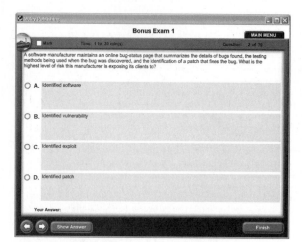

Search through the complete book in PDF!

- Access the entire *CEH: Certified Ethical Hacker Study Guide* complete with figures and tables, in electronic format.
- Search the *CEH: Certified Ethical Hacker Study Guide* chapters to find information on any topic in seconds.

Use the Electronic Flashcards to jog your memory and prep last-minute for the exam!

- Reinforce your understanding of key concepts with these hardcore flash-card-style questions.